2010 Women in Leadership Program
Do not follow where the path may lead.
Go instead where there is no path and leave a trail.

IVORY

BASEMENT

LEADERSHIP

IVORY BASEMENT LEADERSHIP

power and invisibility
in the changing university

JOAN EVELINE

UNIVERSITY OF WESTERN AUSTRALIA PRESS

First published in 2004 by
University of Western Australia Press
Crawley, Western Australia 6009
www.uwapress.uwa.edu.au

Publication of this book was made possible by funding assistance from The
University of Western Australia Business School.

National Library of Australia
Cataloguing-in-Publication entry:

Eveline, Joan, 1940– .
    Ivory basement leadership: power and invisibility in the changing
    university.

    Bibliography.
    Includes index.
    ISBN 1 920694 21 8.

    1. University of Western Australia—Administration. 2. Education,
    Higher—Australia—Aims and objectives. 3. Education,
    Higher—Australia—Administration. 4. Women in higher education—
    Australia. 5. College administrators—Australia. 6. Women college
    administrators—Australia. I. Title.

378.00994

Cover: Frank Hurley 1885–1962, *University of Western Australia through arches*,
Frank Hurley negative collection (1910–1962), ref.nla.pic-an23197653.

Produced by Benchmark Publications Pty Ltd, Melbourne
Consultant editor: Jean Dunn, Melbourne
Series design by Robyn Mundy Design, Perth
Cover design by Sandra Nobes, Tou-Can Design, Melbourne
Typeset in 9½pt Garamond Light by Lasertype, Perth
Printed by McPherson's Printing Group, Maryborough

CONTENTS

PREFACE

Controversy about gender matters was in full swing at The University of Western Australia (UWA) in 1996, provoked by a review of the position of academic women. I was new to the staff, and many of the women and a number of the men I met that year were party to those debates. I found myself participating in, or at least being a keen observer at, several lively meetings. Consequently, I joined one of the women's networks that were pressing for some equitable outcomes from the review.

Several factors eased me into connecting with those gender equity discussions. First, the 'politics of advantage' framework that I had developed in earlier research had been used in the controversial report, and I was interested in its reception. Secondly, a book I was editing included a chapter from the vice-chancellor of the time, Fay Gale. Her necessarily short narrative of leadership sparked my interest. What was the story behind the story? Zest was added to my search for answers when I became a faculty representative on the university's Equal Opportunity Advisory Committee and, shortly after, that committee's representative on the Leadership Development for Women planning group. From interest and necessity I asked the newcomer's questions, read relevant documents and kept notes on what I observed. Since observation, note-taking, and participation are what an ethnographer does, I felt comfortable in that role—having started with a study of women miners fourteen years earlier.

During the next two years I grew fascinated by the practical, everyday instances of leadership that I saw on those committees and elsewhere. I pondered a number of things. Why was the leadership of women so often hidden from public view? Why did equity issues gain more attention when a man took the lead and promoted them? Was there any room for 'post-heroic' leadership at the coalface of work units? How were women faring in departments, faculties and labs?

I was never alone in asking such questions. The women I met on committees and in teaching or support networks were forming similar queries. These were based on the message they were receiving that, in departments and faculties at least, gender was once again a non-issue. Women feared not only that the gender agenda had stalled but also that the representation of women (in decision-making and 'power committees' etc.) was on the decline. By early 1999 a group of us were talking about the need to record, for the sake of history and any future threat to established equity provisions, what gains had been achieved for women during the 1990s.

A decade earlier, Trish Crawford and Myrna Tonkinson had published a book called *The Missing Chapters*, which showed the hazards for women who tried to place their issues, and their history, onto UWA agendas. A sequel to that book seemed timely. It was evident that equity policies and procedures had undergone big changes during the 1990s. The symbolic and strategic influence of a supportive female vice-chancellor, the efforts of other leaders, managers and stakeholders, and external pressures for equal opportunity and quality measures had all played a part. But to what extent had this activity reshaped a workplace formed by, and designed for, men?

The timing was right from another angle. Western Australia was gearing up to celebrate the deeply ambiguous Centenary of Women's Suffrage—ambiguous because Aboriginal women, and men, were denied that vote until much later. Major events, memorials, mementoes, films, plays, songs, books and histories were planned. As my project seemed appropriate to that commemoration, I submitted a proposal for research assistance to the Vice-Chancellor's Strategic Initiatives Fund. I am profoundly grateful for that support. It enabled the original idea of mapping a decade of equity policy to be expanded to an ethnographic study looking deeply into the cultural and gendered dimensions of organisational change and leadership.

By the time the study was underway, diversity was complementing the gender focus of equity concerns, and a new question was incorporated into the research. Would the growing emphasis on diversity make inclusion easier for those whose first language was not English, who had Indigenous or working-class backgrounds, or a disability, or were gay or lesbian? That question helped take the study into the diverse realm of ivory basement work.

A wealth of invisible basement work has been invested in this book—by colleagues, friends and family. I am deeply in their debt.

Over four years the original small team has expanded in several directions. For two years it incorporated intermittently a team of part-time research associates—Frances Rowland, Judy Skene and Rachel Robertson—who gathered and sorted data, organised groups and interviews, compiled categories, sifted the literature and wrote data descriptions. Genevieve Calkin conducted further interviews, did preliminary data analysis, chased literature and edited chapter drafts, while Josh Hogan completed the bibliography. I am especially appreciative of the efforts, insights, commitment and good humour of these ivory basement workers.

The original advisory group of Maria Osman, Sandy McKnight, Barbara Goldflam and Jan Stuart played a crucial role in supporting the ideas for research design and data gathering. Along with Jen de Vries at a later stage, they offered specialist advice on a range of issues to do with the university's functioning, plus a rich source of experience-based feedback on managing the pleasures and perils of collaborative leadership in the lee of the ivory basement.

By the time this book was being shaped, framed and written, Maria and Sandy had moved on, and Jen de Vries was taking an increasingly active role. At crucial points, all these colleagues discussed the data, examined proposals and sometimes read and commented on drafts. Particularly significant was the contribution of my partner, Michael Booth, who read, shaped and made suggestions on every chapter, and typed additions, especially while I was fighting the cancer bug in 2002. I call this assembly of collaborators the Gender Matters Collective. For their intense faith in the project, their generous friendship, their willingness to contribute and their ability to lighten the often solitary task of writing a book, I offer a heartfelt thank you.

I think of the group-within-the-group as my 'collaborative supervisors': Jen de Vries, Barbara Goldflam and Jan Stuart. All steered an insightful path through the mass of early drafts. Jan drafted a chapter, and added her expert editing skills to the whole. Jen helped compile the feminist wish-list in the Conclusion and commented on drafts of other chapters. Barb and I wrote an early version of the Conclusion, which failed to make it into this book but gave us some fun times and a conference paper to boot. The companionate leadership of their unstinting time and effort have given this book a shape and integrity which I could not have achieved alone.

I am especially grateful to two other women, each of whom was generous with time and expertise. Trish Crawford offered a touchstone of experience, a rich knowledge of the context and theory, unwavering interest during the life of the project and, in the early period, helped steer it away from some political and intellectual pitfalls. Fay Gale saw the value of the project from the beginning, drew tirelessly on her personal records and memory to assist the data gathering, provided significant insights on leadership, UWA and the broader context, and showed powerful forbearance as the manuscript underwent many reshapings. Both women read early drafts and offered advice and encouragement. I greatly value their intellectual support and friendship.

In addition to the project's research assistants, three other women facilitated affinity groups: Pat Klinck, Marie Finlay and Maria Osman. Their expertise ensured useful and precise data, and I am most appreciative. I also wish to thank the following people for their valuable contributions. Jan Burrows, Steve Robson, Judy Skene, Lorraine Hayden and Gen Calkin variously undertook the long job of transcribing tapes, while Liz Hutchinson, Rob McCormack and other university archivists supplied figures and information on specific issues. Bev Hill and Malcolm Fialho made useful comments on one chapter, while two members of the Limina Collective formatted early drafts. Women's groups on campus gave generously of their time to arrange and attend affinity groups, as did members of university committees and other staff groups. An amazing and delightful feature of the research was that no one who was approached for an individual interview declined. It was a pleasure to work with these generous people and I thank them all sincerely.

Anne Pauwels, and UWA Press readers Alison Mackinnon and Jan Currie, deserve special thanks for their careful and constructive criticisms of manuscript drafts. I enjoyed immensely the final stage of working with and against their comments, and trust that their suggested additions and enthusiasm have been woven into the book. As publication drew nearer, two further groups provided funds for the final stages. I thank sincerely the Leadership Development for Women Program's Special Project fund and the UWA Business School.

At UWA Press, Jenny Gregory, Maureen de la Harpe and Janine Drakeford have efficiently supported the book and its production. Jean Dunn provided meticulous and insightful editing. I thank them all.

It is always an inadequate thing to thank family and friends for their forbearance and support during the long haul of writing a book. A joy for me has been their acceptance and love throughout, coupled with the welcome provision of meals, shopping tasks, a supportive ear and many big hugs. This was especially the case from daughters Terri and Jen, sons-in-law Shaun and Bill, and grandkids Josh, Joni, Lauren, Georgia, Sarah and Ben. On the household front, Michael Booth took over all cooking and cleaning for long spells, particularly during the later stages. These tasks he coupled with unerring faith, love, intellectual stimulation, research expertise and many hours spent poring over drafts.

Behind it all, the UWA Vice-Chancellery gave generous public and personal support. Deputy Vice-Chancellor Alan Robson (1994–2003) and Vice-Chancellor Deryck Schreuder (1998–2003) ensured the main funding and then gave time and knowledge in advising on who and what should be included in the study. Alan Robson, in particular, championed the project. He provided wise counsel on UWA's diverse cultural mix of disciplines and work groups; he maintained faith in the project's worth; he read draft chapters and sponsored several seminars and reporting opportunities from which I gained useful responses. My very warm thanks and appreciation.

Joan Eveline
Perth

Editorial note

Direct quotes from participants in our study are distinguished from other quoted material by the use of *italic type*.

Abbreviations

ANU   Australian National University
LDW   Leadership Development for Women programme (UWA)
UWA   The University of Western Australia

Introducing the Ivory Basement

What does 'the ivory basement' mean to you? The answer differs, I find, depending on the audience.

It's what's left when the tower has been demolished, replied a divisional dean at a forum for senior managers.

A description of our workplace, was the guess of a female administrator at an international gathering on leadership.

I suspect it's going to be about us, offered the academic chairing papers at the annual conference of industrial relations scholars.

Few university employees see themselves occupying an ivory tower, yet accounts of the university as an institution employ the metaphor as the supreme—if crumbling—symbol of university life. This irony reflects an outdated mind-set of many inside and outside the academy, which fails to mirror the significant changes within universities in recent decades. It leads to questions. Are universities relevant? Have they become too managerial? Have academics lost their prestige? Can university work remain autonomous? Are universities providing the innovations needed for sustainable and competitively advantaged communities? By shifting the lens to encompass a view from the ivory basement, a complex and comprehensive set of questions and answers is revealed.

Urgent questions of power, leadership and change agency lie at the heart of the shift. This book examines those questions through the experience, leadership and reshaping activities of workers in the ivory basement: tutors, casual workers, administrative staff in front-line positions, research assistants, lower level academics, and women and men who seek to generate an equitable and diverse workforce. It is about leadership and innovation as much as it is about 'lower' levels of university life.

Ivory basement leadership is largely invisible. All those who occupy the basement have to make important daily decisions—about grading, about how to design a document while dealing with volatile personalities, about the disciplines they teach and about the wider society—which have implications for the present and future work, creativity and thinking of that society. Yet this basement life remains hidden from the university and the broader society alike. The tutor responsible for twenty students, for example, takes the lead in shaping discussion and minds—yet the system rarely defines that everyday work as leadership. The work that produces the minutiae of taken-for-granted leadership is judged extraneous to the main game of branding and marketing products that will increase the university's market share. This book challenges that misconception.

Significant fears about our changing universities dominate higher education in most OECD (Organization for Economic Co-operation and Development) countries. Universities as privileged sites of knowledge production are rapidly becoming casualties of seemingly irreversible forces: globalised economies, new technologies and the mass growth of higher education. For Brooks and Mackinnon, such dramatic changes turn the university into 'a strategic site' where 'processes of globalisation can be studied'.[1] This book follows their lead in charting that highly contested terrain. Yet an ivory basement perspective extends earlier debates. If the changes shaping universities are to be mobilised so as to equitably enrich our wider communities, then the work cultures of tower and basement must be faced and understood. The stress here is on universities as places of work. Moreover, analysis starts from the premise that the symbolic, hierarchical and changing work of tower and basement is deeply gendered. This idea is by no means uncharted territory. The argument that organisations are gendered began as a marginal dialogue between feminist and organisational scholars in the 1980s[2] and has since become fertile common ground for a large and growing research field, which crosses disciplinary, national, theoretical and methodological borders.[3]

Recent studies of universities have made good use of the notion of gendered organisation. Valuable enquiries have illuminated the big picture—mapping how broad political and economic forces have shaped the gendered régimes of universities.[4] Yet a university, in tower and basement, is a place of work—where the interests of employees and employers meet but also clash. And it is within specific workplaces, each with its own history, culture and resources, that groups and individuals develop their skills, strategies and gendered identities.[5] In Australia, changes in workplaces have brought us job insecurity, increased our hours of work and reduced the time we spend with loved ones and in leisure pursuits. Within our workplaces, men and women adapt, interpret and challenge the pressures to do more and be more. Within universities, the ways in which we adapt to those pressures shape our jobs and professions, and the pleasures and rewards we gain from them. Our current responses are producing deep inequalities of work and rewards, which are strongly patterned by gender.

Through an ethnographic study of one of those workplaces—an 'old' Australian university—this book maps the micropolitics of change in a bastion of masculine privilege. Despite the current obsession with youthfulness, being old is no handicap to the university. A source of pride for those who occupy the ivory tower is its history as one of the oldest organisational models in existence, having survived from the middle-ages—though carrying centuries of sexism and gender bias as baggage. Yet it is now obvious to most that a postmodern and globalising world poses a serious threat to this antiquated organisational model. At a time when old securities are fast disappearing and new ways of managing are in vogue, this book asks how women and men of varying backgrounds, fields, occupations and status 'do' gender. As they occupy and perform their jobs and professions, how does gender reshape or renew their values and influence everyday work practices?

Academic organisations have traditionally seen themselves as places where lessons of integrity, professionalism, creativity and leadership inspire the autonomous doing and teaching of science, humanities, law, technological innovation and arts. Yet even as they treasured their organisational longevity and secured autonomy, universities were simultaneously 'organizations like no other...institutions where the principal product is *dissent*, or opposition to received wisdom'.[6] An important question for our study is the extent to which dissent is available to the more marginalised groups of university work. For, as Morley makes clear, the micropolitics of the university means dissent has different consequences for different groups.[7] Can a study of the ivory basement tell us what we need to know about the health of core university values: creative and courageous leadership, innovative and responsive teamwork, use of dissent to build relevant teaching and research communities, oppositional strategies for challenging unfair or declining standards?

Ivory Basement Leadership addresses each facet of that question. In so doing it follows Morley's example and 'turns the feminist theoretical offensive' back onto the gendered university itself.[8] A primary goal is to shed new light on the unseen but essential labour that underpins academic research, teaching and administration, the unspoken rules and values that create inequitable rewards and spaces, and the unrecognised forms of leadership that people enact in those spaces. To that end, the metaphor of the ivory basement is used not simply to signify structural inequalities but, most crucially, as a symbol of the relational work that is hidden, ignored and unseen.

Studying the work of the ivory basement—and the practices that conceal it—has implications for how we understand the local processes of managing change in universities in particular, and in a global knowledge economy more widely. Most Australians report that they are satisfied with 'life as a whole'.[9] Yet few of us escape what Connell calls the 'panic' effect of pressures for globalisation,[10] as we watch those around us, in universities as much as in other public sector workplaces, striving to combat deteriorating standards, declining wage relativities, fewer jobs, inequitable reward structures and reduced professional prestige.[11] Given that such pressures are endemic to the organisation of workplaces throughout at least most OECD countries, the view from the ivory basement has wide relevance.

A design for voice and visibility

Context, complexity and comprehensiveness were crucial to the design of the project that underpins this book. A major finding from feminist and diversity researchers is that different sub-groups experience work and its problems in different ways.[12] This presents a critical issue for those who want to ensure that difference is not rubbed out by insensitive methods which may refuse them speech and visibility. As Rimmer and Palmer suggest, 'Diversity research will need a strong ethnographic aspect to come to grips with basic issues such as differences in social identity, perceptions of power and fairness, and alternative modes of social action'.[13]

Some studies of higher education are based on wide-ranging but necessarily surface comparisons of the effect of global forces on a national or international scale.[14] This book is different. In a search for lessons about innovation and creativity, it turns to how such forces and responses shape universities from the *inside*, concentrating to a great extent on one institution. It digs deeply into cultural, institutional and leadership patterns in that organisation, and teases out specific themes to show how gender and diversity are, central. Many comparisons are made with other universities.

The approach of *Ivory Basement Leadership* is ethnographic. Writing an ethnography is a way of telling a story that represents experience and can jog half-forgotten memories. The authority for telling that story comes from the insights the analysis conveys to readers, based on the flesh and blood accounts of participants and filtered through the lens of theory. This study was mainly qualitative, assisted by relevant statistics. 'Qualitative research gives the power back to the human voice'[15] and ethnography helps us to know a socially constructed world from the inside out.[16] A research team of four gathered the material, mainly through focus groups and semi-structured interviews. To place the oral material within a research context, the team reviewed statistics, searched archives, observed meetings and procedures, and reviewed organisational, feminist and equal opportunity literature. An account of the diversity and number of interviews and focus groups is in the Methodology Appendix.

Most ethnographies are conducted over an extended period, often with a high degree of observation and/or organisational participation.[17] This study was no exception, ranging across five years of interviews, participant observation and feedback sessions. With such a method, both the wealth of data and the worry that the researcher might 'go native' (lose critical distance) need to be carefully managed.[18] Taking a scholarly approach helps both to disentangle participants' differing perspectives and views and to keep a reflective distance from the data for the writer.[19]

Nonetheless, this analysis is necessarily a partial one. No sociological text can legitimately claim to offer a definitive reading of interviews and observational notes. Rather, it is 'but one reading among many possible readings'.[20] The same holds true for history: 'Every history offers a version of the past, although some discourses masquerade as *the* history'.[21]

To recognise partiality as inevitable can threaten deeply held beliefs, but it is indispensable to contemporary scholarly reflection on a complex organisation. I deal with the problem of partiality by making it clear that this story is anchored in a feminist perspective, which means it is always concerned with power: how it works, how to challenge it. In that I follow Haraway, who argues that the scientific way to deal with the issue of partiality is for a researcher to make her or his situated knowledge explicit. Her approach challenges claims that objective impartiality exists (she calls it the god trick view from nowhere) and gives visibility to voices from the margins.[22]

The voices from the margins in this case are those I link with the ivory basement: mostly women, of various cultural and ethnic backgrounds, plus lower level academic and general staff.

The data to generate a feminist view of and from the basement was achieved through the composition of the seventeen affinity groups,* and through the spread of interviews. Women comprised the majority of participants, with academic and general staff evenly balanced. Affinity groups included five with formalised university committees, several with informally organised but longstanding women's groups, plus several others drawn together for the occasion, such as grounds staff, casual teachers, a lesbian group, equity advisers and doctoral students.

A primary aim was to gain a sense of how people at all levels, both men and women, were responding to equity and diversity issues. To some extent we balanced the over-representation of lower to middle ranking women in the affinity groups by interviewing senior academics and administrators. As these were mostly men, we included every woman holding a senior administrative position. Individual interviews were conducted with ninety-seven people, with the final spread of participants giving some voice to all levels and to most stakeholders.

With ethnography, the writer is often also interviewer and observer. This study was different. Four people shared the interviewing, six people facilitated the affinity groups and four categorised, sifted and analysed material in preparation for the end stage of writing up. As participant observers, the research team attended faculty meetings, Teaching and Learning workshops, staff development sessions, union meetings, women's group meetings and events, staff selection committees, and sundry faculty and general staff workshops, meetings and networks. A different team of three colleagues advised on the drafting and writing of this book, with additional input from an advisor not employed by the university. In tune with the methods of ethnography, collaborative data gathering and writing

---

* An affinity group is a focus group in which participants know each other. Researchers who use the method believe that people who know each other through common interests will be more comfortable speaking together about 'what could be sensitive and controversial issues' (S. Austen, T. Jefferson, and V. Thein, *How Much Further?: Women's Progress, Goals and Status in WA*, Perth, Women's Economic Policy Analysis Unit, Curtin University of Technology, 2001).

support became a feature of this project—weaving a rich complexity of views and insights. I trust that complexity illuminates the text, in spirit if not always in words.

Conclusion

The library shelves of management studies are laden with books that argue how, at a time of seemingly endless instability, creative collaboration and sensitive people-management are the essential ingredients of survival and success. They focus on the work of people called 'manager', 'leader' or 'executive'.[23] This book turns that focus on its head by emphasising the symbolic realm of the university's ivory basement. It reviews how people at all levels manage instability and the reshaping of workplaces in creative and sensitive ways, ways essential but unseen.

Importantly, the study reveals diverse groups and individuals challenging the grip of masculinist norms on the power effects of privilege.[24] Loosening that grip is never easy. Yet here, a regular pattern of mobilising by and for women appears to have furnished a number of potentially transformative practices. I chose a particular organisation—a prestigious Australian university—because it prom-ised insights and examples of the possible at a time when innovative actions are looking less viable. In that sense, the book has something to say to people in many workplaces, particularly those in universi-ties. Pressures on universities show every sign of increasing, and we need to know if past successes and failures can offer us tools for managing the future. The rich insights of a concentrated case study give depth and substance to those lessons.

CHAPTER 1

The New Knowledge Economy

...standing in the way of...the chill winds outside the ivory towers were the forms of collegial organisation which derived from the idea that the university was a community of scholars—professors with deluded ideas about their traditional authority; faculties who believed in peer review; departments who wanted elected chairs; students who thought they were more than customers.[1]

While 'ivory tower' often signifies a group of scholars sadly out of touch with the everyday world, academics have never been too disturbed by that implied irrelevance. After all, the underlying values captured by the notion—of a protected space for producing knowledge and imparting wisdom to eager students—are what attracted them to universities in the first place. They crave a place of privilege, quiet and beauty where their important thinking and reflecting can be done. As their haven has become more integrated into society, many have resisted the imposed administrative routine and kept a sense that scholarship and collegiality should be maintained. For the larger mass of those sharing these institutions, the 'chill winds' have affected them in complex and unequal ways.

In the midst of these pushes and pulls, most of those involved in the proliferation of university work—part of the new knowledge economy—have shown contradictory responses on how to construe their own roles. While several voices today are predicting the demise of the protected space, some have been sanguine about the prospect.[2] Many across the English-speaking world argue that goals of efficiency and cost-cutting have been taken too far—they foresee the undermining not only of the existing university system but also of the economic and cultural viability of national economies, at least in the long-term.[3] Yet university work, while widely held to be poorly paid, is still highly regarded professional work.

The problem with most of the literature is that it scrutinises the upper dimensions of the university workspace and ignores the ivory basement. The blindspots of that top-down perspective present universities, and the communities that need them, with two problems. The first is that the important work of persistent precision and community building is overshadowed by a concentration on quick results and entrepreneurial zeal. The second is that much of the talent needed for comprehensive and innovative planning consequently drifts off into other sectors.

Rapid change of unprecedented scope confronts not only the university as an institution but also the vast majority of the workplaces of today's workers, professionals and managers. The link between globalising economies and a 'frenzied search for new and better management practices'[4] is well established in critical studies of corporate change.[5] Two decades of increasingly powerful Asian competition sent gurus in English-speaking and many European contexts scurrying for solutions—the most popular being downsizing and organisational restructuring.[6] One consequence is a growing polarisation of Western workforces—a few highly paid jobs at the top, a large number of low-paying and insecure jobs at the bottom, and fewer jobs in between.[7] Universities in a number of countries, but particularly the United States, are like many other workplaces in polarising workers into haves and have-nots.[8] In the case of universities, this shows as an increasingly demonstrable basement and a smaller symbolic 'tower'.

How global economics and politics affect higher education in Australia is therefore an essential backdrop to our study. Both locally and globally, the university is having to redesign itself in institutional terms in order to find its niche in a new stage of human development. The change taking place is not simply at the institutional level—with new systems of meaning defining the university's role in the wider community—but at the level of the university as *organisation*.

Globalisation

Perhaps most worrying about the shift to globalising economies is the danger that growing inequities can appear inevitable to governments, voters and corporate managers alike. Whether the effects are lost jobs, destroyed cultures or damaged environments, political and business leaders around the globe talk of 'managing' sweeping change rather than attempting to challenge the neo-liberal economic practices and ideals that drive it.[9] Local protests and global demonstrations seem to have missed the critical moment to suggest radical change.

Yet, while élites accept globalisation and even distant shows of force, activists in a variety of movements take to the streets to express dissent. The evolving radical views can, therefore, be pro-global or anti-global. What is clearly evident is that corporate and political élites tend to place a positive spin on globalising economies and their militaristic imperatives, while the left lines up with the growing numbers of families, church groups, activists and movements that are increasingly critical—and political. Proponents of globalisation lean toward a unified view: economic and technological developments have furnished a world of increasing interconnectedness, in which nation-state boundaries are deemed largely irrelevant. They couple this with claims that global markets bring international equality and that the rise of 'global culture' means that all local cultures must grapple with multiculturalism on an equal basis. They highlight diversification of tasks and services, cheaper consumer goods, the flexibility of occupational mobility, the joys of life-long learning, the relaxing of cultural, economic and political barriers. Critics of globalisation are diverse in the features they challenge. Currie et al., for example, emphasise a significant erosion of national, political and economic autonomy. They list three crucial features of globalisation: (a) removal of barriers to free trade coupled with deregulated banking; (b) increasing power of transnational corporations, able to locate their production plants wherever they can gain the cheapest labour and the best governmental support; and (c) dissolution of national cultures and national economies.[10] Connell exemplifies a second group of critics, who wish to puncture the hype over globalisation. He argues that globalisation is the 'panic factor' through which 'the market agenda has gained its stranglehold on politics', and suggests that the 'hype and loose talk has created some strikingly false impressions'. Connell looks to history and to recent sociology to set the record straight. He challenges claims that globalisation 'is something radically new...has already integrated local economies into a monster world economy...(and) has necessarily overwhelmed the state, and local, national and regional social forces'.[11]

While many social scientists agree with Connell that governments are over-reacting to the threat and/or promise of globalisation,[12] such awareness does little to allay their growing concerns about the damage and dangers of a concentration of power in the hands of a few. The headquarters of the huge multinational corporations, along with the centres of finance, are in a handful of cities—New York, Tokyo, London, Paris and Munich. This concentration of economic power has been part of the historical advance of capitalism, but it has grown apace since World War II. With the exception of the United States, which was the outright economic winner of that cataclysmic war, the political structures of earlier imperialism were dismantled in the second half of the twentieth century.[13] In their place we have what sociologists and historians call 'neo-imperialism'—a global set of economic institutions which frame the policies of individual governments.[14]

The economic and technological forces propelling national economies into one global marketplace bring governments increasingly under the influence of international monetary and regulatory agencies. Such institutions as the World Bank, World Trade Organisation and International Monetary Fund apply pressure on national governments to 'conform to the economic orthodoxies of small public-sector expenditure, balanced budgets and production for export rather than domestic demand'.[15]

The General Agreement on Tariffs and Trade (GATT), which operated until 1994, proved inadequate to eliminate government restrictions on labour conditions and tariffs. By contrast, continuing criticisms and mass demonstrations against its replacement body, the World Trade Organization arise from its rapid success in achieving neo-liberal goals. Consequences of that success are unsafe and substandard working conditions for workers in many countries, coupled with wide-ranging environmental damage and the destruction of local cultures, industries and workplaces.[16]

Changing work practices accompany globalisation, but the costs and benefits are unevenly spread. The great losers, caught in the processes of those challenging globalisation, are the poorer nations, with transnational corporations exploiting their economies and labour markets. Those same free market policies have also forced the demise of earlier manufacturing industries in the OECD countries, and raised the question of where stable jobs will come from. For countries such as Australia, one answer has been to increase access to, and performance of, higher education, with the goal of replacing subsidised manufacturing with high technology and innovative research and development. Marceau argues that taking that OECD route 'maximises higher-skilled, higher-paid employment and improved living standards'.[17]

The shift to knowledge- or innovation-intensive economies, emerging in most OECD countries, grows out of a consequent jockeying for competitive advantage in global markets. Universities lie at the centre of this shift in knowledge production. Paradoxically, their status as élite producers of valued knowledge is simultaneously being eroded.[18] Universities are caught in the paradox that global changes requiring them to show strong growth are simultaneously weakening them and suggesting irrelevance.

The global knowledge economy

A number of research projects have clearly shown the negative effects of globalisation on universities. In examining changes to higher education in Britain, the United States, Canada and Australia, Slaughter and Leslie note a drift in all four countries 'towards national "wealth creation" rather than a traditional concern with the liberal education of undergraduates'.[19] Similarly, critics write of 'the new knowledge industry' in which knowledge is corporatised, privatised and commodified.[20]

Yet higher education is not simply a *casualty* of globalisation. Higher education is also an architect of the technological and research expertise that marks the globalised production of knowledge. The expansion of post-secondary education has helped to lay the groundwork for the diffusion of scientific, technical and research competencies throughout Western societies. University-generated knowledge has underpinned the drive for more initiative and innovation,[21] and created a mounting market for new cultural products.[22] Questions of economic and political power are just as crucial. As Connell remarks, 'In a knowledge-based economy, knowledge is a crucially important resource, and distortions of knowledge are a crucially important tool of social control'.[23]

The rise of a global knowledge economy heralds the emergence of a new international division of intellectual labour. For Gibbons et al., that division, and the growing inequalities of wealth it sustains, hinges on whether knowledge production continues to rely on a traditional, disciplinary, 'scientific' mode—or whether it deploys transdisciplinary, applied and problem-solving techniques. They coin the terms 'mode one' and 'mode two' to heuristically distinguish those two forms of knowledge production. Moreover, they predict that the world is witnessing a transformation to mode two, which has developed out of new technologies, rapidly increasing cultural products (such as art, music, books) and globalising economies. In mode two the quality review system has a broader social and economic composition, leading to fears of lower academic standards. Economically advanced countries are now using mode two knowledge production to their advantage in the global marketplace, and this, they argue, is further entrenching inequality of wealth distribution.[24]

The combination of technological success and global diffusion of knowledge production has created a rapidly growing market for higher education, although funding has by no means increased accordingly. The management, direction and worth of university-based research is also being reshaped—to its detriment, many argue.[25] 'The process of globalisation', according to Mackinnon and Brooks, 'has fundamentally undermined the traditional position of universities as the primary sites of knowledge production'.[26] The harmful effects of marketising core research are felt throughout the sector. For Gibbons et al., it is clear that to 'a noticeable extent university-based research is threatened by the encroachment of industry and the profit-making mentality'.[27] Such criticisms fall on deaf ears. As Brett notes, 'traditional arguments are proving weak in the face of zealous reformers convinced that increased competition will lead to enhanced performance'.[28]

Gibbons et al. use the term 'massification of education' to capture the shift in higher education since World War II that has resulted in increased student numbers, relatively fewer staff and decreased status for traditional academic values. Contributing forces include the democratisation of politics and society; the growth of new welfare states needing a larger educated class to staff a growing public sector; and industrial economies deploying increasing numbers of highly skilled and educated employees. Subject to these forces, the 'massification of education' is 'now a strongly entrenched phenomenon, it is international in scope and is unlikely to ever be reversed'.[29] Caught in this whirlpool of change, universities have lost their earlier image—that calm assurance of their worth and work as a public good—of being quiet places for thought.

The university is both beneficiary and loser in the 'massification' of education. On the one hand it has experienced considerable growth, as the numbers of graduates flowing out of higher education continue to increase. On the other, these graduates are potential knowledge producers. The many who apply their skills in the knowledge industry now pursue their craft 'not only in universities but also in industry and government laboratories, in think-tanks, research institutions, consultancies etc.' As a result, 'universities are coming to recognise that they are now only one type of player, albeit still a major one, in a vastly expanded knowledge production process'.[30] The loss of their élite status means that universities are no longer the sole determinants of what counts as excellence in research.

According to Gibbons et al., university managements have not fully grasped the implications of mass higher education. Many fail to see that 'to the extent that universities continue to produce quality graduates, they undermine their monopoly as knowledge producers'.[31] Now that their quantum additions to knowledge may no longer be so outstanding, universities need to re-examine themselves and their role in knowledge production and to develop a new self-image and justification. In line with the new form of knowledge production, traditional demarcation lines between academic life and corporate life are breaking down. Universities are pressured to adopt corporate values, to encourage the careers of new, entrepreneurial academics, and to abandon their tradition of collegial consensus in favour of new 'tough' strategic planning and career management.[32]

Above all, the changes demand new and complex forms of management. Brooks claims that 'the management of change and the emergence of new work environments' are central to 'the process of globalization and the framing of a global knowledge economy'.[33] Division between academics and management is increasing, with administration redesigned along 'sleeker corporate lines'.[34] Moreover, as Karmel suggests, universities 'have been encouraged to adopt modern management techniques, such as strategic planning, the development of research management plans, and equity programs'.[35]

Most worthy of note in terms of management practice is the relationship between central control and individual response. Whether the unit of analysis is the relationship between university and government or that between university employees and their administration, a complicated process of self-management is brought into play. For Blackmore and Sachs, self-management is 'a process by which academics internalize organizational and system-wide objectives through the work practices of self-managing institutions'.[36] These insights on managing change, managing identities and image management make a significant contribution to the debates over universities in globalising economies. However, they leave us with unanswered questions. Can 'self-management' be used to provide a better understanding of the ways all university employees, not simply academics, cope with their changing work environments? Can the concept cope with questions of agency and collective action? Do answers to those questions suggest a new niche for the university? Can university work still command respect and a unique place within accounts of the economy of knowledge production? Such questions of subjectivity, place and image are central to this book.

The Australian context

The 'massification' of higher education has been as dramatic in Australia as in other OECD countries. In 1972 the federal government took over from the Australian states the responsibility for funding and managing higher education. Karmel writes that in 1987, when university students numbered 78,000, the Dawkins Green Paper suggested a target of 125,000 students by 2001.[37] Subsequently, in 1988, the government created the Unified National System (UNS) of higher education. The UNS replaced the binary divide through which universities (which were funded for research purposes) were distinguished in funding and status from technology institutes and colleges of advanced education.[38] Equity of resources for higher education institutions was an expressed goal of these changes, along with access to university education for all Australians. Equity goals would be accomplished within 'an environment of productive competition'.[39] In the event, student growth has surpassed the wildest expectations of those 1980s policymakers. In the 1950s there were less than 40,000 students in Australian universities; by 2001 enrolments had grown to 600,000.[40] According to Karmel, Australian 'participation in higher education has risen to the point where close to half the population may be expected to become involved at some stage of their lives'.[41]

Resources for knowledge production is the key marker of inequity, and the Relative Funding Model (RFM) introduced by the federal government in 1990, has tended to entrench the resourcing inequalities that existed between institutions prior to the UNS. As Currie et al. note:

> Research allocations have consistently favoured the older established universities with greater financial reserves and longer research traditions. Indeed the idea behind the reforms is that the already strong should be rewarded, ensuring that 'research funds go to those best able to make effective use of them'.[42]

In similar vein, Marginson outlines how disciplinary inequalities and a lack of awareness of what is needed to develop new knowledge are perpetuated under the RFM:

> Because of resource concentration it is difficult for new areas of strength to even begin to develop, while within established fields, tried and tested ways are retained at the expense of new ones, and new researchers are dependent on the sponsorship of chief investigators to an unhealthy extent.[43]

Despite the huge leap in student numbers, equity of access has also suffered with the development of a user-pays philosophy. After fourteen years of free higher education, a short-lived policy of up-front payment accompanied the imposition of fees in 1987. Two years later the Labor government introduced the Higher Education Contribution Scheme (HECS) through which deferred fees could be paid through the tax system. The conservative Coalition government has since further privatised the system. This has been done by lowering the income threshold at which loan repayments commence; by introducing fee increases within a three-tier system of cost-recovery; by tightening income tests for student support schemes; by permitting universities to charge full-cost fees to overseas students; and by allowing universities to enrol a tightly regulated proportion of full-fee paying Australian students.[44] In 1996 the proportion of students unable to obtain government support was 61.9 per cent, almost double the figure for 1984.[45] Moreover, by world standards the

35–40 per cent of operating costs that are left to students to cover is 'a relatively high proportion for people attending publicly supported institutions'.[46] Equity may be failing, but government measures of productivity show considerable gains. In 1975–76 government spending on higher education as a proportion of gross domestic product was 1.5 per cent. Since then, there has been a steady decline to 1 per cent.[47] Governments have increasingly offloaded taxpayers' responsibility for higher education onto business and other sources. In 1981 universities obtained 90 per cent of their funding from government sources; by 2001 that proportion had dropped to 55 per cent.[48] According to Karmel, between 1997 and 2000 the Commonwealth government cut higher education spending by 6 per cent, leaving universities to face a gap in their budgets of 'around 13–15 per cent'. Staff numbers, which have been significantly reduced, have borne the brunt of the funding gap. From 1988 to 1996 student load increased by 49 per cent, but academic and general staff numbers increased by only 26 per cent, giving an increase in productivity of 18.5 per cent.[49]

The growing complexity of the permissible fee structure is one way in which the paradox of a 'self-managed' university system plays itself out. Talk of unfettered markets and freedom of choice provide the rationale for neo-liberal reforms. In a critique which indicates the falsity of that narrative of freedom, Harris identifies three forms of interlocking control to which Australian university staff and students have been subjected.[50] The first, she suggests, uses an appeal to self-interest, through incentive/penalty schemes. The second applies highly detailed forms of surveillance and assessment, such as HECS and the Relative Funding Model, to individuals and institutions alike. The third uses coercion, in the form of job losses, funding cutbacks, forced amalgamations and programme closures. Each practice is set within a narrative of 'personal choice', an effective camouflage for a carefully manipulated system of command and control. After outlining those interlocking control mechanisms, Harris and her co-researchers comment on the difficulty of contesting them: 'The intersecting and obfuscating nature of these claims makes the composite whole hard to challenge, the more so as they engender a climate of divide and rule and personal alienation'.[51] Similarly,

Marginson notes that 'one of the means whereby the underlying tensions are kept implicit' is through 'the ubiquitous use of competition as an organising device'.[52]

The problem for Australia, according to Marceau, is that the direction in which federal policy is pushing higher education—into block grants for research funds for example—is exactly the opposite from where we need to go. In part, the problem stems from Australia's history of industrial development, since a 'low technology industrial structure inherited from the past...discourages business investment in research and development'. Whereas many others are arguing that Australian universities, and those who work within them, are stretched beyond their limits, Marceau wants to see more output, at least in terms of research. 'More not less knowledge is needed', she claims. She goes on to argue that the organisation of teaching and research 'no longer go well together', and that Australian universities should move to an open, organisational schema of ever-flexible global networks, built upon the practices of international collegiality already usual for academic researchers.[53]

I would argue that in many ways Marceau's model of ever-changing networks describes a system of organised labour which already exists on university campuses, not simply in research complexes. It has long been acknowledged that universities are structured along the lines of a 'loosely coupled' system of administration, as described by Weick.[54] In calling for universities to face up to the challenge of creating, nurturing and developing 'flexible networks', Marceau fails to see that the fluid networks she notices in international and national research are also at work in teaching and administrative practices, albeit more localised, particularly at the lower levels. It could well be that in fixing her sights on the ivory tower, Marceau misses what goes on in the basement.

Focusing the micro lens

Australian higher education includes a group of six so-called sandstone universities. They gained that title because, as the first universities founded in their respective states, their oldest buildings are of hand-quarried stone.[55] The prestige of tradition envelops those sandstones, but they can also be viewed as élitist, with entrenched hierarchies. Another form of higher education prestige is bestowed through the criterion of research intensity, with inclusion in the Group of Eight being the definitive badge of success.[56] The fact that the subject of this book—The University of Western Australia (UWA)—qualifies for the select group of five that belong to both prestigious groups can be a source of pride to those who manage it, and a means of retaining relative power and privilege.

A medium-sized university, employing around 1000 academic and 1500 general staff, UWA has a robust tradition of academic excellence, linked with a strong focus on science, technology and the (male dominated) professions. It is noted for an ability to attract high-achieving school leavers, gaining more than 70 per cent of the first preferences of Western Australia's prospective undergraduates. For many years UWA enjoyed a reputation as one of the wealthiest universities in Australia, although recent stock-market downturns may have affected that position. Nonetheless, most of its 16,000 students[57] live within 5 kilometres of the expensive riverside suburb in which its 65 hectare main campus is situated. Given its favoured history, the university's longstanding reputation for élitism is perhaps not surprising.

The University of Western Australia is no exception to the 'loosely coupled' organisational system through which universities have traditionally been administered.[58] UWA has a governing body, the Senate, composed of representatives of the community nominated by the state government, the graduate body (Convocation) and the staff. In 1999 the chief executive officer—the Vice-Chancellor—took on the dual title of President, while the Deputy Vice-Chancellor gained the extra title of Provost. At the same time, a multi-million dollar deal with Motorola was signed, which has since delivered a multi-storey enterprise to the campus, linked to UWA research and teaching. The additional titles signalled that UWA was moving closer to the system of administration favoured in the United States, in which the President provides 'big picture' leadership while the Provost shapes the internal direction of the institution. A Registrar and a Finance and Resources Vice-Principal head the general staff, and hold responsibility for all administrative matters. In 1999, when our study began, men filled all those senior roles, although the institution was led by a woman vice-chancellor between 1990 and 1997.

UWA was a collection of many diverse departments in 1999, each with its own one-line budget. They were grouped into six faculties (divisions), each headed by an executive Dean. All but one of the deans were men. Faculties showed varying degrees of agreement and compliance with the vision and direction of 'the centre'—the Vice-Chancellery. The devolution into divisions under a 'lean' central management had occurred in the early 1990s. By 2002 a three-year restructuring process had dismantled the departmental system, along with their one-line budgets, and had relocated teaching into 'programme groups' located in nine faculties comprising thirty-one schools.[59] Funds for teaching, research and administrative support are now distributed at school level, led by a Head of School appointed from among the academics. The majority of school heads are men. At the same time, a new level of administrative management has been installed, with the title of School Manager, who holds responsibility for overseeing the administrative staff of each school. Women comprise almost half of these new general staff positions.

Despite the restructuring, the administrative form is still largely that noted by Crawford in the late 1980s: 'Decision-making at UWA is a complex process based on a committee system'.[60] An Academic Board with a large and unwieldy membership of professors and elected representatives is nominally responsible for all final decisions on teaching and research matters. Coupled to that is an Academic Council, with a membership of twenty, which meets more often than Academic Board and makes interim decisions. Numerous committees deal with university-wide issues of finances, utilities, promotion, teaching and learning, research funding, travel guidelines, equity etc., although some streamlining of these has occurred during the most recent restructure. Many of those committees are duplicated at the school level, thus stretching still further the degree of administrative service that academics and general staff above a certain level are expected to maintain.

The paradox of decision-making within universities, spelt out in this book through stories at UWA, is that administrative committees contribute only half the story. Collaborators in their local settings are still primary instigators of cultural conformity or innovation. They are not simply followers of senior management directives. Whether in departments or programmes, academics in particular often see themselves in opposition to 'central control' or 'central interference'. And that can mean their own senior administration, or the directives that come from governments through ministries of higher education and their administrative agencies.

UWA is not alone in having academics who are notably resistant to top-down management. Marginson describes research management as a process of 'flying the butterflies in formation'.[61] Those in the basement talk of 'herding cats'. Our UWA data show disciplinary groups of scholars, each seen as experts in a discrete field, doing their own thing. When our study began, departments had considerable autonomy over their research, teaching and finances. In the newly formed schools, systems being developed may dispel some of that diversity.

UWA's schools and programme groups also demonstrate other features of the paradoxical system of university governance. Research is accorded more promotional and selection weight than teaching, yet structural descriptions are oriented around undergraduate teaching. Deference is paid to decisions on teaching and research by Academic Board or Council, while grading decisions are left to individuals at the periphery unless they are contested. The major portion of funds is allocated through a centrally determined formula, but one-line budgets convey considerable autonomy. Above all, a clear status division into 'academic' and 'general' staff, and a gendering of that division, cuts across the whole hierarchical ordering.

In Australian universities, 'general' staff means all those who do not qualify as academics. Academics are mostly those who both teach and do research, although top-level administrators such as vice-chancellors and their deputies are included, as are research-only staff at senior levels, as well as casual tutors who are not expected to do research as part of their duties (although many are also research students whose research output is credited to their school). The 'general' staff category covers a wide spectrum—from registrar and resource management to front-office receptionists, secretaries, security, maintenance, library and legal staff—but it also includes lower-level research assistants. The gender division operates both horizontally and vertically, with more women at the lower levels and on the general staff, while most men are found in the higher levels and among academic staff. Even within the academic category, however, gender patterns are shifting, with women now holding a majority of positions among research-only middle-level staff, often in insecure and contract jobs. Since ethnicity, sexuality and disability intersect those gender patterns, our study found that gender differences and commonalities varied according to the time, issue, level and space we scrutinised.

As most ivory tower initiatives have outcomes determined by the local structuring and relational work of the basement, an ethnographic study focusing on the basement is more likely to overcome the contradictions generated by equating university and ivory tower. This book will take a critical but optimistic look at how people within the basement manage instability and change. In so doing they shape the identities of both their institution and themselves. This focus on the ivory basement, by contrast with Marceau's on the ivory tower,[62] reveals that collaborative internal networks are an indispensable part of everyday university activity.

CHAPTER 2

The Search for Answers

A century ago, Sigmund Freud posed a question that was supposed to
have puzzled generations of men and which, in any case, rehearsed
the now controversial view that women and men were fundamentally different. He asked, 'What do women *want?*' The women we
interviewed produced some significant and revealing answers: to
be equally valued and fairly rewarded for all facets of their work,
to have time to balance their lives, and to feel they did not have to
continually prove their worth.

To assume that those answers have no relevance for men,
or to Australian universities and workplaces more broadly, is to be
blind to the realities of the twenty-first century. In 1998 the World
Bank identified personal depression as the second greatest global
problem, which the world must face.[1] Youth suicide is just one facet
of the hidden social costs of inequalities in working lives. Longer
and harder work for those who have jobs, and growing numbers of
unemployed, are coupled in Australia with soaring divorce and crime
statistics and a declining birth rate. Those inequalities are shaped and
reflected through gender relations and underpinned by the persistent
maldistribution of caring labour. As Pocock's comprehensive study

reveals, the strains and costs of that maldistribution are seen in workplaces, bedrooms, kitchens and streetscapes. She concludes, 'Our institutions and cultures lag behind the changes in our lives'.[2]

Some would like to turn back the clock. Yet to tell women to return to kitchen and nursery is to misrepresent a much larger problem. Indeed, that solution reproduces the problem. It nurtures old myths about women as the source of social ills, and deflects attention from the outcomes of decisions, made in the halls of transnational and governmental institutions, that are based on economic and political greed. As Pannikar notes, misconceived deflection of focus is 'like looking for darkness with a torch'.[3]

Theories can allow us to 'see' what, like darkness at night, may be under our noses all the time. As carefully crafted tools of analysis, theories can help us frame our questions and make sense of the answers in ways that 'reveal the hidden assumptions which pervade the taken-for-granted web of social reality'.[4]

Social reality is never fixed but is continually constructed through systems of meaning, embodied in institutions such as family and work, and in the rules and sets of practices that organise our workplaces and households. A key tool of analysis used in this book is the theory of gendered organisations.

Gendered universities

To demonstrate how an organisation can be gendered, feminist organisational theorists turned to a politics of the body. Work by Acker[5] and Hearn and Parkin[6] has been particularly influential here, in showing how a type of embodiment associated with the male body is taken as the standard for measuring suitability and potential for success. In the words of Acker, 'it is the man's body, its sexuality, minimal responsibility in procreation and conventional control of emotions that pervades work and work organizations'.[7]

This book shows how the gendered university is shaped by a set of assumptions—constructed by and for men—about the necessary attributes of an academic career. Two examples are the belief that academic success means giving total priority to one's work, and the assumption that the best scientists are competitive and assertive, with curiosity and persistence taking second place. Such beliefs and assumptions are bundled together in an image of the ideal academic:

> the academy is anchored in assumptions about competence and success that have led to practices and norms constructed around the life experiences of men, and around a vision of masculinity as the normal, universal requirement of university life.[8]

To give clarity to a view of how the university is gendered, one needs a 'gender lens'.[9] A gender lens can show not only the masculine values underpinning the institution, but also the feminisation of ivory basement work that keeps the hierarchy of tower and basement in place. A fresh Australian government report shows the continuing strength of that gendered hierarchy: 'women remain concentrated at the bottom of the academic hierarchy, while men still account for more than 80 per cent of the most senior academics in Australian universities'.[10] As this book indicates, the gendered university is shaped through the assumption that the relational and emotional labour of women requires no reward or recognition; through the separation of work and family responsibilities into home lives and work lives; through the ways we view, enact and reward different forms of leadership; through assumptions about what is valuable, practical and normal underpinning our employment and promotions policies; and through entrenched masculinist norms and allegiances of the 'men's club'. All of these can shape patterns of inclusion and exclusion, and set in train access to and separation from both key information and decision-making.

Doing gender in the workplace[11]

A persistent problem for those who use a gender analysis are the widespread misconceptions that surround the use of the term itself. If we examine many of our equity policies, for example, we will see that they treat gender as something people *have* rather than something people *do*—in interactions with others, and in the rules and sets of practices we apply to our lives. The idea of 'critical mass', for example, assumes that getting more women into powerful and status positions will provide the answer to gender inequality.[12] Gender is not simply an attribute of persons and things. It is embedded in power relations, operates through our enculturated perceptions of self and others, and is created and modified through everyday interactions.[13] That understanding led feminists to focus on the practices that 'do' gender so as to highlight gender as a process and as an outcome.

Important for my analysis of the gendered university is the idea of the workplace as a context-specific site for 'doing gender'. For West and Zimmerman it was possible to 'do gender' without necessarily living up to 'normative conceptions of femininity and masculinity', yet one's gender performance will nonetheless be viewed and measured against an expectation of normative standards.[14] In similar vein, Fenstermaker and West argue that gender is an accomplishment, an unavoidable performance that is enacted within diverse contexts by actors who do not necessarily follow the normative script.[15] An example is the woman leader whose assertiveness is seen as unnecessary aggression. In performing the masculine ideal of the forceful managerial body, she is judged as the 'ball-breaker' who fails to perform her assigned feminine gender. As Pringle writes, 'women who have a strong desire to attain an integrated sense of self in masculine workplaces face these contradictions and must "manage their gender"'.[16]

Gender is *done* not only through socialisation within families, schools and the like. It continues across the life-course, particularly through the systems of meaning applied to work and organisational practices. In examining how language, talk, social interactions, reward systems and the allocation of jobs do gender, the analytical frame used in this book is concerned with power relations and meaning systems.

Power, micropolitics, relational work

As the current frenzy of restructuring envelopes our workplaces, feminist-inspired theorists have turned their attention to the question of how change is embodied. A diffused view of power is essential to an understanding of embodied subjects. Individuals can experience themselves as powerful in one context and powerless in another. Power is exercised rather than possessed, by individuals over others as well as on themselves.[17] Morley reminds us that 'the exercising of power in organisations can be overt and identifiable, but also subtle, complex and confusing'.[18] As power is structured through how we respond to others, it can seem as if no power is used at all. A feminist analysis of the micropolitics of organisations can bring to light the distorting and invisible effects of power, and show how power is relayed through seemingly trivial incidents and encounters. Morley writes:

> Micropolitics is about influence, networks, coalitions, political and personal strategies to effect or resist change.
> It involves rumour, gossip, sarcasm, humour, denial, 'throwaway remarks', alliance building.[19]

Above all, the micropolitics of organisations is about processes rather than structures. I take a process view of the ivory basement metaphor, and focus on how the gendered hierarchy of tower and basement is made to appear immutable, and on the energy and resources that keep up that appearance. A process view of change brings to the surface 'subterranean conflicts and differences which are otherwise glossed over in daily routines'.[20]

This understanding of power links an account of the micro-politics of organisational life to the concept of 'relational work' or 'relational intelligence' developed by Fletcher.[21] Her analysis of how organisational norms 'disappear' relational intelligence proved a useful tool for explaining the hidden nature of ivory basement work. In particular, Fletcher investigates how women's pursuit of relational behaviour is prompted by the wish to transform their organisations and work relationships. My study does add a dimension that is at best implicit in Fletcher's. It suggests that the subjectivities of people who practise relational work are shaped by those practices, as they strive for gendered identities that may be based on *concealing* or *downplaying* their transformative actions.

Organising, diversity and identity groups

Entrepreneurialism, branding strategies and new forms of management are the business-like face of today's 'new' system of higher education. And though university employees might voice their complaints in private, they have generally kept their heads down. Compliance occurs both in the name of academic objectivity and because they are too strapped for time to stop and organise. For academics, an ethic of individual scholarship and independent research has invariably swamped the call for active participation in organised labour. In Australia, for example, the industrial relations system has delivered nationally uniform conditions of employment, to unionised and non-unionised staff alike.[22] General (or support) staff are difficult for labour unions to recruit, since their workplace presence is low-status, often transitory, in many cases ephemeral. Managerial levels, too, are rarely conducive to unionisation. Fear that dissidents are more likely to be targeted for downsizing is a further disincentive to highly visible resistance.[23] Undoubtedly, the sense that no one outside the academy appears to be listening is also disabling and dispiriting.

A significant exception to the academic tradition of avoiding collective action is the feminist claim for equality of conditions and voice. Through their writing and their organising, academic women gave strong support to the second wave women's movement, at its height in the 1970s and 1980s.[24] For a time the movement flourished and fed women's studies courses and departments, equal opportunity policies, women's caucuses at disciplinary conferences, and national and international networks of feminist scholars. Although street marches and sit-ins have dwindled, the quest for gender equity remains, now channelled into academic feminism.[25] Academic feminism has been challenged by concern to accommodate within an understanding of gendered power the wide range of identity groups also seeking an equity voice on race, ethnicity, sexual preference, disability, age and Aboriginality. As with gender, these 'all raise issues that have not been well handled in existing organisation...or industrial relations...theory'.[26]

During the 1990s the Australian public sector followed the example set by North American countries and shifted its discourse of equity to one of workforce diversity. Like their counterparts in the United States and Canada, Australian feminists and many equity practitioners were sceptical of how the diversity movement was being translated into a 'managing diversity' frame.[27] Critics point to a lack of rigour in how diversity management is often used, yet the term has many and highly contested meanings.[28] Practical and research examples show it can be utilised both as a smokescreen for managerial lip service and as a way of making stable equity advances—with similar conflicts and contradictions to those encountered by its predecessor, the 'target groups' of equal opportunity and affirmative action.[29]

Challenges to the exercise of power through relations of gender and diversity are risky. In organisations generally, and in universities in particular, such challenges are met with varying degrees of hostility and suspicion. Academia has valued its image as a non-political arbiter. And as Oakley reminds us, 'It has never been possible to speak about women or gender in ways that are *non*-political; some social constructs are indissolubly *about* power'.[30]

Culture

The concept of organisational culture used in this book can be captured by the phrase 'That's how we do things round here'. When people use that familiar phrase they are not only repeating a narrative about the culture they work within, they are also reaffirming that specific practices and values are unremarkably 'normal'. Gherardi opts for an interpretative view of organisational culture, as 'the taken-for-granted and problematic webs of meaning that people produce and deploy when they interact'.[31] She goes on to suggest why she prefers her definition:

[It allows for] Non-material things like values (what people think)...such concrete things as what people say when they meet, but also something so banal as appearance (sex, I would add) and the symbolic message it transmits (the social construction of gender).[32]

To view culture as a 'thing' is to misapprehend its nature. Bacchi makes the point succinctly: 'cultures do not spring ready-made from above; people make culture'.[33] In a university we 'make' culture in myriad ways: our procedures and criteria for promotion, graduation ceremonies, the technologies we employ, the facilities we provide for staff training, and so on. But universities also make culture through everyday practices such as who eats lunch at the keyboard or joins 'the boys' at the staff club; through the jargon, lifestyles and appearances staff and students favour and reward, the rituals and attendance patterns of staff meetings, the meanings we make of our decision-making processes; and through the time teachers provide for students in lectures, tutorials and one-to-ones. Changing any one of those practices involves cultural change, but it may be limited, unseen and with no guaranteed permanence.

Importantly, this analysis seeks to avoid an understanding of organisations as having a unified or single culture. This is particularly important with respect to universities, which are widely regarded as being 'loosely coupled' organisational systems in which different cultural, disciplinary and identity group formations vie with each other for recognition and resources.[34] In fact, this book envisages culture, like gender, as something that individuals and organisations *do*, rather than as something they *have*.[35]

Leadership

Changing entrenched ways of doing things entails a continuing process of renewal and recommitment, operating in many different forms.[36] When the goal is gender equity, it demands what Dahlerup calls 'critical acts' of leadership.[37] These include the acts of leaders in senior positions, such as how much support women and gender issues receive from them. For Dahlerup, critical acts also include whether women are able to support each other and recruit other women to share and analyse experiences; how they develop a language to name the problems they face; and how effectively they network, lobby and intervene as a group.

The range of critical acts widens when applied to the inhabitants of the ivory basement. Women and men may provide information and support each other, sometimes across the horizontal and vertical demarcations of tower and basement, in order to combat discriminatory or inequitable practices. They may extend a helping or welcoming hand to new or stressed students or staff, find a solution to conflicts or dissidence in their work areas, be the anchor or 'glue' for research or teaching teams, take the brunt of initiatives to market new teaching and research programmes to prospective students and collaborators, or provide the relational 'glue' to repair the fragmentation and loss of high-speed organisational networks after radical restructuring.[38]

To the extent that such actions generate cohesion, conviviality and a sense of comradely endeavour, they are examples of the 'relational work' conceptualised by Fletcher.[39] To the extent that the protagonist performs them with the intent of 'making a difference' to their group or workspace, they are examples of 'everyday leadership'.[40]

This study was particularly concerned with how *women* managed the conflicting demands of competition and co-operation, alongside the pressure to act effectively and independently. An act, such as sending a letter of complaint to the dean, might be self-consciously intended to change a decision—and so be an example of everyday leadership. Or it might simply be a show of solidarity with the woman in the adjoining department—and so be a friendly gesture. Yet in the micropolitics of the gendered university, that act is likely to be read either as a woman complaining about nothing or as a woman doing what women are supposed to do: offer support to others. Each of those characterisations of the situation is producing an account of embodied feminisation, but in different ways. Contradiction and ambivalence, therefore, accompany women's experiences of leadership.

Meyerson and Scully's 'tempered radical'[41] is an employee who loyally works within and for her organisation, but also wishes to transform it. There is no doubt they see their tempered radical as an everyday sort of leader, one whose identity is never constant but is formed through shifting sands of ambivalence and marginality. One problem with their account, at least for the purposes of my analysis, is that it deals purely with an individual's change endeavours, linked to an assumption of unitary purpose. Chapter Three deals with that concern by examining collective actions for change in a range of formal and informal group formations.

The message of these studies of organisational reshaping, and indeed the position of most researchers in the field, is that leadership (however defined) is vital to cultural change. However, the behaviours we characterise and value *as* 'leadership' are themselves cultural norms and practices embedded in the exercising of power. In short, the meanings our actions and languages give to both leadership and culture are highly significant. When someone says 'we shared the leadership role' or 'that group organised ways to manage up', s/he is both making a statement about the diversity of leadership and engaging in the gendered micropolitics of conflicts, tensions and power imbalances that shape our everyday lives.

CHAPTER 3

Leading in the Basement

There is something about visibility and invisibility for women leaders. One of the most important qualities of leadership is path breaking—like you are actually creating a new way of being and doing things. But it is invisible.
a female administrative staff member

Unlike the leadership characteristic of the individualised and prestigious decision-maker, 'companionate' leadership focuses on the everyday acts through which people manage changing work practices, take risks to initiate change, and set the pace in reshaping their workplace and work identities. Companionate leadership emerges from collaborative networks. In our study, it was invariably prompted by concerns that certain practices were unfair or exclusionary, whether intentionally or not. Some collaborations focused on changes in higher education; others targeted longstanding forms of marginalisation.

Companionate leadership as practised in the ivory basement is rarely viewed as leadership, partly because it is collaborative, partly because it has gendered associations with the domesticated capacities expected of women, and partly because some of it is hidden. The effort expended is largely invisible, receiving only limited recognition and support. And some of those who practise it prefer that the time and effort they put into it be shrouded from view. They see their companionate practice as something they can manage and control *because* it is largely unseen.

Thus gender, power and pressures for new forms of organisational identity collide around this issue of invisibility, making it difficult to notice how such behaviour provides an important model for achieving core equity goals. The tools that bear on the idea of companionate leadership include the concept of self-management and the idea of relational work, as well as attempts to move to a post-heroic understanding of leadership.

Self-management and relationality

The self-managing university operates in the context of devolved responsibility in a competitive marketplace. Paradoxically, the setting of industry-wide priorities is outside its control.[1] Marginson calls this 'steering from a distance'.[2] Incentives for individualised contracts are linked to economic power located in hard-nosed directives issued from the centres of political governance, which in turn are subject to the forces of globalising economies.

A number of recent writers[3] have drawn on the work of earlier social theorists, from Rousseau to Foucault, to apply the concept of self-management both to universities and to those who work within them. They develop the position that as an organisation changes its direction and values, employees and managers must also change to accommodate its changing needs.[4] Self-management involves a relaxing of direct forms of surveillance and control, coupled with increased requirements for accountability and performance. Contractual capacities, rights and obligations lie at the heart of this reshaped system of management, which Yeatman calls 'new contractualism'. For the university employee, self-discipline, self-government, self-assessment, self-protection and individualised personhood are the contractual rights and obligations replacing 'paternalistic principles of protection in the employment arena'.[5] As Blackmore and Sachs note, self-management is about 'managing within greater rather than less control over the key aspects of identity' as the 'commitment to vocation, to service and to knowledge production' is channelled towards 'national or organizational productivity'.[6]

Blackmore and Sachs add a relational dimension to this notion of individual subject formation in the concept of self-management. In their study of female academics across several Australian universities, they conclude that 'the (managed) self operates in relation to others...there is a collective projection of relationships in which the self is enmeshed: the self with respect to the other'. Their finding that women 'strategically position' themselves 'always in relation to others' for their 'personal, professional and often feminist political projects' frames a view of self as engaged in contesting the distorting effects of power.[7] This concept of self-management can be linked to a growing concern in feminist sociology: that while new forms of management seek to foster and exploit relational intelligence, that same relationality disappears as gender and power collide.

Relational work, in Fletcher's account of women engineers, is the invariably unrewarded work that is both essential to organisational life and is taken for granted to the point of being unseen. In Hochschild's earlier account, 'relational work' is downplayed in favour of the more targeted term 'emotional labour'. I shall build on the more generic 'relational work', since the behaviour we studied covers a wider spectrum than management of the emotional.

In Fletcher's analysis 'the basic tenet of relational theory (is that) growth and development require a context of connection'.[8] Importantly, she uses close observational method to show that when technical processes are always given priority as the essence of an organisation's functioning, the equally time-consuming and highly skilled communicational processes in relational work are treated as if they are an optional extra for a free moment. Her thesis is that relational practices at work are seen as natural outcomes—'what women do'—and are therefore not recognised as highly skilled.

In line with this work, I shall show that relational work is invisible because it is regarded as work that can be taken for granted. Fletcher shows how this happens within a system that devalues 'women's work'. By examining companionate leadership, I further show that women themselves manage the invisibility of their leadership.

The search for 'post-heroic' leadership

The conventional image of the heroic general leading his (sic) troops sits uneasily with many women and with increasing numbers of men. Spectacular corporate crashes, risky boardroom tactics and multi-million dollar handshakes to failed chief executives have tarnished respect for the executive machismo popularised in the early 1990s. As headlines trumpet fresh examples of corporate chicanery almost daily, books on 'post-heroic' leadership are jostling for a place on the shelves of organisational literature. In mapping this change, Bryman argues that we are witnessing a new research tradition. He sees an attempt to supersede the 'visionary hero' characteristic of the 1980s leadership literature, who neglected teamwork, sub-cultural activities and the micropolitics of organisations.[9]

Despite this growing literature, a more inclusive form of leadership may be far from the reality for many organisations. Several studies have looked for new forms of leadership and found them wanting, even missing. Sinclair, for example, found few of Australia's top corporate executives 'doing leadership differently',[10] while Fletcher argues that organisations in the United States find it hard to put the model of post-heroic leadership into practice.[11] In 1999 Blackmore examined Australian schooling systems and drew a similar conclusion.[12] Nonetheless, both Fletcher[13] and Blackmore[14] found significant networking, interdependent collaboration and shared leadership skills among women in professions and in middle levels of authority. The trouble is that such relational interactions are rarely recognised as leadership by those who hand out career rewards.[15] Nor are relational skills classified as core organisational competencies.

In the absence of inclusive models of leadership, feminists have responded by crafting their own definitions, based on their perceptions of (some) women's interactions as leaders. Invariably, these have highlighted collaboration, power-sharing and collective responsibility. In the United States, Astin and Leland, for example, interviewed three generations of women who saw themselves as feminist change agents, and developed a model of leadership for social change. Besides collaboration, empowerment and inclusivity, their feminist conceptual model stresses a passion for social justice and understands leadership as 'an action to make a positive difference to people's lives'.[16] In Australia, Blackmore similarly described leadership as 'to act with others to do things that could not be done by the individual alone'.[17]

At the time it was written, Blackmore's definition held a degree of promise for liberals who wished to generate more equitable practices in Australian universities. The politics of reshaping the tertiary education sector was gathering ground, with management practice and finance as key issues. In the race for survival in the market-driven system, new regulations and guidelines, including equal opportunity and affirmative action laws, propelled universities toward a two-pronged agenda. Primarily, it meant keeping abreast of the increasing competition that Canberra was encouraging. It also meant displaying signs of increasing quality,[18] including greater equity and diversity among students and staff and a broader, inclusive curriculum,[19] although these notions were often relegated to the status of afterthought.

In organisations generally, the demands of the information age and global economy brought a call for new models of leadership.[20] Some of these models reiterated feminist ideas that long-term effectiveness depends more on collaborative practices distributed throughout than on individual, heroic action focused at the top.[21]

The new models signalled three important challenges to the heroic paradigm.[22] For a start, they sought to undermine the myth of individual achievement, by identifying a vast network of support and collaboration. Secondly, by envisaging leadership as a collaborative, egalitarian process, they challenged the efficacy of old images of command and control. Lastly, by defining leadership as the capacity to create the conditions for continuous improvement and collective learning, they moved the skills base for senior leadership from technical expertise to what is commonly called emotional intelligence.[23] Fletcher's work indicates, however, that the notion of relational intelligence is more useful, since the emotional is generally thought of as something individuals *have* rather than *learn to do in alliance with others.*

Blackmore and Sachs caution against a 'discourse which "feminizes" change agency and people work, thus positioning women as middle managers where they can do the emotional management work of systems under stress' while leaving the 'dominant masculinist images' of leadership intact.[24] It is important to take note of such warnings, but they should not lead us to ignore or silence examples of relational work. The work of women in gendered workplaces has always been enacted through contradiction and ambivalence. When their relational work is driven through values of collegiality, a wider sense of the public good, and political resistance to their devalued position, it is in the interest of all to elaborate those contradictions.[25] I will suggest five categories of collaborative alliances, within each of which a specific model of change is assumed. All are reliant upon some aspect of co-operation or collaboration, and each incorporates what Fletcher identifies as relational work and reveals a shared sense of strategy based on collegial values.

The local context

More so than most men, women have a specific investment in changing the male-ordered culture of universities. Universities were formed by men, who kept women out for centuries.[26] For much of the twentieth century, the few women who gained access to the academic enclave were concerned to be treated as non-gendered people rather than as women.[27] With the large increase of women students from the early 1970s, and the influence of the reawakening women's movement, women staff began to realise the power of networking. They began to act collectively by consulting, persuading and influencing.[28]

The University of Western Australia was no exception. In the late 1980s Crawford and Tonkinson show that it was clear to many women staff that the recent introduction of equal opportunity laws had done little to improve their position. Women held only 15 per cent of academic posts in 1987, almost half of them as senior tutors and below.[29] Sex segregation of work was rife. Most women were employed as so-called non-academic staff, where they still earned less than their male counterparts. Women also obtained few promotional opportunities, although general staff women gained access to the same superannuation conditions as male general staff in 1983.[30]

It is indicative of the university's poor record on women that there were none in senior management and only two female professors in 1990. Between 1990 and 1997 the number of women professors jumped to sixteen, and five women took up positions in senior management.[31] In comparative terms, that increase was substantial. It owes much to the efforts of Vice-Chancellor Fay Gale and to the team she built around her, yet pressure for gender equity was coming from other quarters as well. The awareness generated by the equal opportunity movement, itself an outcome of the human rights movement that stemmed from the 1960s,[32] played a role in this, as did government regulations and the efforts of women in unions.[33]

Networking leadership

None of UWA's current self-organised women's groups existed before the era of equal opportunity in the 1980s.[34] Our study found that membership of those groups varies over time and in response to what is occurring in the university environment. Although most of the women's networks are not part of the formal university structure, the administration generally provides a small level of support by allowing the use of communication and meeting facilities, stationery and the like. It also funds what has become one of the major sources of women's networking, the Leadership Development for Women (LDW) programme. The women's groups provide an alternative to the informal male networks, most of which tend to gather at University House (the staff club).

The oldest and most proactive of the women-only groups is the Status of Women Group (SWG). Formed in 1983, SWG plays both a social and lobbying role, and is open to all women staff on campus as well as to women postgraduate students.[35] From the outset, its formation was significant in providing women with a safe space to talk and a forum in which to network:

> *I reckon the boys always did that...still do, you can see it in that they...stand there, they have a few drinks, they lobby. We lack a natural forum for networking, I don't want to be in the bar of University House to meet...We don't have a place where women can meet that is seen as special women's space.*

The introduction of equity procedures and practices in the late 1980s raised expectations of what the administration might do to develop the position of women. As those developments became more accepted, SWG moved to being more strategic and proactive. Its efforts had been crucial in employing an equal opportunity co-ordinator in the mid-1980s.[36] In the early years, members would form working parties to deal with specific issues, write submissions, build a case to lobby central administration, write letters to particular faculties or organise a social event. Although such activities were pursued on behalf of the group, the individual acts from those Astin and Leland call 'instigators'[37] were invariably important in how well the group's messages were sent and received. As a woman on general staff noted:

> *I send out fairly regular e-mail updates about what is happening with enterprise bargaining. We have found that things come into heads' and deans' offices and don't actually flow through to staff.*

Four ongoing working parties provided the basis for SWG activities between 1997 and 2001. They kept a watchdog role, suggested initiatives to central administration and/or particular faculties, and generated social events to keep the membership alive and interested. Members had significant input into major developments such as the Leadership Development for Women programme and the highly visible and controversial reviews of the position of academic women (1995) and women in general staff (1997). In the relatively more woman-friendly environment of the mid-1990s, a combination of a supportive vice-chancellery and pressures for equal opportunity through the federal government's quality rounds were brought to bear on women's issues. Yet lobbying for those outcomes had been a lengthy process.[38] A woman professor recalled those beginnings:

> *I can remember I think it was in the late 1970s a group of women we had lunchtime meetings, this is pre-SWG. We sent a submission about something—we never even got a piece of paper saying your submission has been received. I grizzled about that to one of my colleagues who in the end said 'Don't just wait for the response, ask for it to be heard before the c'mmittee'. So we didn't initially know what you did and we have got smarter I reckon.*

By 1994, the new deputy vice-chancellor had signalled that he was prepared to champion gender equity. The SWG membership learned to use that support strategically. Members no longer simply prepared submissions or made a case on an issue; they now lobbied senior management directly. In 2002, SWG continued to raise and monitor gender-inclusive issues, such as rapidly increasing workloads and the anxieties surrounding departmental and faculty restructuring. The viability of such groups is broadly issues-based. Increasing workloads, a lack of burning gender issues, and alternative sources of networking have reduced the turnout for SWG meetings since 2001. Nonetheless, the group retains a member on the university's Equity and Diversity Advisory Committee, chaired by the deputy vice-chancellor, and members sit on other influential committees.

Because such alliances are issues-specific, new network clusters will necessarily arise to meet contemporary needs. [39] The Administrative Staff Group (ASG), a networking alliance of administrative staff, is a case in point. It was a significant source of support and information sharing for general staff, who often find themselves left in the dark in their work units, particularly in those groups that customarily exclude administrative staff from planning meetings. ASG first met in 1989, when it went by the title of Administrative Secretaries Group. By the mid-1990s it was holding monthly meetings.

Although theoretically open to men, no one can remember any attending meetings. The Review of Women General Staff (1997) was the catalyst for a more direct political stance by the ASG, which until then had placed mutual support at the top of its list of priorities:

> *You can be quite isolated when there are only one or two women in a department. But in ASG there's the general support of knowing somebody you can ring and say 'Look, what are you doing about this?', especially over the last little while with the various systems that have been introduced and the changes that are coming with restructuring.*

ASG membership has declined since the review was completed. Members gravitate to other networks, decide they can manage the micropolitics of their work units without group support, find other networks of more interest, or that their opportunities for networking are limited as demands for learning new systems and technologies cut into their time.

The stories that SWG and ASG members tell about how their groups pursue equity issues describe an implicit model of change. I call it 'networking leadership'. That model of change assumes a link between two instigational actors: in this case senior management and the network of lobbyists and activists. Networking leadership is necessarily companionate, since the effectiveness of its lobbying depends to some degree on the advocates' claim to represent (numbers of) women.

In the process of formulating and negotiating their group's claims these women enact leadership, for as Astin and Leland note, leadership emerges from 'the critical interplay of personal values and commitment, special circumstances…and personal events that motivate and mobilise people's actions'.[40] Nevertheless, women in the groups shy away from any claim to be leaders, on ethical and political grounds. The collaborative ethic of their group is a key factor, but so is their understanding of the politics of the collective voice. Yet in the context of the gendered university, their non-individualistic and collaborative politic feminises their actions through the expectation that women are happy to play the subordinate role of the follower. Thus their actions 'do gender' in ways which put them and their roles in an ambiguous and contradictory light. Managing those contradictions in the minutiae of everyday lives is the ongoing task of the woman who wants more than the subordinate role that a gendered university allocates.

In their analysis, Astin and Leland code women as either 'instigators' or 'inheritors' in their styles of leadership, and they further distinguish between positional and non-positional leaders. Despite those differences, they make the point that there are striking similarities between the factors that propel all women's leadership. If I were to use their model, I would single out members of the women's groups and categorise them as either 'instigators' or 'inheritors', and point to the vice-chancellor and deputy vice-chancellor as positional leaders. That model would work quite well, provided I limited the analysis to the big events of change management, such as the instigation of the Leadership Development for Women programme and the generation of the reviews of women's position. Yet highlighting big wins cannot cope with the everyday small changes that women make to their workspaces and to their work identities,[41] in which a form of companionate leadership simultaneously emerges.

Do-it-yourself leadership

In *Tempered Radicals*, Meyerson sifts through the deliberate acts of everyday leadership of those who want to cautiously change their organisations without jeopardising a hard-won career.[42] She argues that fresh ways of doing leadership are within everyone's reach. The do-it-yourself (DIY) leadership observed in our study of UWA is characterised by an understanding that work units and work practices are not as fair and equal as they could be, and that the best thing to do about it is to negotiate the needed change at the micro level, usually through conversation and collaboration with others. I prefer the term 'DIY leadership' to Meyerson's 'everyday leadership', because it makes the doing and the self-management aspects of the leadership act more explicit.

Companionate leadership was evident in the sense of shared experience and information that women gained from their networking groups. It appeared to offer a vital source of affirmation and confidence-building. Observation and affinity groups showed several examples where a DIY approach to problems was part of the group dynamic. Members told each other stories about the micropolitics of their work areas, then gave each other advice on how to deal with the conflicts, imbalances, exploitations and manipulations. Take for example the following excerpt from an affinity group transcript. A general staff participant outlined an issue she faced in her department and asked the group's advice. Others joined in to say what they had done about similar problems. The result was that some women gained important new information about UWA's Human Resources policy. That information had not been made available to them through departmental information flows:

> A: *How do you cope with the workload? We've lost two staff and yet there's more students...I'm working till 6:30, 7:00 at night...*
>
> B: *I arranged with my department head for a morning each week to work at home. I get a clear run [on the paperwork] that way.*
>
> A: *Can anyone do that? Is there some kind of rule or something?*
>
> B: *As far as I know it's open to all general staff [to do]. Providing your work station's approved and such like, and your department agrees...*
>
> C: *That wouldn't suit me. I like to keep home and work separate.*
>
> D: *Me too, my boss agreed I [can] have a room and close the door for two mornings each week. I hang out the 'don't disturb' and that's it.*

Useful information was generally accompanied by women encouraging each other to be assertive, decisive and determined. At times that encouragement took the form of spoken urgings, but more often than not it involved some women modelling the changes in their own working lives and identities, and passing on tips to the others about how they might improve their situations.

Some women were well aware that they were engaging in a version of collective organising in giving each other advice on the minutiae of organisational micropolitics. For example, in another affinity group (comprising academic and general staff), a similar problem-solving discussion took place. One woman urged the others:

> *Go and ask for it, be strong...we have to be strong and stand up for ourselves and say this is what we want. I think this group really supports you to do that because we all sort of talk about different things. And then we can go back and say 'Look I know 20 women standing up to this'.*

Ackroyd and Thompson label such organisational behaviour 'self-organization', and describe it as a key aspect of worker resistance to overwork and tighter controls.[43] Our study did not set out to assess the extent to which individual women drew on the idea of a collective voice to resist overwork, non-recognition and exclusion. Nonetheless, the research team found that some women built an idea of strength through numbers into their accounts of how they coped with challenges. Moreover, through the face-to-face negotiations they described with bosses and co-workers, other women indicated that they were not averse to using the gains made by women in other departments as a way of arguing that they should receive similar treatment.

It is fair to conclude that the DIY leadership operating at UWA *acts on* the assumption that the triggers for change are the critical acts of the individual networker,[44] backed up when necessary by the collaborative power and shared corporate know-how of the networking group.

Distributive leadership

Gender equality is as much about men as about women. It is well known that a male administrator sympathetic to women's concerns can carry considerable influence with a staff member who sees no wisdom in gender equity strategies.[45] Knowing this, women wise to gender politics look to encourage the input of helpful males. The efforts of particular men have been crucial to the success of most equity initiatives at UWA, but none more so than the Leadership Development for Women programme. As mentors, champions and allies, a number of senior men have played significant roles.

By 2000, when the then Deputy Vice-Chancellor (Alan Robson) proposed a one-line budget for the women's leadership programme, he was a keen supporter. When interviewed in 1999 he expressed the view that the LDW programme was the most crucial of all the gender equity strategies that UWA had supported:

> *I actually think establishment of the Leadership Development for Women and the way in which that has developed has made a huge difference to the position of women here. I would say that is the most significant thing we have done when I think about it. I want to see it extended to all women staff, and I don't see why we shouldn't look at something like that for postgraduates. We should make sure that our postgraduate women want to stay on here—stay in WA.*

The LDW programme differs from the other campus women's forums in that it receives mainstream funding through UWA's Centre for Staff Development. However, it was generated by the concerns and efforts of women's groups and the Equity Manager, who gained funding in its initial years through a federal staff development grant. Significantly, since gaining its own one-line budget, the programme's planning group has taken care to retain the original design of women-only participation, along with a feminist-inspired, community-building focus.

Since its first intake in 1994, the programme has gradually relaxed its criteria for participation so that any woman employed at UWA on a 12-month contract or longer, and at half time or more, can apply. By early 2003 over 300 women had completed the year-long course. Overwhelmingly, participants place networking near the top of the benefits they gain from participation.[46] As well as providing information about the mechanics of the university's systems, LDW workshops are designed to raise participants' awareness of how the gendered culture operates and to build their collective and individual strategies for combating systemic discrimination.

In interviews with the original planners of the programme, a memory they had in common was that they set out to design an initiative that would 'raise awareness' and 'give women a chance to develop and share strategies'. The early outlines of the programme show three listed aims: (a) networking that would foster collective action, (b) awareness raising and (c) a university community more open and welcoming to women.[47] It was important to these instigators that LDW was more than a training programme, because training was instrumental and individualist—a model that suggested counting success simply by the numbers of women trained. Instead they wanted qualitative relational development, in a similar vein to the shared leadership they had encountered and fostered in proactive women's networks.

The model of change underpinning the LDW programme aims to distribute the incidence and values of a gender-aware model of leadership. In effect, it formalises women's networking in the interests of distributing their relational and leadership skills more widely, yet in so doing it provides a planned program of personal and institutional development. The strategy is to take up the lessons about gender politics that women learned through sharing stories and strategies within their DIY networks, and to situate them in the formally organised role of staff development. I call this a 'distributive leadership' model because its primary aim is to circulate the skills of gender-aware leadership among women. The long-term goal, ratified in the programme's mission statement, is to reshape existing leadership practices in the interests of creating a more inclusive culture.

Multiplying leadership

A few women had concluded by 1997 that none of the existing women's networks were focusing sufficiently on diversity issues. Consequently, they formed their own group for support, information and collaboration, calling it the Women of Diversity (WoD). In a 1999 interview, a woman in the WoD network made the point that diversity had become as big an equity issue as gender, and that at UWA there had been too little effort to recognise this:

> *I still have that feeling of wishing the Status of Women Group would identify that the brown women are not there and make some positive moves to ask them in.*

The network was meeting on an irregular basis during 1999–2001, mainly as a support group, and occasionally voiced concerns about their marginal status. The women came from diverse cultural or linguistic backgrounds. They believed that white Anglo-Celtic women at the university often excluded and overlooked the voices and experiences of those who did not fit that category. Several held the view that the perspectives of most white women (like most white men) had not enlarged to appreciate the challenge and the benefits of cultural difference. As one member said:

> *This [university] is an environment where circles of power form and thrive, and this includes among white women as well as men.*

By late 1999 positional leaders at UWA were responding to such concerns and looking to formulate and implement a diversity strategy. The first step was to employ a diversity officer. The officer's role was to increase the number of culturally and linguistically diverse staff and to liaise with staff responsible for the needs of students with disabilities and Indigenous students. A Workforce Diversity Strategy was established in 2001 to create jobs for people from three identity groups: Indigenous Australians, people with disabilities and people from culturally and linguistically diverse (CALD) backgrounds. By October 2002 the Diversity Strategy had placed 52 candidates in jobs (34 women and 18 men) and UWA had gained the Prime Minister's Award for its diversity efforts, specifically for employing people with disabilities.

Embedded in the idea and implementation of the Diversity Strategy was a model of change that I classify as 'multiplying leadership'. It recruited multiple project leaders in various work units. Each was responsible for ensuring that the newly placed employee was given encouragement, technical backing and a collegial welcome (including support from co-workers). Project leaders (mainly library, grounds and cleaning staff) were themselves given training, awareness-raising and support if and when needed. This included access to a network of project leaders and other supportive people. In turn, the new employees were encouraged to develop their own networks for mutual support and the sharing of practical tips for coping with new jobs and co-workers.

This multiplying leadership model differs from models of change described earlier. The instigator here is neither the senior positional leader nor the marginalised group nor a combination of the two. Rather, the identified pressure points for change are the growing band of project leaders, who use their positional authority to shape positive perceptions of diversity among a widening group of employees. In effect, the Diversity Strategy attempts to reduce reliance on the goodwill of senior leadership and to draw support from the mainstream. It also addresses the lack of designated organisational authority among those who practice DIY and distributive leadership.

Alliance leadership

The Ally Network, launched in June 2002, extends the implied model of change in multiplying leadership. It is an informal association of staff and students who identify as allies to gay, lesbian, bisexual, transgender and intersex (GLBTI) staff and students. The task of an ally is twofold: to offer a safe place to people who seek confidential information, support, empathy or friendship on GLBTI issues; and to raise awareness of GLBTI people, their issues and concerns, and advocate for them. The collaboration of an ally is deliberately made public. Allies show the Ally Network logo prominently on their office doors, and are given a badge to be worn as wished. They include a strong proportion of senior and prominent staff including, since 2002, the deputy vice-chancellor. From the outset, the Ally Network grew out of a straight/gay alliance for change.

Like the Diversity Strategy, it seeks to multiply people with positional authority who might shift the awareness of others. However, as the name suggests, the Ally Network goes one step further. It makes very visible and public the *collaborative alliance* between allies from the normative heterosexual group (often with organisational authority) and the marginalised GLBTI group they are supporting. In a sense, those who designed the Ally Network appear to have built into their model of change salient features of earlier models used at UWA. The alliance model includes recognition of the need for commitment from the top, the collaborative force of the network, the taking of responsibility (as in DIY), and the value of gaining formal legitimacy for a specific network (as in the Leadership Development for Women programme). The designers of the Ally Network, a combination of GLBTI and straight men and women at mid-levels of academic and general staff, as well as students with positional roles in the Student Guild, drew on models operating in universities in the United States and Canada.

Most importantly, the Ally Network includes raising public awareness in its goals for change, and shows promise of significant success. At its launch, there was standing room only, with staff across all levels and areas rubbing shoulders with students, politicians, senior public servants, and members of the community and various professions.

This turnout contrasts sharply with the launch of its precursor, the Rainbow Project, in March 2001. There is evidence that many GLBTI staff were fearful of attending that launch, because their attendance might identify them. As the first sexuality-based project funded by UWA, the Rainbow Project aimed to 'determine the campus climate with regard to sexuality and to identify key issues with respect to gay, lesbian, bisexual and transgender students and staff'.[48] It was funded by UWA's Diversity Initiatives Fund, managed by a straight/gay coalition of staff and students, and broke new ground by conducting research on the level of awareness of the issues facing GLBTI staff and students. Key recommendations were that a network of advocates for GLBTI staff and students be established, and that staff development programmes address sexuality. The Ally Network was the initial response to those recommendations.

Invisibility in the ivory basement

In describing these groups and their identified missions, I emphasise the networks, alliances and sense of group agency that ensure a relational approach to change. This grows out of an experiential understanding that the task of making a difference is a collective, often companionate, activity from which leadership emerges. Such actions are usually guided by employees' concern that certain university practices and policies are unresponsive to their needs or to the needs of other groups on the margins. Although their actions are often construed as running counter to the status quo, these groups gain legitimacy from equal opportunity and diversity discourses, which are circulated as much through policy directives from governments and upper levels of management as from the human rights and women's movements that inspired them.

The analysis so far gives a sense of group identities formed around specific constellations of goals, needs and resources, and pursued in a companionate manner. But the research can also tell us a story about the simultaneous pleasures, constraints and passions of those who engage in relational leadership work while negotiating their place in educational institutions.[49]

Focus on the ivory basement adds a dimension that is at best implicit in Fletcher's study of relational work. It indicates that the subjectivities of people who practise relational work are shaped by those practices into identities based on concealing or downplaying their transformative actions. An example is the practice of networking leadership described above.

Another example comes from a group of thirty women who assembled for a feedback session midway through this research project. I described some critical acts,[50] most particularly by women, that had played a part in transforming workplace behaviours, rules and policies. Most of the examples were similar to the ones in this book. In addition to challenging discriminatory or outdated practices, such actions showed the range of behaviours that Fletcher characterises as relational intelligence: empathy, collaboration, facilitating, listening, welcoming, smoothing conflict, enabling, solving problems.

Women in the feedback session generally agreed that the study's evidence of companionate leadership rang true to their experiences, and that the nature of such contributions was that they usually went unnoticed and unrewarded. They also intimated that as part of the pleasure of their work was to engage in such activities, in that sense there was no need for reward. Moreover, some expressed qualms about going public with the findings.

Most of the women who expressed concern were in middle to lower levels of general staff, and at lecturer level and below among academic staff. They gave two reasons for their ambivalence. One group aligned their concerns with the woman who said that 'if we let management know that we do this sort of thing, they will stop us from doing it'. By contrast, the second group suggested that the relational intelligence needed for problem-solving and conflict management enhanced the culture and development of the university's strategic goals. For exactly that reason, they said, it would be dangerous to give companionate leadership public exposure, because 'management will put it in our job statements and *expect* us to do it'.

Further questioning clarified the thinking that lay behind this double-edged disquiet. For a start, it revealed that these women saw themselves as operating beyond a purely instrumental set of values. Secondly, it showed that their qualms related to a belief that they would lose their autonomy over how, when and why they engaged in companionate, transformative actions. Within their jobs a growing culture of management was changing the meaning of formal responsibility from a sense of self-direction to a realisation that there were few elements of their work that were not subject to processes of accountability, surveillance and tighter control. Whether that control entailed joining a team-teaching exercise in which they had to match their rhythms for preparation and assessment to those of slower colleagues, or learning new computer skills, or spreading their capacity to service someone else's needs around ever-enlarging groups of academics or students, it represented a limitation on self-directed autonomy. Their response was to bolster a sense of themselves as effective, powerful, self-managed individuals by the control they exerted over when and why they acted to make their workspaces and working relationships more satisfying, equitable and non-instrumental. Not surprisingly, they surmised that an opportunity to exercise (relative) power—so essential to a pleasurable sense of a self-managed identity—was reliant upon their relational actions remaining tacit.

Individuals are linked, sometimes globally, through their networking and relating. Yet in a global knowledge economy, self-management is 'a process by which [people] internalise organizational and system-wide objectives'.[51] This in turn implies an organisational expectation in which 'Is it true?' and 'Is it just?' become reduced to 'Is it efficient?' and 'Is it marketable?'[52] The invisibility of companionate leadership in the ivory basement is in part due to the actions of those who would protect from the current swirl of instrumental values a secure sense of place in which truth, justice and autonomy can be pursued, felt and enjoyed as a human benefit rather than as practices to be dissected in a job description. Yet the gender performances of women are scripted through systems of meaning that signify support, relational skills and subordinate silence. In that sense, companionate leadership as a hidden activity is 'doing gender' even as its exponents contest and challenge the masculine norms that advantage men.

CHAPTER 4

Tacking in the Tower

[At UWA] the women spoke behind closed doors. It shocked me. In Adelaide I was the first woman professor and the first chair of the academic board and so on, but I never felt the level of fear and isolation those women must have known.

First impressions can burn deeply into our memories. For eminent Australian academic Professor Fay Gale, arrival as Vice-Chancellor at The University of Western Australia in 1990 was one such time. Her words above create a vivid image of academic women at UWA as cloistered, cautious and few, whose concerns were never aired publicly. A little more than a decade later, UWA can boast significant change in the profile and recognition of women and their contributions. At times, recognition comes through national awards for quality output such as the 2002 Equal Opportunity for Women in the Workplace Agency Employer of Choice for Women Award. Occasionally it comes through public statements by senior university leaders. In an address to the university's 2002 Leadership Development for Women graduation dinner, Deputy Vice-Chancellor Alan Robson symbolised the appreciation now given to new, feminised forms of leadership and, in particular, to how these linked with women's contributions as leaders:

> *The very best leadership is what I call 'organic'. Lao Tzu, the Chinese philosopher, is one of the people who know how to describe that way of leadership. He wrote: 'Leadership is best when the people say: "we have done this ourselves"'. Having worked with several women who are very good at that style of leadership, including Fay Gale, I can say that's what we want to encourage at UWA.*

Such awards and statements indicate a genuine appreciation of women's contributions, a sincere promise of action and evidence of equity advancement. We might expect that women would gain from this valuing of relational models of leadership in the literature and the rhetoric of management. Yet a glance at the statistics on women in senior positions, at UWA and elsewhere, is salutory.[1] Why are more women not enjoying the 'female advantage' that Rosener[2] and others predicted would follow the rise of 'new leadership' thinking and practice?

With regard to universities, Bond argues that the answer lies in the personal and professional price exacted from women who take on positions of senior academic leadership. Based on data from 1200 women and men, Bond questioned why the numbers of women in senior management in Canadian universities had plummeted to pre-1990 levels in the late 1990s. Her study concluded that a woman taking on senior leadership faces a situation that is much more dangerous to her welfare than it would be to a man's. For women, such a move often led to social isolation and loss of health.[3]

Gender, power and lack

Dame Leonie Kramer, then Chancellor of the University of Sydney and one of Australia's most senior academic women, told the press in 1995 that selectors had good reason to overlook women for university leadership because 'women go limp when the going gets tough'. Kramer's association of women with a lack of capacity to keep it up reflected and shaped some deeply held assumptions about women's lack of sexual, personal and institutional power. Her opinions drew justifiably angry reactions from other women.[4] Yet even as her words were actively 'doing' gender, Kramer was inadvertently demonstrating how normal it was to characterise women as lacking the necessary.[5]

Fletcher adds another view about how masculinised privilege is normalised. Behind the doing of gender, she argues, lurks the tendency to see 'the social world as being separated into two spheres of activity':

> the public spheres of paid work where we 'produce things' and the private sphere of family and community where we 'grow people'. This way of seeing the world is so natural that we rarely think of it or question its influence.[6]

In practice, men are active participants in the family sphere and women participate in paid work. Yet these idealised images of two very different forms of effort shape in powerful and gendered ways our expectations of how women and men should act at home and at work. The double bind for women is that conventional femininity is associated with nurturing or relational skills, which means that women can often (and are expected to) practise those skills more easily. However, relational skills are also associated both with the domestic sphere and with servicing the needs of the more powerful. As Fletcher notes, 'strong, societal beliefs about individual achievement and meritocracy' ensure that in the workplace relational skills are unconsciously associated with 'a *lack* of power'.[7]

Fletcher's analysis is based largely on her study of women in engineering, a male-dominated occupation. Given the preponderance of men in upper university management, her analysis has relevance for this book. Furthermore, another study, comparing women and men in male-dominated occupations more widely, adds an important dimension to her work. Through research on Australian industries, Gardiner and Tiggemann reported in 1999 that men in male-dominated industries gained rewards from following a personally oriented leadership style, while women leaders in the same industries were penalised through pressure to drop their personal orientation and adopt a more masculine style.[8]

If we consider the findings of Fletcher together with those of Gardiner and Tiggemann, we might surmise that deeply embedded gendered associations have powerful effects on how and when we recognise and enact leadership, and on the uneven visibility of women and men as recognised and positional leaders. Crucially, we can assume that, in the case of women in male-dominated occupations, relational, empathetic effort is tainted by an association with weakness and powerlessness. For their male contemporaries, however, a quite different standard may apply. Such findings have significant implications both for individual women and for the gendered organisation of male-dominated occupations. For the purposes of this book, they raise questions for those women leaders in male-dominated fields whose self-management incorporates a personally oriented, companionate approach to leadership. These women are likely to be symbolically associated with a lack of power and authority that translates as a lack of leadership.

Much has been written on the power and influence of leaders and executives, and most of it assumes that leadership is gender-neutral. Yet both executive power and leadership are gendered and sexualised. Aligning women *with* power (whether at the top of an organisation or not) is invariably a highly contested task. In the words of Sinclair, 'even before they open their mouths or act, men are likely to be endowed with power and the potential for leadership'.[9] The examples, language and concepts that most researchers use effectively associate organisational power with men, and leadership with masculinised ways of knowing (such as tough-mindedness, emotional detachment) and doing (such as assertive self-promotion, making 'hard' decisions and disconnection from family responsibilities). Normative masculinisation, albeit disguised as gender-neutrality, is what identifies leadership as gendered.

The feminisation of change agency

The traditional literature on the subject sees change being driven from above. Yet in managing fundamental change in the public sector, there is a scarcity of managers who can claim unqualified success.[10] Writing in the context of Australian higher education, Yeatman argued that 'women who show management and policy talent' are likely to be recruited into senior roles 'Precisely because of their lack of loyalty to the established way of doing things—and to the established masculine elite of the institution'.[11]

Yeatman's forecast reiterated earlier claims that the feminisation of management was here to stay. As globalising economies sparked the notion of organisations in crisis, fuelled ever since by frenzied restructuring,[12] organisational sages predicted that women would come into their own as leaders and managers.[13] Why? Because, it was said, women's relational skills, their higher concern for the collective good, and their ambiguous authority status made them better at handling the insecurities and resistances that the promised changes would bring.[14] As much subsequent feminist research has shown, such narratives of doing it differently can contribute to a construction of women as 'necessarily "different"—always against the grain...ironically reinforcing the reality of a "mainstream" occupied by men'.[15]

In the context of universities, Yeatman argued that a number of senior academic men were inclined to be supportive of talented women and indeed were likely to champion equity goals more broadly. She outlined two reasons: that their institutional positioning both affords them some understanding of the centrality of these objectives to the institution's growth and development, and negates any threat in these few women's advancement into senior positions'.[16] Yeatman's reasoning was to prove somewhat prophetic, in the Australian context at least, with the numbers of female vice-chancellors jumping from two in 1995 to ten in 2001 (more than a quarter of the total).

Although it is rare to hear autobiographical accounts of how female vice-chancellors manage their leadership, a number of women in middle management (heads of schools, deans, vice-chancellery assistants) in English-speaking countries have been prepared to analyse and publicly share their experiences.[17] Commonly, these writers shape their identities as university managers by positioning themselves as attuned to equity and diversity, and as leaders who manage collaboratively. As middle managers in New Zealand universities, Munford and Rumball, for example, note that they strive to 'facilitate processes that encourage collaboration'.[18] Key terms they use to describe their management practices are 'inclusivity', 'diversity', 'equity', 'participation', 'accessibility', 'power-sharing' and 'pastoral care'. They also position themselves as change agents, discussing how they continually 'push the boundaries' by 'challenging the focus on efficiency, effectiveness and competition and the need to be output driven'.[19]

To what extent is such self-positioning a politics of difference? Do women reclaim the notion of gender difference in order to distinguish themselves from a male-ordered set of behaviours? Although they were obviously careful to name their strategies in line with the accepted language of innovation and change, Munford and Rumball were nonetheless keen to suggest that they were doing leadership differently from the expected, masculinised, standard. Similarly, in a comparison of women's experiences as university managers in Canada and Australia, Wyn et al. suggest that difference is 'a source of pleasure and accomplishment for these women as they have learned how to move from a situation where they were defined as "other" to a "non-oppositional" mode of difference'. Simultaneously, they prepared themselves for 'the necessity to be confrontational at times'.[20] The task for women leaders, as Sinclair concludes, is to shape their identities as 'bi-gendered'. That double-sided identity means they must show themselves capable of 'doing it like a man' while simultaneously projecting as 'woman'. Women, in sum, must be seen to lead in conventional terms, which signify masculinity, as well as to empower others in ways which signify femininity.[21]

The conundrum of women's leadership is exacerbated by changing views and modes of management, which position women in leading roles in highly contradictory ways. In universities, Wyn et al. conclude that 'a single event (promotion, for example) may be both positive and negative, welcome and problematic, inclusive and marginalizing'.[22] A similar contradiction accompanies the social expectation that women will be the nurturers of human relationships. Most of the women leaders in the study of universities by Blackmore and Sachs held 'a concept of leadership tightly tied to teaching, service and care'.[23] Yet, in an echo of the findings of Gardiner and Tiggemann mentioned above, the demeanour required of them carried the message that 'care was out and strong leadership was in'.[24] Moreover, women were embodied as effective change agents, but often overlooked when it came to filling upper-level positions. In short, Blackmore and Sachs argue that university restructuring uses women but inevitably favours men.

Importing 'new' leadership

When Fay Gale became vice-chancellor in 1990, controversies over Canberra-driven change were heating up.[25] As well as shaping new meanings and directions for their universities, positional leaders had to reassure internal critics that none would be disenfranchised; neither would academics be expected to change too quickly or too much.

During Gale's eight-year term, the university moved from the bottom to the top of Western Australia's gender equity index (an evaluation tool used by the WA Department of Equal Opportunity in Public Employment). It also won, in the second half of the 1990s, several awards for equal opportunity, and was consistently placed in the top band for all categories in the Commonwealth Government's quality review process. Those shifts owe a debt both to various incentives from Canberra, driven by pressures for affirmative action for women, and to the influence of a vice-chancellor with considerable background in gender equity.

With the removal of the binary system in the late 1980s, some older universities had the advantage of amalgamations with teaching institutions in which the proportions of women staff were substantial. This was not the case at UWA. Given the institution's longstanding reputation as a bastion for male, white and class privilege,[26] the shift in gender profile is notable.

Professor Gale's witnessing of entrenched privilege in action initially inclined her against the job of vice-chancellor. After meeting some of the team with whom she would be expected to work, she told herself, 'this will kill me, I don't want this'. Indeed, such thoughts helped her speak her mind about UWA's institutional arrangements during the selection interview. She apparently criticised the complacency that was likely to drive the university into an academic backwater, and showed herself to be even less impressed by the institution's wealth and tradition, telling a questioner that the Number Two Account (a portfolio of investment and endowment funds) 'is probably your biggest moral hurdle'. Gale also made it plain that the well-known painting of a nude hanging in the interview room[27] took her out of her comfort zone. She shifted seats so that the subject's bare breasts no longer 'framed the head of the Chancellor'. Overall, she gave what one eye-witness described as 'the most impressive presentation I'd ever heard'.

In overcoming her doubts and taking on the job, Gale was responding in part to the expectations placed on the woman in the public eye. Those expectations sustain the gendered organisation in ways which, for women, sometimes blur the layers of status between ivory tower and basement: 'If I said no, they would have said it was because a woman couldn't cope with the pressure, the task, the stress. It is quite different when a man opts out; people see that as simply an individual man who cannot cope, not a statement about all men.'

Gale built a team whose efforts propelled the university into top quality review ranking and to the top of the 1997 *Good Universities Guide* for research and teaching. Documents reveal that her team pioneered a responsive new senior management structure and prize-winning performance-based funding for research and teaching, fostered transparency in procedures and operations, developed new frameworks to reward and train staff, launched a successful international student programme and registered important productivity gains.

The 'great men' version of history delights in the listing of historical firsts, but feminist historians generally eschew such categories. Celebrating achievements is, however, something that women should do more often—if only because results can too often be short-lived. Gale gained distinction as the second female vice-chancellor in Australia and the first (and to date only) woman to lead the Australian Vice-Chancellors' Committee in its eighty-year history. Gale made good use of her wide national and international networks to substantially increase UWA's national standing, including strategic outcomes for gender equity. The significance of that legacy is captured in the tributes from dozens of UWA women, presented to her on a hand-inscribed scroll, when she completed her term in 1997. One inscription reads:

> *I admire Fay so much for the way she has stuck to her commitment to equity in the face of considerable opposition by a very vocal minority. I have been at UWA for nearly 20 years and, as a woman in academia, I at last feel this is a comfortable place for women to be.*

Around Australia, high-ranking university women celebrated what this vice-chancellor had achieved. The National Colloquium of Senior University Women convened a women-only testimonial in early 1998 to honour Fay Gale's contribution to the scholarship and leadership of Australian universities. In presenting the tribute, Vice-Chancellor Jan Reid of the University of Western Sydney spoke of what Gale had achieved for women:

> Fay has never been reluctant to speak plainly about the position of women in universities and of putting in place processes in her own university that ensure good women are recognised and rewarded.[28]

It is often the fate of incoming leaders, women and men, to encounter resistance to their goals and antagonism to their ways of managing. Like the women who have followed her into Australian vice-chancellorships, Gale differed from earlier generations of vice-chancellors in that she was a woman in male territory, and she was expected to negotiate the quite dramatic changes to higher education that Canberra was driving. Her appointment provoked some unrealistic expectations from women staff, and a flurry of parochial responses from media and die-hards. A local press headline, for example, greeted her with 'Gale Blows into UWA'.[29]

Feminist research has comprehensively documented the contradictory mixture of expectation and misogyny that invariably befalls the woman who breaks new ground in male-dominated hierarchies,[30] and Gale's experience provides a further example. At the outset, an active minority of staff positioned the new vice-chancellor not only as an outsider to Western Australian culture but also as the usurper of masculine privilege. Despite the evident success of her leadership, the antagonisms that had simmered among a small group from the beginning boiled over in 1996. The Sunday tabloid of the Western Australian media attacked Gale's managerial competence and leadership credibility. In the end the challenge failed and Gale stayed on.

The first two women to become Australian vice-chancellors— Professors Fay Gale and Di Yerbury (Macquarie University)—were, as Reid noted, both 'targeted maliciously by those who feared and resented their presence and what they stood for': that women could and would take on university leadership. She described 'a deep anxiety and antipathy towards these two women whose appointments signified a break in the natural order of things'. By 'deflecting, withstanding and transcending the ire of their detractors' Gale and Yerbury 'set a standard for the resilience, determination and skills of women CEOs in universities, and showed us that we could survive the slings and arrows of outrageous foes'.[31]

Professor Di Yerbury was the first of twelve women to become university vice-chancellors in a period of almost twenty years, and in 2002 nine of Australia's thirty-eight universities were led by women. Besides Gale, the only other woman to preside over a sandstone institution was Professor Mary O'Kane, who chose to resign from the University of Adelaide after lengthy disagreement with her senior managers. To what extent is there accuracy in Jan Reid's claim that the experiences and achievements of Gale and Yerbury smoothed the way for other female vice-chancellors? That question is impossible to answer with any certainty, despite anecdotal evidence that individual women have benefited from the counsel and lead of those pioneers.

Simply posing the question confirms the normative expectation of the woman who breaks new ground. Moreover, such expectations tend to minimise the extent to which organisations are not only gendered but are 'doing gender'.

Two other female vice-chancellors, both of whom took on their jobs during the second half of the 1990s, have since 1999 agreed to an anonymous interview for our study. I draw on that material to throw some light on how a later cohort of female vice-chancellors may depict their experiences. Although there were considerable differences in the challenges of management and leadership described by those two women, each intimated that she felt no added pressure on the basis of her gender. That made their depictions of self quite different from that of Gale, who saw gender as the major factor in how others saw and treated her authority. Although their accounts also conflicted with the findings of Bond's Canadian study, it is important to note that responses from two women cannot be compared with the hundreds surveyed for that study.

Male senior managers in Currie et al.'s study were virtually united in their acceptance of 'being set apart' from their lower-level colleagues in academia. Indeed these men saw apartness more or less as a badge of honour, coupled inevitably with a sense of isolation.[32] The data from my three female vice-chancellors shows less agreement on those two points. Gale, for example, moved in and out of a sense of isolation throughout her term, depending on the context of events around her, and she challenged at various times the sense of being set apart from other university staff. Like the males in Currie et al., both the second-generation female vice-chancellors accepted that the role demanded they be set apart from former colleagues. However, neither saw isolation as inevitable. Unlike Gale, who had only one female peer to relate to, one of these women spoke of the value of having a range of women vice-chancellors in other states with whom to swap stories and strategies. The other was more similar to Gale, in that she spoke of male peers (vice-chancellors or ex-vice-chancellors) who had offered useful advice. Unlike Gale, however, she felt she gained sufficient support from those interactions. The recognition and power that came with being vice-chancellor also countered any sense of isolation: 'when you are the V-C you are actually there. You don't have to prove yourself all the time and that's a very important thing'. In that respect her experience was very different to that of Gale, who felt she could rarely rest on her role as vice-chancellor with a secure sense that her authority would not be challenged.

Like Gale, one of these women depicted herself as paying special attention to gender issues, particularly in relation to more women in senior positions. The other claimed no special developments on that score and instead spoke of the difficulties of recruiting senior women, 'who these days could virtually name their own price'. In response, she had surrounded herself with 'honourable men'.

All three vice-chancellors fielded questions about their leadership by moving between situating gender as a personal attribute and a sense of the shaping of gender in the working institution. The vice-chancellor of a post-Dawkins amalgamated university remarked:

> *I'm often under attack, sometimes by women as well as men, so it's not simply a matter of gender—though gender is something that like any woman I've had to deal with it's not that simple any more...as anyone can tell you I have no problem with assertiveness, I can talk so they have to listen, and I can even shout when I think it's called for. Sometimes it's like putting on an act, sort of calculating—but not only that—but you have to be careful how often you use that.*

This vice-chancellor, who said she had been called on to make 'countless hard decisions, and that's why they employed me', nonetheless found the 'very strong feeling of them and us' that permeated the relationship between the academic community and the administration 'deeply depressing'. Like her second-generation counterpart and the senior males in Currie et al., she felt herself set apart from the blissful ignorance of most academics as to how the 'external environment' was exerting unceasing pressures on the direction of universities:

[Twenty] years ago the V-C was a respected academic. He was always a man, he had the respect of his discipline and was elected by his professoriate. Now the funding is insecure, the orientation is about service to the community rather than to the disciplines, and those personal qualities that have nothing to do with your scholarly background are much, much more important. So much of it comes down to how well you can lobby the politician, how appropriately you can package a deal with the community, with industry, in international networks.

This awareness of a historical shift from respected academic to community leader, or at times supplicant or salesperson, featured also in the second vice-chancellor's story. As the head of a smaller university, she spoke of the jolt she experienced in coming to terms with what was expected of her. She was not quite prepared for the continual surveillance of the public figure, along with the unceasing demand for political acumen:

It's really a shock when you get into the position, because you know what to expect in your head but now you actually have to live it. I have very few personal attacks on me but in a purely management sense, as with enterprise bargaining, I'm the one who gets blamed if it goes wrong. Nobody ever asks you about that in a selection interview. You know—your political skills, your public relations skills, your ability to give appropriate speeches, motivation speeches at the drop of a hat to all sorts of communities.

Women at middle levels of university management deploy various techniques of managing gender as they attempt to reshape their identities as teachers and researchers.[33] That reshaping is both prompted by and facilitates an academic system bent on forging ever-new and more marketable university identities under a system of growing accountability and surveillance. The narratives of the two vice-chancellors I have quoted, when linked with the story told by Fay Gale, reinforce the scenario painted by Yeatman—that the task of feminised change agent is being built into the role of positional leader in the university. In Australia, such feminisation is evident in the growing numbers of women chosen to act in that high-level capacity. Furthermore, the gendered qualities of ivory basement work—such as service orientation, ongoing surveillance, adaptability and loss of autonomy—may simultaneously be seeping in to colour managerial decision-making in the university tower. Whether the Australian experience will show a similar trend to that of the Canadian is a significant question that only time will answer.

What are some of the personal effects for women? According to Gardiner and Tiggemann, the double standard applied to women and men who opted for a more feminine or personally oriented leadership style had negative effects on the health of the women they studied but positive effects for the men.[34] There is little or no comparable research on Australian university leaders,[35] although ill health or exhaustion among high-flying academic women leaders is not unusual. Indeed, the directive reported by female middle managers in Blackmore and Sachs' study, that 'care was out and strong leadership was in' points to such pressure.

While Fay Gale did more than merely survive her term of office, the pressures of a parliamentary inquiry, alongside media controversy about whether she should be commended or vilified, did take its toll. Perhaps because pioneering women often seem to weather storms that would sink many of lesser fortitude, we expect invincibility. In writing about women managers in Australian and Canadian universities, Wyn et al. note:

> It may be that these women are the survivors, the ones with the stamina to cope with the stresses of the academy, and their positioning as senior managers reflects that fact. Yet, for some, the cost has been high. In addition to discussing specific illnesses, some spoke of burn-out and of the pressing need to find 'time for me'.[36]

Managing authority

As UWA's governing body, the Senate was crucial to Gale's success or failure. In her view, she lost remarkably few motions because she rarely moved a proposal unless the groundwork had been fully developed. Occasionally, however, Senate resistance proved difficult to predict. In 1991, for example, when she tried to make the Equal Opportunity Officer a full member of the Appointments Committee, key members of the Senate opposed her strategy. Their rationale indicates how women leaders are shaped as ultimately responsible for all aspects of gender equity, and therefore as the source of additional, lower level work effort. 'Why do we need a woman on all selection committees', they asked, 'when we have you?' A compromise allowed an equal opportunity officer to sit on all professorial appointments committees, but only as an observer. A Senate member who supported the original motion recalls the discriminatory practices of the earlier procedures:

> Before Fay made the changes we didn't even have agreed criteria against which we were selecting candidates. There was no linking of advertisement and selection criteria. We gave each candidate a different interview. We didn't have representation of both sexes on panels, and comments that I would have regarded as biased were made in deliberations.

Gale saw her role as being to institute structural changes that would affect equity practices, before overtly directing attention to specific gender equity programmes. It took five years, for example, to steer equitable procedures for academic promotion and tenure through the governing Senate and the Academic Board. Gale decided that gaining the support of Senate for amalgamating the two 'money' committees—the Finance Committee and the Investment Committee—had to come first, so that strategic management of financial policy could be developed to include equity and productivity incentives. She also needed the support of Senate to overturn archaic selection procedures, and prioritised that need over other gender equity procedures. One of the female Senate members described the process by which Gale brought the Senate into line with her thinking:

> *Fay wasn't someone who tried to do things rapidly and dramatically. She tried to do it from the bottom up through consulting and getting people involved and owning change...It felt to me like it took a long time, but she got support for radical changes in the way the selection processes occurred.*

The lengthy leadership process of 'bringing people along' was not a style familiar to committees and administrators, and men who used and admired confrontation and unilateral decision-making did not see Gale as an authoritative leader. On a late Friday afternoon at University House, the regular group of senior males stopped laughing as she approached. One told her they had been grading her leadership on a scale of zero to ten, adding: 'I gave you five—you never make up your mind'. They construed 'bringing people along' rather than overt command and control as procrastinating or dallying.

Through such encounters, women in male-dominated fields are given the message that they need to conform to a macho image of leadership. Gardiner and Tiggemann suggest that men do not face the same treatment, which leads us to question whether a double standard operates in this regard. Certainly, one-upmanship is an accepted feature of male-defined academic debate. Yet it would be interesting to know if the men in the University House bar would confront a male vice-chancellor in the same manner. Historically, discourses of educational leadership have forged links between masculinity, knowledge and power dependent on the 'othering' of the feminine as incapable of authority.[37] Some of that is changing, with women in authority becoming more accepted at lower levels. Yet the idea that such powers belong in the basement, leaving the ivory tower to men, is deeply entrenched. When women take up senior positions, masculinist assumptions readily come to the fore, placing the woman leader under a critical surveillance similar to that which circumscribes basement work.

Nonetheless, our study shows a marked overall respect for Gale's leadership. As one male interviewee said, 'at an operational level she got to hearts and minds rather than being seen as a figure-head'. Others found security in her professional fair-mindedness:

> *at a personal level you knew where you stood, she was someone who said it as it was. And I think she was tactful, she worked the numbers like everyone who has to work the numbers.*

Here we have a view of authority as a negotiated and ultimately social relationship. Socially, Gale was described as a 'superb mixer', although she sometimes raised eyebrows with the people she threw together. In parties at the large vice-chancellor's house, she broke with tradition in mixing guests from all walks of life. One female professor interviewed remarked: 'I was surprised to find myself sitting next to the cleaning lady'. Invited to elaborate, Gale recalled:

> *What worried me was that UWA was very hierarchical and very status conscious. It was expected that senior administrators only talked to professors, and the grounds staff you took for granted and you didn't speak to them. My plan was to try and mix people up to say we are all a team, this is what a university is about, everyone plays a different role. So I had dinner parties like a send-off for the cleaner when she left.*

Building an inclusive culture

Building relationships with general and grounds staff could also provide a strategic advantage. When a leader commits to building an inclusive organisational culture, it is crucial to 'walk the talk'. As a step to building a diverse student base, Gale met with the Student Guild monthly so that its members could brief her on what they saw as the issues and needs of the student body. In one of those meetings in 1991, female graduate students confided that they were afraid to walk from their departments to their cars or library buildings at night. A rape in nearby Kings Park was prompting more fears. Gale promised to make campus safety a priority, yet several obstacles stood in the way.

The grounds were extensive, with unlit or dim tunnels leading out to the colleges. Overhanging the footpaths that criss-crossed campus were plantings that looked magnificent by day but became dark spots where potential assailants could lurk at night. Some of the more striking shrubbery was floodlit, but walkers were blinded by the glare. Unlit steps were a hazard for the unwary. Removing the shrubbery would mean convincing the environmental group whose charter was to protect the heritage nature of the grounds, and gaining the agreement of the gardeners. Upgrading the lighting would mean requisitioning substantial funds, for which there was no budget provision. The Vice-Chancellor did not then have the annual fund that later in her term she could use for strategic purposes.

Gale began by inviting the head gardener for morning tea. She listened, they negotiated and she gained his provisional co-operation. The Vice-Principal (Finance and Resources) was sympathetic but unconvinced of the urgency. When Gale offered that 'I am going to hold you personally responsible if there is a rape on campus', he organised grounds and finance staff to walk with her, well after dark, through the campus.

At first blush the group, all men, could see no problems with either the gardens or the lighting. Undeterred, the Vice-Chancellor led the contingent back and forth between teaching, research and library buildings, pointed to the glare of spotlights and adjacent dark patches, bushes overhanging walkways, unlit steps and tunnels. The men peered into dark exits and unlit lobbies, while she suggested they imagined what it was like for a woman walking alone at night. A couple of hours later, the high cost of new lighting had been agreed for tunnels, steps and major paths. The gardeners' representatives agreed to keep cherished shrubbery regularly pruned. A series of meetings with the security administration negotiated the installation of buzzers in office blocks, and night security staff to escort women to buses or cars when called upon. Finally, the student body agreed to help draft maps that would encourage students to use only the patrolled areas of campus. Professor Gale recalls the outcome:

> *We didn't ever have the problem [of sexual assault], but it seemed to me that it could have happened. It wasn't only to stop the possibility of rape, it was also to show this was a campus on which women could feel welcome.*

This story, which recaptures but a minor part of a busy vice-chancellor's schedule, is told for two reasons. Firstly, it illustrates everyday elements of companionate leadership and demonstrates that leadership in basement and tower do not have to be so very different to be effective. Second, it supports the idea current since the late 1980s that leadership in today's complex organisations requires negotiation and collaboration, shared local knowledge, and the capacity to listen and learn.[38] The community-building leadership enacted by Vice-Chancellor Gale served also to shape the work identities of administrators, gardeners and security guards as self-managed planners, organisers and leaders.

Yet it would be unsound to wipe the effects of positional authority from this story. A senior manager's ability to control strategic directions through funding resources and information flows, performance measures and procedures for selection and promotion should not be underestimated.[39] When a vice-chancellor invites the head gardener to 'stop by my office for morning tea', it will be interpreted quite differently from a peer saying the same thing. Nonetheless, Gale's capacity to exercise that power was diffused and distributed to others, whose authority as collaborative decision-makers was established in the process. As with all social interaction, leadership is an enactment of self in tension with a given context.[40] That enactment is necessarily shaped by our interactions with others. In this case, as in other actions attributed to Gale, leadership becomes what I call companionate. Rather than removing enactments of power and authority, it reshapes them in ways which signify collaboration and respect.

Tacking in the tower

The symbolic effect of a woman at the top can prove a powerful mechanism for raising women's expectations and aspirations. One female senior lecturer pointed to revitalised women's networks:

> *All of a sudden people had a reason to actually stand up and push something forward because it was like we were charged to do this...Whereas if you just try to do it on your own...it is more difficult. But this is like Fay Gale saying: 'Well I am giving you the space to do something'.*

Such expectations of a woman leader can also prove unrealistic. A female professor recalled Professor Gale addressing the Status of Women Group in the early days of her vice-chancellorship:

> *I remember how disappointed we all were. We had the feeling that she was not going to back any of the major things we wanted to see happen...It's easy to see how naive we were to think that such changes could be straightforwardly driven from the top...we were blown over by having a woman up there. We were quite unrealistic.*

How observers in different positions viewed Gale's vice-chancellorship provides a clear example of gendered associations creating a double standard for women and men. For many, the female leader symbolises an expectation of sensitivity, caring, equity and new direction. Yet women would rarely pin their hopes for any of those things on the leadership of a new *male* vice-chancellor. The gossip that surrounds any highly visible leader means that many onlookers have a fixed view of the object of their inspection even when they have scarcely met. For the woman leader, the level of surveillance is even more acute. The price for some feminist observers at UWA was an initial feeling of disappointment, and a tagging of Gale as lacking in reliable 'feminine' attributes. By contrast, colleagues who worked closely with Gale suggested her leadership exemplified an effective and innovative style. As one male executive said:

*Fay was interesting in that she really didn't direct anyone
to do anything. Working with her you knew what the issues
were and you would develop your own momentum. At
least you thought it was [yours]. There were times when I
thought something was my idea and later realised it was
part of something she'd earlier said or written.*

Two other senior male managers told similar stories. One, a
yachting enthusiast, likened her style of 'getting people to run with
the ideas' to the act of tacking:

*I said to her once, 'Have you done much yachting?'
Because she would tack out way past anyone else I ever
saw. She would be right out here, tacking back and forth
until everyone else was steady up to the line. It worked. But
it meant people never knew how much she did to make it
happen.*

From her closest colleagues, then, we have an image of a
vice-chancellor whose actions made a difference to the collaborative
relationships around her, and whose leadership style was 'different'
to the masculinised norm. While her companionate leadership is
credited as a valuable form of people management, it is nonetheless
presented as lacking the characteristics of the standard model.

These stories of a female vice-chancellor in a particular era of
Australian history show that subtle dynamics of gender and power
shape our understandings of leadership. It would be a mistake to
suppose that the story was not one of considerable agency and prag-
matism. What one of Gale's former deputies referred to as 'a wonderful
capacity to be opportunistic' enabled her—like many other women
at work—to manage the constraining effects of gendered power.
Referring to what she had learned about working on equity issues
at Adelaide, she recalled that 'people would listen if I got a man to
put the proposition. If I put it up unaided I'd probably have a fight
on my hands.' Gale's technique of tacking was probably as much
an attempt to overcome the gendered conundrums of the female
leader as sensitivity to the mind-sets of others. In fact the two are

entwined in the gendering of women. Yet it would also be wrong to assume that a capacity for 'bringing people along' meant that Gale (as perhaps all successful positional leaders) was not also tough-minded, competitive, self-promoting and as remote as she was accessible.

Importantly, the second-generation vice-chancellors I discussed earlier also claimed to find leading-from-behind procedures useful to generate support and consensus. One remarked, 'You are in the meeting, so let other people shine—as long as what comes out is something that you want'. As the era of the self-managed university was taking hold, management of self entwined with management of others. For women at the top as well as in the basement, the micropolitics of the gendered organisation ensures that when leadership is companionate, it is likely to be concealed *as* leadership. Furthermore, the woman who practises companionate leadership in a male-dominated field is likely to be pressured to adopt a more masculine style. One technique of gender control of women in the public eye is to judge any evidence of people-orientation as non-leadership. Hence the words of one middle manager: '[Gale] was not what I'd call a leader. She listened to too many people so it took her too long to make up her mind. Besides, she took the focus on women too far.'

Conclusion

When a woman inhabits the ivory tower she will face pressure to be both the 'feminine' nurturer who supports and sponsors other women and men, and the warrior/leader who can not only survive the slings and arrows but also forge a clear path in times of radical change. Professor Gale's leadership identity was shaped through her people skills, ambition and untiring commitment to attain the goals she set for herself and the institution. At times she enacted a form of companionate leadership that can be rendered invisible as readily as ivory basement work. For a woman to succeed in that context, the task can become the near-impossible one of tacking between the hidden dynamics of the inclusive, collaborative leadership that characterises invisible ivory basement work, and the public face that signifies strength and unchallenged authority.

CHAPTER 5

Inside Agitators?

I never used to say anything at staff meetings, I just used to sit there thinking 'Oh, I can't say that—I'll get shouted down'. Well, you do get shouted down, but I learnt not to take that to heart and to be quite calm about it. Taught me a lot about the physical managing of these things as well as being able to say 'that is inappropriate behaviour and please don't do that again'.

a female lecturer

But the main benefit is women being more proactive and more confident and working together and helping each other.

a female administrator

A unique feature of the second-wave Australian women's movement is its history of feminists entering government bureaucracies, intent on changing them from within. The distinctiveness of the 'Australian experiment'[1] was that these women, soon known as 'femocrats',[2] were recruited to provide a feminist analysis in advancing women's interests. In the suites and offices of federal and state bureaucracies, the femocrats were charged with gender-specific policy and programmes on issues ranging from health, child care and job training to education, sexual violence and affirmative action. In examining a specific case of women's insider action at The University of Western Australia, I shall draw parallels with the 'inside agitator' role of the femocrat.

In the first half of the 1990s a number of universities mounted initiatives for developing women's leadership. National pressures for change included union responses to award restructuring and federal government initiatives for affirmative action to counter the lack of senior women. Key pressures at the organisational level, at UWA at least, were a campus women's group motivated by renewed expectations of affirmative action, and a supportive vice-chancellery. A significant outcome was the establishment of the Leadership Development for Women programme.

The political context

From the early 1970s Australian femocrats worked with, and sometimes through, a decreasingly visible women's movement to generate major legislative reforms. What they achieved for women fascinated feminist political theorists for the two decades in which 'state feminism'[3] was in the ascendancy.[4] Yet ambivalence, contradiction and debate swirled around these women, from right and left of the political spectrum.[5] As both Sawer and Eisenstein demonstrate, the contradiction was that gains made by the femocrats on behalf of their female constituencies also served the interests of their political masters. It did not take politicians long to see that women's policy was in many cases delivering the women's vote to governments wise enough to take the counsel of their feminist advisors and to promote women's issues and interests.[6] Where those governments proved not so wise in implementing change, it was the lot of the femocrats to minimise the electoral damage, which sometimes brought conflict with parts of the women's movement. Feminist analyses of the role of the femocrat have provided important lessons about the ambiguities of trying to change an institution from within, and recent work on the gender and diversity dynamics of organisational intervention is indebted to them.[7]

Neo-liberal pressures for rationalisation of the public sector were becoming more attractive to governments in the OECD countries by the early 1990s. In Australia as elsewhere, agencies in which women's policy was located were being dismantled, 'downsized' and 'mainstreamed'. Perhaps the last resounding example of the strength of the alliance between femocrat and women's movement came when Ann Summers, a former director of the federal Office of Status of Women, was commissioned by Prime Minister Paul Keating to formulate a policy package attractive to women voters in the 1993 federal election. The media duly reported that the Women's Electoral Lobby and several other national women's groups had given the package a public vote of approval. The election result was a narrow win for the Keating Government, based on a major proportion of the women's vote.[8] For a short time this increased focus on women's issues had a flow-on effect for women in universities, playing a part in affirmative action targets.

The early state advocates of feminism viewed equal opportunity and affirmative action legislation as key strategies for equality.[9] Once those laws were passed and support agencies in place, the stage was set for a less senior type of 'femocrat' to find her way into organisations—the Equal Opportunity (EO) officer or manager. In most Australian universities by the late 1980s these roles were dedicated positions, usually with an emphasis on policy and outcomes for both staff and students.

Like her high-flying femocrat counterpart, the EO practitioner in those initial intakes invariably had links with the women's movement and developed policy from a feminist perspective. Like the femocrat, she too had to serve two masters—the need to protect her employer from discrimination laws and build a positive image of equity support, and the need to further the interests of women and other 'target groups'.[10] In practice, this meant that, in fostering proactive measures for change, she often relied on taking an opportunistic approach to organisational and government initiatives.[11] It was in the context of quality rounds in higher education, coupled with the emphasis on staff development that the education and employment ministry in Canberra was encouraging, that the idea of specific leadership programmes for women began to take hold.

Encouraging women's leadership

The federal election campaign of 1993 gave some impetus to affirmative action in the public sector, and the lack of women in senior positions in universities made them a target for political concern. The government's 1988 plans for reshaping higher education included award restructuring, which was introduced under the August 1988 and August 1989 National Wage Cases[12] and continued until 1995.[13] During this process, women in university unions and staff associations campaigned for places on national union forums, where they formed an affirmative action committee. On some campuses (for example Flinders and Newcastle) equity officers 'were involved directly in the Award Restructuring Implementation Committees, set up as joint consultative committees between the unions and administration'.[14] The establishment of the Commonwealth Staff Development Fund was directly linked to award restructuring.

In 1990 the national union of the time, the Federated Australian Universities Staff Association (FAUSA), reported that section 5 of the award restructuring package established the provision of staff development and training to all academic staff 'where this is appropriate'.[15] Consequently, the national affirmative action committee of FAUSA stressed that the needs of women were primary in staff development, and eventually negotiated specific funds for women's programmes.[16] With the near absence of women in senior positions in universities, the idea that women needed training in leadership had also become popular. A number of universities, often through the work of their equity officers, women in unions and women's groups,[17] applied for staff development funds for women's programmes. The cross-organisational networks of equity practitioners are coalitions of interest akin to academic research networks, and are just as important as intra-organisational ones for ensuring that policy ideas developed in one place are taken up in another. Their most striking formalisation with regard to women's leadership programmes is the inter-university ATN WEXDEV programme,[18] a collaboration between the five Australian Technology Network universities.[19]

The first women's leadership programme in Western Australia to be funded through federal staff development provisions was not, however, in the technology network but in the state's newest university—Edith Cowan University (ECU). In late 1990, the year ECU gained university status, its new equal opportunity officer applied for and gained funds from the Cathie Committee[20] for a 1992 women into leadership programme. This programme was designed to upgrade women's skills, promote their collegiality and networks, and thus help them move into leadership roles. But it also encompassed the more radical goal of altering the structure of the organisation to make it more conducive to female career progression.

A core planning group developed a conceptual framework of leadership to oversee programme delivery, long-term strategy and guidelines for improving poor outcomes for women by developing viable career paths.[21] Although the group applied for and gained funds for successive years from the Cathie Committee, support for priority from university decision-makers grew harder to obtain every year.[22] Attention shifted to other programmes in which assumptions of gender-neutrality prevailed, with their consequent outcomes of invisible affirmative action for men. [23] After most of the core group left the university in 1994–95, the programme moved away from sessions devoted to developing women's proficiency in seeing and challenging gender bias. The new training model left aside the earlier aims of changing the structure and culture of the organisation itself.[24] The optimism of the early proponents of this programme was to inspire a group of women at UWA to formulate a 1993 proposal for women's leadership.

Murdoch University's women's leadership programme, initially funded through the federal staff development fund for 1994, was less ambitious than ECU's. Offered in the same year as UWA's first Leadership Development for Women programme, Murdoch's initiative gave junior academic women time out to complete their PhDs or gain publication credits. For the following year, a joint application with Curtin University was rewarded with funds for a mentoring programme, again for junior academic women. Liaison between the project developers, the equity officer, the chair of the Academic Staff Development Committee, and the Academic Services Unit[25] ensured a further application with Curtin. The 1996 programme, Scaffolding the Careers of Academic Women, in part continued Mentoring Junior Academic Women of 1995. It also included a senior management programme, in which up and coming women were paired with senior men and women on campus to develop management skills and promote greater understanding of the organisational culture at senior levels.

When federal funds for such programmes ceased at the end of 1996, Murdoch's programmes ceased also. At Curtin, however, a programme for senior women continued, as part of the WEXDEV collaboration. For senior women only, WEXDEV supports nationally organised conferences and seminars, with occasional national training modules. In 2000 Curtin's programme was extended to include all women staff. In similar vein to the original ECU programmes, Curtin aims at 'transforming both individual capabilities and institutional cultures'.[26] It targets five streams, including a network for Indigenous women and support for women in professionally isolated areas.[27] Apart from the University of South Australia—which has had a workshop, mentoring and collegial group programme for academic and general staff women at all levels since 1996, and a Women's Indigenous Network since 1998—Curtin appears to offer more comprehensive development strategies than other WEXDEV collaborators.[28]

The case of UWA: planning and promise

The conviction that leadership is a skill that could be taught is now widespread. It developed with theories of socialisation in the 1970s,[29] bringing talk about leadership style into fashion. Around the same time women began moving into managerial positions. A few even took on the mantle of senior leadership, including the Australian femocrats. In public and private sectors some leadership training programmes were designed for women only, but they usually followed the training formulas generated by and for men. The planners, supporters and most of the alumni of UWA's Leadership Development for Women programme claim that it broke with that tradition in important ways, without sacrificing the credibility it needed for enduring support.

The Status of Women Group had since the early 1980s urged UWA to address blatant gender bias, mostly to little avail. Under Professor Gale's sponsorship, new search procedures and internal promotions increased the numbers of women professors, the Promotion Committee made changes to criteria, and the university funded better child care. But affirmative action to rectify women's lack of visibility and voice had no public face. As at the other universities, UWA leadership was persuaded to tackle a leadership programme specifically for women. This shift took place in the context of Canberra's funding incentives, which deflected any threatened backlash against affirmative action away from local initiators. The success of the Edith Cowan model helped persuade both equity office and vice-chancellery to offer strong support.

With infrastructure costs guaranteed by vice-chancellery funds, a leadership programme for women was one of three proposals submitted to the Commonwealth Staff Development Fund in 1993. Of the two subsequently funded, its budget was small by staff development standards, but sufficient to employ a part-time co-ordinator for a year, as well as occasional consultants to run workshops and training sessions. As with many initiatives for women, the initial funding was never designed to be permanent. For the following two years the programme's Planning Group applied for and received similar funds, after which no further federal monies were available. Between 1997 and 2000 the programme was funded from the Vice-Chancellor's Discretionary Fund. Since 2001 it has had its own one-line budget and is an integral part of UWA's staff development programmes.

The LDW planners, well aware of the need to develop broad ownership of the programme within the university, established at the outset a Planning Group comprising academic and general staff from various areas of the university as well as representatives of the Equity Office, unions, Human Resources and the Centre for Staff Development. A key strategy was to generate extensive networks of support, and the Planning Group was actively supported by the senior administration. Campus leaders, from the vice-chancellor down, gave time and expertise to make workshops and seminars buzz with information and practical tips. Their input emphasised not only the importance that senior administration placed on the programme but also that collaboration, networking, mentoring and fresh perspectives were as significant to women's development as training in specific skills such as meeting procedure and budgeting.

The committed group of women who founded LDW and served on its planning group in the early years view their efforts as a success. Its popularity ensures that it is over-subscribed every year; the university is attempting to model its other leadership programmes on LDW's offerings; and the great majority of its graduates are highly appreciative of how the programme developed their professional and personal lives. LDW is run at no cost to participants and is held in high regard by senior staff, many of whom have been part of its mentoring team. At the 2002 Leadership Development for Women graduation dinner, for example, Deputy Vice-Chancellor Professor Alan Robson described the programme as:

> ...the most significant contributor to the development of leadership in the UWA community, and to the fine performance of that community itself.

It is perhaps crucial to LDW's success that in the early planning and development stage it had no need to rely on support from the predominantly male Academic Board or the university's overall budget. With one-off federal funding each year until 1996, the planners were able to define the programme's content and philosophy in a form which reflected women's interests.

The key role of evaluation

The model developed for the LDW programme has shown it can stand the test of time, having run continuously since 1994. The one-year programme consists of a two-day core, a series of skills development workshops, information sessions, a mentor network, career development workshops, and a series of forums and informal networking opportunities for those who have completed the initial year. Open to all women staff, academic and general, with a half-time appointment or more, the programme also targets women in isolated professional fields. During the first few years an Action Learning Project was offered.[30] In 1997–98 an Executive Development programme for more senior women was also trialled, and has since become a Senior Women's Network with meetings and more casual networking.

A series of evaluations show success on a number of vital yardsticks, including personal and professional empowerment, participant opportunities and organisational effectiveness.[31] The differential between the promotion rates for academic staff who have participated and those who have not continues to be high (see Table 1). To March 2003 a total of 126 of the programme's alumni had been promoted, which is 48 per cent of graduates overall.

Table 1: Comparison (%) of Leadership for Women (LDW) promotional success with other female, male and total staff promotional success, 31 March 1994 to 31 March 2002, for the 1994–1996 and 1998–2001 cohort groups. There was no comparable LDW cohort in 1997.

	1994	1995	1996	1998	1999	2000	2001	2002
Academic staff								
LDW group	**74**	**47**	**38**	**25**	**40**	**43**	**13**	**21**
Other female	23	19	18	20	21	14	11	3
Male	27	27	27	27	24	18	13	7
Total	27	25	25	25	23	17	13	6
General staff								
LDW group	**64**	**50**	**30**	**29**	**40**	**45**	**44**	**36**
Other female	13	20	20	20	19	19	16	12
Male	19	22	19	18	17	14	12	9
Total	16	21	20	19	18	17	15	11

Note: 'Other female' staff excludes LDW participants.

In addition, the retention rates of LDW graduates are consistently higher than those for the total staff population. The rate for 1994, for example, is 84 per cent, compared to 39 per cent for other female academics, and 48 per cent for academic males. The figures for general staff were 64 per cent, 33 per cent and 32 per cent respectively. A major evaluation in 1998 noted:

> LDW participants…are much more likely to be promoted and more likely to remain employed at UWA. They self-report significant changes in their working lives that they attribute to their programme involvement. As a result the university has more women in more senior positions contributing to decision making.[32]

This survey also found that of those LDW participants who applied for promotion, 59 per cent felt their decision to apply was influenced by the programme, and 82 per cent felt that the quality of their application was influenced by their participation.

Findings in other universities[33] as well as in earlier periods at UWA[34] indicate that academic women tend to suffer both a sense of isolation and a lack of encouragement with regard to promotion. The 1998 evaluation showed that LDW had directly addressed those two concerns. Academic staff ranked 'participation in UWA networks' (96 per cent) and improved 'quality of their applications for promotion' (87 per cent) as the biggest impact that the programme had had on their working lives.

Because general staff have a different system of promotions, their responses to the 1998 evaluation were different. Promotion did not figure, but all those who achieved secondments attributed their success to LDW, as did 90 per cent of those 'being offered/applying for special projects'. General staff joined with academic staff in giving a high rating to increased networking participation (89 per cent).[35]

Making the programme part of the system

From the start, LDW's effectiveness was monitored and participants' evaluations sought after every seminar and workshop.[36] Extremely favourable results, and the large number of potential participants, enabled the Planning Group to build a strong argument for the project's continuation. By 2001, LDW had generated sufficient university-wide support to persuade the deputy vice-chancellor that a proposal to the Finance Committee for a mainstream budget could prove successful. Senior staff, including some who had mentored LDW participants, argued for and secured that one-line funding.

LDW had over 300 alumni by early 2003, with 30 women a year enrolled since 1994. A further 60 were undertaking programmes in 2003. From 2001, to cope with opening the doors to women at all levels of general and academic staff, three courses have run every two years, resulting in an intake of 90 women per period.

By expanding participation beyond the senior levels, LDW's planners broke with the tradition of most other university leadership programmes. The original funding was for academic women only, but negotiations between the vice-chancellery, the equity office and the programme's planners ensured the inclusion of 10 general staff in the group of 30 participants. Since 1995 the groups have each represented 50 per cent of the yearly intake. Other early restrictions were to academic staff working half-time or more at lecturer A or above and general staff at level 6 or above. Funding has enabled the Planning Group to progressively lower the eligibility ceiling, so that general staff at all levels are now invited to apply, provided they hold a 12 month or more contract at half-time or greater.

Of the 38 public universities in Australia in 2002, 16 offered mentoring programmes specifically designed for women.[37] One-quarter of these charged for the service.[38] A major strategy of LDW has been the careful matching of participants with a senior member of staff in a mentoring arrangement.[39] At the outset, mentors were mostly men, but in later years alumni who have achieved seniority have taken on mentoring responsibilities, and by 2001 there were as many women as men. Some senior men have repeatedly acted as mentors, and there is a widespread view that the programme's success is linked to their support. Drawing men in as mentors was a deliberate strategy of the early planners, as Professor Gale has explained:

> This was done on purpose. It was important to involve the senior males in the process so that they would own and support this affirmative action programme. It was very interesting to see how enthusiastic the male mentors became and how positive they were about a number of other equity issues as a result...There are just too few senior women and these are already stretched to the limit. There are so many more males to draw from.[10]

Quality of work environments and relationships

The idea of using women's development as a tool for organisational change is not unusual. As noted above, it was a primary goal of the programmes at both Edith Cowan and Curtin universities. The Leadership Development for Women programme at UWA has produced cumulative change, with its alumni demonstrating successes in promotion, secondments and career advances. Women who have undertaken the programme see more than a quantitative effect on their individual careers. For many, including this senior lecturer, their participation generated a qualitative change—a feeling of belonging that was previously missing:

> I have always, from a very young age, wanted to be in a university environment rather than being in the commercial world, and I always had my doubts like 'Do they want me there?'...the LDW programme has given me the idea: there is a place for me here.

Other women identified how the programme had enabled a sense of community. It opened networks to them, through the information it gave about how the university committee and decision-making systems operated. It offered training in speaking out on issues and speaking up for themselves. Respondents commented on the value of knowing where to go for information when an unexpected problem arose, of utilising their new links across both general and academic staff and between central administration and academic departments. Networking among participants was the key to overcoming a sense of isolation in a specific department or professional field, particularly for women in departments where men were more numerous or where women were physically removed on satellite campuses.

'An oasis'

Leadership programmes for women have drawn criticism from some scholars on the grounds that they simply teach women to 'fit in' to the existing culture[41] while leaving intact the traditional work environment—extended hours of work and lack of support for family responsibilities—modelled on traditional male careers.

There are strong indications, however, that most LDW participants would say that the programme has done more than help them to 'fit in'. A common view expressed by the women we interviewed was that a key strength was that it was mounted for women only. They saw it as particularly significant not because it taught women to find their way around and within a set of rules and structures designed by and for men, but because it legitimated a women's space in an affirmative action sense. One administrator said that LDW formed a 'cell of protection' around her and women she knew, and another saw it as 'a kind of oasis in work time'. A lecturer claimed LDW 'would never work [well] if it wasn't a women-only space' and a counterpart in engineering noted how it taught her that 'I am not alone, that other women have the same problems, that there are solutions to the problems we face'.

In programme evaluations and in our focus groups and interviews, women claimed that they looked forward to LDW events and workshops. One said that 'taking time out with other women is a valuable learning experience that leaves me feeling stronger and less isolated',[42] another that 'I feel normal when I'm at LDW' and a third that 'plotting with other women fills up my well, I go out and face whatever'.

The symbolic effect of a women-only space with top-level support is also described in other evaluations of the programme. For example, one woman's response to the 1998 evaluation was that LDW had allowed her to acknowledge that 'I am proud that I am a woman. Coming here reminds me that women are amazing.'[43] From this perspective, LDW provides an enclave for women to reassure each other, to build networks, to gain practice in difficult face-to-face encounters and to open possibilities for collaborative practices of leadership and innovation.

Human geographer Massey writes of the 'politics of space', and suggests that cultural struggles can ensue over how and whether the 'realm of the spatial' is politicised.[44] In similar vein, Mitchell argues that an important political strategy for marginalised groups is to restructure public space into 'spaces of representation'.[45] Clearly the participants in the LDW programme were invoking a new sense of power in defining a space specifically for women. Such symbolic space-making can, however, be subjected to hostile responses from men who see it as an unfair or unnecessary use of university resources.

'Secret women's business'

As with most affirmative action projects, claims by minorities to 'spaces of representation' are subject to backlash and punishment. One woman spoke of a 'boys' club' which tended to characterise the LDW programme as 'secret women's business'. Others saw such men as annoyed to see this space for women turning an advantage that was men's alone into one that must be shared:

> There is a degree of harassment that takes place in the
> departments of women who are vulnerable. Some women
> are criticised for coming on the programme, for taking
> 'too much time off work', even though staff development is

work...a fair amount of unpleasantness around—depart-mental stuff that happens over morning tea.

One Head of Department, he just flatly refused and said 'No, you are not doing it—I don't see how it is going to benefit us'.

Interviews with heads of department and executive deans support women's descriptions of negative reactions by some male managers. In response to a question about how he viewed the LDW programme, one male head of department said: 'X is the only woman in our department and she's done very nicely without such things'. There *were* other women in that department, on general staff, but most were below Level 5 and at that time did not qualify for LDW. A male executive dean in a faculty with more women than most at UWA said, 'I don't believe the best women here want to be targeted like that, particularly the younger women. No need...we're all equal here.'

It was clear that the topic of affirmative action, or targets, can sorely try the patience of a minority of middle-level staff. Two of the six executive deans in 2000 refused a request by the deputy vice-chancellor to set targets for recruiting female staff, on the grounds that targets were 'unfair' and 'not necessary'.[46] A gender pattern emerges in this middle-management group, which included deans and departmental heads. We interviewed sixteen people from this group.[47] The data shows a lack of agreement between women and men on the topic of support for LDW, and broad disagreement on the topic of affirmative action. All five women spoke favourably about the programme; only one expressed some concern about policies designed to counter entrenched advantage for men. Two of the eleven men spoke in favour of it, while comments from the rest were either non-committal or critical. And all but one of the men were either ambivalent or against affirmative action for women.

For one head of department, in a group with no women above lecturer level, the LDW programme symbolised a bitter gender war. This war was driven by 'political correctness', ensuring that men were now disadvantaged. Echoing the words of two other males we interviewed, he claimed that 'It all went too far under Fay Gale':

> *The person who really needs that [training] in this depart-*
> *ment is a man who's never applied for promotion. I've*
> *tried [to persuade him] so have others. But X [the woman*
> *who used to head the department] did nothing about that.*
> *He's the one that needs something to give him confidence,*
> *not the women.*

The most strident critics of this women-only leadership programme considered participants to be bent on occupying the university's centres of power. Moreover, affirmative action gave them an unfair advantage. The fact that a woman or two had entered the heartland of organisational power was proof that all women were now on an equal footing with men.

The women and men who devised and now support, maintain and guide the Leadership Development for Women programme point to such stories as proof of why the programme is needed. Essential to the development of all women are considerations of how to counter antagonism and lack of interest, and how to overcome lack of under-standing of how gender patterns affect opportunities.

'Whose culture?'

The LDW programme has sponsored a number of women from diverse cultural and linguistic backgrounds. Most of those we inter-viewed said they gained from their participation. It led some to join other informal groups for mutual support. One such group was a response to LDW, which its members saw as having inadvertently demonstrated for them a lack of sensitivity to the issue of ethnicity. Four women, among the first from non-mainstream backgrounds to do the programme, claimed that they raised in feedback sessions the question of the ethnocentrism of the programme and its 'culturally specific' notions of leadership. For example, they said, the focus on teaching women to speak in the ways of the dominant culture (i.e. assertively and rapidly) may indirectly have resulted in women of diversity being punished for being 'too pushy'. Because race-based stereotypes often assume that women of certain ethnic groups act quietly and non-assertively, those who fail to conform to type are characterised as strident, outlandish or aggressive. These four women were not confident that issues of cultural difference and of racism had been addressed adequately in the workshops and training, and one said: 'My words about that fall on totally deaf ears'.

Despite these concerns, two of the women considered that LDW had improved their level of assertiveness. Members of the group sought a better understanding between all women on campus, with one remarking that their network was committed to improving the relationship between the various groups, such as Status of Women and LDW. One said that she would not necessarily recommend the programme to women from diverse backgrounds because it did too little to counter dominant assumptions about what constituted leadership. The group wanted to see the programme educate all women on a range of equity fronts (including anti-racism and diversity) by looking at how leadership is perceived and enacted in different cultures. At present, they said, the programme is geared to help white women 'get on' in a highly establishment and racist culture. Lesbian women echoed this criticism of lack of inclusivity, albeit from a very different perspective. One woman made the point that LDW sends a message that it is helping women to deal with an unwelcoming culture, yet itself deals inadequately with a most important question: 'Whose culture are we talking about?'

Such comments and criticisms are a necessary reality check for LDW's planners, and encourage a renewed effort to meet the needs of a greater diversity of women. Since 2001 there have been two programmes, running year about, from which women can choose. One deals more with the development of higher level leadership skills: the other (a double intake) places more emphasis on issues of personal development and building relationships across levels and differences. The photographs taken at each year's graduation dinner show faces representing a range of cultural and ethnic identities, although it is rare to see an Aboriginal woman among them. So the problem of universalising programmes derived from white, Anglo ethnicity remains an issue. UWA has few Indigenous staff, and almost all senior roles in Indigenous teaching and research are filled by women. Aboriginal women consider that a leadership programme suitable to their needs should not single them out at all, but should be open to Aboriginal men. Resourcing and management issues both in the programme and in Aboriginal education itself have prevented such a development to date.

The change agent within

The symbolic effect of a leadership programme for women depends upon how it is supported, portrayed and harnessed by competing interests. The supporters and planners of LDW readily admit that the primary goal is to give women the necessary skills, confidence, networks, training and experience to fit more easily the criteria of success that UWA fosters. The first objective of the programme's mission statement is 'To enable women...to develop leadership skills and knowledge in order to increase their participation in the university's decision making and to facilitate their leadership at all levels'.[48] On that count, as the figures on promotion prospects show, the programme has been remarkably successful.

Has it delivered outcomes which go beyond the 'fix the women' approach critiqued by Kolb and Meyerson?[49] Has it realised the vision that inspired the original planners? The first programme handout, in 1994, gives some clues. First, it highlighted a key cultural goal: 'a better understanding in the University community of gender differences and equity issues in the working environment, and recognition of women's talents and contributions'.[50] Where that cultural goal differs from a 'fix the women' approach is that, as the founders and organisers would argue, LDW aims to do more than advance the career chances of individual women. Nor is it designed simply to give women tools of assertiveness so they can cope with gendered norms and rules. Rather, it focuses on changing the wider culture of the organisation.

Importantly, interviews with members of the original planning group showed they wanted shared leadership development, along the lines they had known in earlier women's networks. Two made it clear that LDW was never designed to be a training exercise. One claimed she wanted the programme to 'generate a sense of community that welcomed women's contributions', and another believed the programme would 'help women overcome their fears'. A third envisaged 'workshop facilitators with a strong feminist understanding', and believed the programme would 'soften the male dominated environment' and develop 'the type of leadership that increases women's comfort zone'. In short, these planners envisaged a companionate leadership model.

The idea that the programme should take on the task of reshaping the gendered university is clearly revealed in the list of objectives and expected outcomes drawn up for the first intake in 1994. A major heading in that document is 'New concepts of leadership', and there is emphasis on a collective politics as the driver of change. Listed among LDW's ten 'Expected outcomes for UWA' is 'the emergence of a proactive group concerned with women's issues'. To a feminist ear that goal sounds remarkably like a plan for the development of 'inside agitators'. Yet to turn those qualitative goals into measurable outcomes the planners had to translate their feminist-inspired ideas into what Fraser defines as readily acceptable organisation-speak.[51] Thus the second objective of the mission statement is 'To contribute to a culture change in the University'.[52]

A vital way in which LDW aims to achieve that 'culture change' is by developing UWA's cultural literacy. Common sense ways of seeing the world can inhibit a view of how the gendered university operates. Some LDW workshops use a 'gender lens' to help participants see beyond two of those blinkered perspectives. A gender lens insists that the first trap is to operate from a 'fix the women' strategy, which tends to treat women as the problem, rather than the gender effects of entrenched norms and practices. The second trap is that the answer does not lie in simply 'valuing the feminine',[53] which can simultaneously position women as part of the ivory basement—i.e. as support troops for the main game played by men. A clearly focused gender lens can help women to determine what their work units need to do if they, their colleagues and students are to develop in fair and equitable ways. As promotion and retention outcomes clearly show, a focus on cultural literacy simultaneously helps realise individual career goals. Outreach is also an important tool for reshaping 'how we do things around here'. Sponsored seminars and awareness-raising gatherings draw together LDW's participants and graduates, and the wider communities of university work.

Responsibility for change?

The LDW programme enjoys a reputation as the university's core driver of cultural change on gender matters. Professor Bob Wood, who chaired the Review of Women Academic Staff in 1995, identifies LDW as the most viable source of that change process. He explained in 1999 why a key recommendation of the review was that the women's leadership initiative be continued, with funding from the university purse:

> We thought if we go directly for some sort of programme that forces men in more traditional departments into some training, it would invite reactions that would make things worse in the short term...Rather than change the male-dominated culture directly, because that [would] invite reactions, what we decided to do instead was to fund an activity that we saw as being very effective in building a support network and developing female leadership so that they could then exert an influence over culture.

That decision endorsed LDW as a significant factor in women's professional development, and simultaneously as a preferred source of the change needed to counteract the gendered university. Most women who have been through the programme endorse that view.

There is a problem, however, if the effect of that decision saddles LDW with sole symbolic responsibility for what is clearly a mammoth task. First, it is vital that other important programmes and areas of management are not let off the hook. Secondly, the decision should not leave the onus for change with women, with no required training for men to update their understanding of gender issues. Thirdly, the programme has neither the financial resources nor the structural support to shoulder the full burden of 'culture change'.

Conclusion

The Leadership Development for Women programme's success has been recognised in important ways.[54] It has provided the university with good reason to showcase its effective and comprehensive women's leadership programme at Australian and overseas gatherings.[55] Within UWA, that success has encouraged senior leadership to ensure its financial security and thus extend it to women across all university ranks. Importantly, LDW has proven that women across the university spectrum will seek advancement and new ways of contributing if there are signs that the organisation encourages their expectations. By highlighting the success of the programme in various ways, UWA's leadership has enabled a reshaped identity for the institution itself—from one seen as harshly unwelcoming to women, to one that more women and most men now see as more inclusive. Most of the women who have been through the programme speak of a new sense of self, of feeling 'part of the action' and confident about claiming a space and a voice for themselves—as women.

Perhaps the secret of LDW's longevity is that it provides support and development for women, alongside leadership insights and a pleasing list of triumphs for the men and women who support it. No doubt the early planners—who viewed LDW participants as potential agents for change—will watch with keen interest to see whether the programme's graduates will shape not only their university's culture/s but also its future directions.

CHAPTER 6

The Elasticity of Academic Merit

*The concept of merit is so elastic. In effect we've had an
affirmative action program for men in the past and we
used the concept of merit to justify it.*

a former UWA deputy vice-chancellor, 1999

'Chilly climate' is a phrase that Australian academic women were
beginning to use by the mid-1990s. It had gained currency in overseas universities from the early 1980s as shorthand for women being
frozen out of the status and reward systems in their institutions. Like
the weather, the notion of climate conveys an environment that is
'all around us and nowhere in particular'.[1]

When Dame Leonie Kramer made her now infamous remark
that 'women go limp when the going gets tough', it was not too
difficult to see that her words were contributing to the chilly climate
for academic women. But so, too, is the renowned scholar who
welcomes the cohort of new PhD students with a story about persistence—how he had haunted the pub every night to meet and 'land'
his high-profile potential supervisor—a more difficult strategy for
women candidates. Another contributor is the university teacher,

male or female, who interrupts women more often than men students in class discussion, or allows others to interrupt women but sometimes insists on hearing out certain men in the class.

Coming from Australia's most senior university woman of the era, Kramer's public pronouncement was potentially damaging to the advancement of women academics. Yet, partly because of the publicity it generated, it was rapidly discredited as a public gaff by scores of influential women.[2] By contrast, the senior scholar's story of persistence in the pub may have a greater covert effect, however benignly intended. Like the everyday sexism of the teacher, it is a subtle and routine expression of the thinking that tends to advantage men in ways we seldom notice.[3] Both practices are normal to the extent that they appear inconsequential. Hall and Sandler, who coined the term 'chilly climate', argue otherwise.[4] In their report on gender dynamics in North American universities, they conclude that 'subtle and/or inadvertent incidents can sometimes do the most damage, because they often occur without the full awareness of the [people involved]'.

Such incidents shape people's understanding of academic merit. If the criteria for senior university management include the ability to avoid 'going limp', and if women are stereotyped as lacking that ability, then men are more likely than women to be seen as meritorious. If the criteria for effective seminar participation include jumping in to speak, then students trained to politely wait until they are asked to speak will be seen as lower in merit. When it is normal to find that eighteen out of twenty senior managers are men then, as Cockburn argues, that very normality implies that being male carries more merit for senior management than being female.[5]

This pattern of accrued advantage to men[6] increases the likelihood of men in the tower and women in the basement. There is considerable literature on the respective reputation of women and men in a variety of fields. For instance, in a study of organisation research, Martin and Collinson note that 'men cite men more than they cite women, whereas women cite women and men about equally'.[7]

Psychologists have shown, since at least the 1970s, that putting a male or a female name on a piece of written work for merit assessment invariably reveals a bias in favour of males. In 1999 a group of psychologists in the United States copied early and later forms of a woman's curriculum vitae and sent them to members of psychology departments across the country. The first stage of the CV was when the woman had gained departmental lectureship; the second when she had gained tenure. The researchers put a female name on half the documents and a male name on the others. They asked respondents if they would (a) hire the person with the early CV and (b) give tenure to the person with the later CV. The question of hiring revealed a large gender gap. Almost two-thirds of the respondents (men and women) said they would employ the male, while one-third said they would employ the female. On the issue of tenure, the gender gap disappeared.[8] The researchers attribute the response on tenure to the quality of the CV—the candidate was well above the credits normally required for that level. Revealingly, however, they pointed out that respondents were four times more likely to write cautionary comments when the candidate for tenure was a woman, such as 'I would need to see evidence that she had gotten these grants on her own'.

Such attitudinal studies show that merit is shaped by social stereotypes that normalise gendered occupational segregation and hierarchy. In organisations framed around the lives and interests of men, a male norm operates at the unseen level of everyday thinking to favour men.[9] Because the discriminatory behaviours are so normal, it is usually difficult to see them as anything but natural and it takes a particular study or task to reveal the bias. Such biases are shaped not only through a devaluing of women's roles in the domestic sphere[10] but also through the relegation of most women to support roles in their jobs. Janet Finch is vice-chancellor of a medium sized university in the United Kingdom and chairs the steering group of the prime minister's Equality Challenge in Higher Education, established in 2001. She suggests that the greater role played by women in devalued support work—as secretaries, caterers, cleaners and in personnel—helps shape a devaluing of women's contributions to academic disciplines. Finch stresses how male advantage is normalised from one generation to the next in universities: 'young people are learning...that...women are valued less highly than men...when the vast majority of people who deal with students from a position of authority and responsibility are men'.[11] Such comments show increasing support for the insights of the 1980s that led feminist researchers to argue that universities are 'social institutions where gender is done'.[12]

Practitioners and researchers in the field of equal employment opportunity argued from the 1980s for redefining merit in order to remedy inequitable and stereotyped judgements.[13] Their arguments prompted a backlash, with the guardians of the old system arguing that any change to the merit principle would result in a *lowering* of standards. The literature, by contrast, suggests that the redefining of merit in the criteria for selection and promotion requires a *raising* of standards.[14]

Perceptions of merit

The merit of a university employee, student or written product is viewed as being assessed on objective, rational criteria. As judgement made solely on merit is considered a key indicator of a fair and reasonable academic organisation, the notion of merit as a product of social and political organisation is therefore ignored. A male departmental head put it like this:

> *Traditionally there has been a very powerful sense that merit drives this university and all its internal policies and nothing should interfere with that.*

For some men it was crucial to keep the traditional construction of merit from being tarnished by equity considerations. One senior male thought that the circumspect behaviour of women's groups on campus had enabled UWA to avoid that disaster:

> *Women's groups handled the changes round equity issues well. They haven't set out to violate some of the principles of merit that drive the university.*

Several heads of department considered merit a reliable source of equity. Some suggested that this equitable tradition is so embedded in the culture that there is little need for any formal policies for ensuring equity:

> *If you actually have people who are in the major positions searching for candidates and sensitive to emotional issues, then you are probably going to get about as many women as you can anyway without the formal thing.*

For other male heads, equity practice was a threat to merit:

> *We just want the best candidate. I would not pick the second best just because she is a female. It is based on merit.*

As always with such judgements, it is assumed that there can be no doubt about what constitutes merit. Those making the decision use 'Of course we got it right!' as a hubristic smokescreen for doing just what they were inclined towards. And thus the idea that equity is irrelevant to questions of merit is perpetuated.

Selection procedures

Establishing merit is usually described as employing a scientific approach. Quantitative evaluation is deemed fitting for such judgements, and therefore the number of publications and/or the quality of publishing in certain categories is attractive as a 'best' method of establishing career achievements. By contrast, people wanting to see more equitable selection practices argue for a more detailed analysis of careers which deviate from the accepted norm. As one woman noted about her experience as a member of a 1999 selection panel:

> *I talked about all of the ways that we need to recognise the hidden selection bias, to be aware that women have different career patterns. And then this very senior male*

completely undid whatever I had said by talking about
how you work out the worth of a publication list.

Yet women too are encultured into the belief that academic merit is earned by countable achievements. As individual effort and talent is what counts, so teamwork, teaching and even administrative wisdom run a poor second to the recruitment of one's disciplinary peers (editors and journal readers) into a responsive cheer-group. It comes as a rude shock to some women to find that there is a social and gender dimension skewing the concept of individual merit:

> *I find it rather depressing, because my idea always was*
> *that my career was about me. It was about me going out*
> *there and getting the qualifications and doing the work...*
> *But when you see the stats, the numbers are against you*
> *and the policies are too dependent upon interpretation.*

Nonetheless, at The University of Western Australia there are signs of change. For some senior academics, taking on the task of examining equity outcomes can produce insights about merit. A former deputy vice-chancellor provides a good example. In chairing the Review of Women Academic Staff he sifted through the submissions, listened to interviewees and collaborated with his team of reviewers, all of which taught him about the elasticity of the merit concept. Another senior academic said he began to doubt the efficacy of relying on the merit principle when he correlated the gender pattern of those who had been selected as senior academics:

> *We recently went through how we'd employed a number*
> *of people, and by the time we added up our selections for*
> *those jobs we looked and we had not one woman. So we*
> *could see how we were judging people on all the crite-*
> *ria we were supposed to, we were following the policies*
> *exactly, doing all the things to ensure merit—and yet not*
> *one woman. That process became visible to us because we*
> *looked at a whole lot at once. If you do it one at a time it*
> *just passes unnoticed.*

These senior decision-makers had learned what equity agents had been trying for several years to teach.

Redressing gender imbalance at work requires that the procedures developed must shape a new understanding of merit. The complacency with which merit has been understood in the past must be acknowledged, and the observer led to question earlier assumptions. Yet despite a greater awareness by some of the administrative group of senior males, recent figures indicate that after performing better than most universities during the mid-1990s, UWA is again falling behind the average in increasing the number of women above senior lecturer level.[15]

The previous chapter described how the affirmative action committee of the national academics' union had some influence on government approaches to gender inequalities in universities. Once women with an equal opportunity agenda had secured places on the National Tertiary Education Union, the NTEU encouraged individual staff associations to target affirmative action selection and promotion procedures through award restructuring and then enterprise bargaining.[16] Such claims were supported by Vice-Chancellor Fay Gale, who in 1992, for example, sponsored search plans to recruit more senior academic women. In Western Australia, UWA was not alone. Murdoch University developed similar plans through its award restructuring process.[17] Edith Cowan University set a 1994 target of five promotions for each faculty (division), three of which had to go to women,[18] and Health and Human Sciences gave all five promotions to women. However, this one-off affirmative action round was never followed up. As one of the sponsors of that initiative remarked a year later, 'it was almost as if that had never happened'.[19]

Collaboration between equity managers, key human resources personnel and the staff association at UWA led to guidelines that focused on four aspects of the selection process: job clarification; advertisement preparation; appropriate distribution of information about the job; getting and keeping applicants interested. The search plans aimed to identify individuals to be approached directly. For senior positions, these search plans were submitted to the Search and Screen Committee, and thereby the vice-chancellor for consideration and finalisation.

These procedures proved successful, particularly in the first half of the 1990s. They played a strong role in raising the complement of women professors from 2 to 16. A small number of women were recruited into general staff above level 10 or promoted into professorships. Yet those small wins had their price. A woman who had worked at UWA for fifteen years in a number of general staff positions spoke of the backlash:

> *For this institution the changes might have moved a bit too quickly...there was a bit of a backlash...It came from the blokes, and because people didn't understand the process it sometimes seemed as if these women had been parachuted in. None of them were, but it seemed that perhaps they were being favoured, which wouldn't have been the case because there was a promotions committee or selection committee.*

For academics in the ivory basement, however, the search plan may not prove as effective. The requirement for search procedures was not formalised for all new academic staff until May 1996, in a memo to all heads of department from the human resources director:

> Changes to selection procedures now make a search plan a requirement when recruiting new academic staff. Developing and using a search plan broadens the field of applicants and is helpful in attracting well qualified women candidates. It involves going beyond the normal advertising procedures and using less formal networks to inform potential applicants about the vacancy.

We found that understanding of the search requirement was rather patchy, with a number of male professors who had chaired selection committees seeing it as illegal to 'discriminate' in favour of women. One said he 'always felt it best to wait and see who had applied'; another that 'it was illegal to inquire about the sex of applicants, so you don't know who you've got until you decide to interview them'. Nonetheless, whether search procedures were used adequately or not, female appointment into tenurable positions rose from 10 per cent in 1990 to almost 40 per cent in 1997.

Search procedures and the micropolitics of merit

Despite the initial success of the search procedures in relation to women professors and upper level administrators, it was clear by the late 1990s that a number of women interviewed for our study were concerned about backsliding. One respondent, a senior academic herself, described the lack of search plan activity for a senior position in 1999, citing lack of interest by the chair of the selection panel:

> He did nothing to make sure that some women were on the shortlist to be interviewed. He said, 'We shook the tree and none fell out'. He should have been going around to some of the senior women and saying 'You would do a good job, I notice you haven't applied—can you tell me what would make the job attractive to you?' That isn't to say that you would shoe a woman into the job, but he didn't even think about the women.

Another senior academic woman reported a similar observation:

> For the selection of professor positions the selection com- mittees were nearly always predominantly male and they nearly always had very male ways of operating. There was a recognition of the search processes to get candidates, but in a number of disciplines there was only lip service paid to the principle, and to an outsider looking in it didn't appear that there was a real search for female candidates. It depends partly on who chairs the committees.

For many women academics in our study, a crucial step to enlarging the understanding of merit is to have a significant number and proportion of senior women academics. They spoke of the need for role models and mentors for other women; of the need for women in decision-making roles, who would bring a more complex perspective to all university issues; and of the impact high-profile women could make if and when they spoke out publicly on gender issues:

> *Because Fay Gale was a very senior woman, she was automatically on those power committees. So I think we miss her in terms of that. I am often the only woman now. I think we don't have enough senior women and the minority of senior women have too many demands on them.*

With such small numbers of women at the top levels, two or three more can make a large percentage difference. When women professors or senior administrators left and were not replaced, alarm bells sounded for those concerned about equity issues:

> *We have lost a few women professors. It highlighted just how few women professors there were, that if you lose two then everybody notices, whereas if we lost two male professors then nobody would feel bad. [When a man leaves] the gender balance isn't being threatened in any way.*

Selection committees which try to address the gender-biased nature of merit encounter frequent problems. When merit is construed as inherently fair, reasons are found to explain why clear gender inequities continue to exist:

- Budget constraints
  If you want targets, I would love for the Vice-Chancellor or whoever to give me a budget to hire fifteen women professors in our faculty.

- Faculty culture
  I'd like to, but the academics in my department wouldn't wear it.

- Low turnover
  Our department has always had a great deal of difficulty in attracting and hiring females, so the question of background, training, those sorts of issues were really never on our agenda...But other departments have been desperate to get people regardless of who they are.

- Difficulty in attracting applicants to Western Australia, due to the tyranny of distance and the small number of universities:
  It is actually hard to recruit people in Western Australia in general, and given the number of dual career people these days it is even harder going. In any other job when you are hiring you are always hiring dual career people, but there is actually some place else for the other person to get a job...making a decision to move to the West for either man or woman is actually harder, they often can't find their partner a job as well.

- Not finding any women
  I have been on a search and screen committee for a very senior position and we worked really, really hard to try and find suitable women. There weren't any at the time. But that wasn't just me, that was the whole committee.

The procedures followed by selection panels were also criticised. According to one panel member, part of the problem stemmed from a lack of time allocated for analysing applicants with different career patterns:

> *You get a wad of papers to read in one afternoon before passing it on to the next person. There is no time to try and find out whether the applicant is a late starter, has had family responsibilities or how well she has performed relative to opportunities. Instead, you just count up what her publications and strengths are and compare her with everyone else on that basis.*

The reality of time shortages and formula-based assessments contrasts with an awareness of the problems at the level of policy, as shown by these comments from a senior male:

The arguments that were used to bolster the idea that we had a merit system—but it wasn't producing great equity—ranged from 'Women traditionally have babies' through to 'Some women don't like doing science' or whatever. So when we looked behind those and looked at the quality of the selection and the types of people, you realised that people just use merit—it's a concept that's almost tautological. 'These people are selected because of merit.' 'How do you know that they've got merit?' 'Well because they were selected.' Under that system you could be as biased as you liked and the process was almost a self-fulfilling prophecy.

And there is room for optimism in the university's committee for promotion and tenure having shifted procedures in recognition of bias and discrimination.

Promotions procedures

A study in the early 1990s showed that such a change was sorely needed. Everett surveyed the demographics of academic staff at four universities, including UWA, in 1978/79, 1984 and 1990. At UWA the discrimination ratios, based on a comparison of men and women of similar age, service, publication and degree qualification, show women held lower rank than they should across all those years. This was strong *prima facie* evidence of consistent discrimination against women in promotion and selection levels. Analysis of the other three universities showed similar results.[20]

The factors that advantage men had been discussed for some time. In a 1980 paper, Fay Gale noted the difficulties inherent for women in traditional academic life.[21] She demonstrated that travelling abroad, networking overseas and within Australia, becoming well-known to journal editors through conferences, and other ways of gaining academic recognition and support were frequently impeded by responsibilities for children or the exigencies of a partner's job location.

Although there is little sign in Australian universities generally that academic promotion criteria were changing to accommodate family responsibilities,[22] there was considerable change at UWA. Since the early 1990s UWA has reshaped these processes, to the extent that a significant minority of the staff we interviewed claimed that there was now no barrier to women's advancement. We then examined documents on the procedural changes, interviewed members of the Promotions and Tenure Committee, senior administrators and academics, and canvassed university opinion. We found that a form of collaborative leadership has had an important influence on these changes.

Statistics give us a way of summarising in clear-cut terms the undoubted success stories stemming from UWA's academic promotion policies. The first notable change was in successful promotion to lecturer for women and men: from 1983 to 1989, 38.5 per cent of women were promoted and 59.3 per cent of men, while from 1990 to 1996 it was 66 and 69 per cent respectively.[23] In 2000–02 women and men applying at this level had an equal success rate of 80 per cent. The annual Equal Employment Opportunity reports show that from 1994 it became increasingly common for female applicants to apply for promotion from lecturer to senior lecturer. Only 10 per cent of these applicants in 1994 were women. This proportion increased by around 50 per cent in 1995 and 1996 until it reached 23.8 per cent, then rose to 34.6 per cent in 1997.[24] Between 2000 and 2002 women applicants in this category averaged 49 per cent. For human resource administrators, these figures were proof that the Promotions and Tenure Committee had been transformed. As one said:

The Promotions and Tenure Committee changed ahead of the rest of the university. The old story of 'Don't bother to apply until you have six papers and two books' has been broken down.

As we look up the levels to associate professor and professor, the proportion of women applicants drops dramatically, although their success rate has risen since 1998.

It is important to unpack the context and practices underpinning this change. The fact that women were not applying for promotion to the extent that would be expected was made obvious to the vice-chancellery, to the equity office and to human resources from the early 1990s by a combination of external and union pressures for affirmative action, feedback from women's groups on campus, and comparative data and research. Over the succeeding decade, the vice-chancellery responded by modifying the promotion criteria to make them more thorough and wide-ranging, broadening the make-up of the Promotions and Tenure Committee, and implementing strategies to increase the gender awareness of that committee.

Most of the dramatic changes to the promotion process occurred between 1991 and 1996. In 1991 the vice-chancellor appointed a professor, who was later to become deputy vice-chancellor, to chair the committee. Strong memories of his own early treatment as an applicant determined Professor Robson to introduce transparent procedures with support and feedback to applicants. In line with union claims in enterprise bargaining, he argued for and introduced teaching and service criteria and, in 1995, monthly consideration of applications.

The Promotions and Tenure Committee (with help from human resources and the equity office) researched and developed the service portfolio and argued for its introduction. They also worked on criteria for the teaching portfolio, ultimately developed by the Centre for Staff Development. Until 1994 there was only one academic woman—a newly promoted professor—on the committee (she joined in 1992). She and another senior female professor have since been appointed to chair the committee. Key changes to the promotions procedures included:

- teaching and service counted as highly as research
- no requirement to be at the top of a particular level before applying for the next

- part-time work and careers hindered for family reasons to be compared to pro rata expectations of achievements
- contract staff able to apply for promotion and, if successful, to be granted tenure
- applications to be considered monthly
- applicants able to seek feedback from the vice-chancellery both during and after the process

Academics who worked in the ivory basement were also given some consideration. The academic award restructure in 1991 required that the criteria for promotion from senior tutor to lecturer be clarified. Positions were renamed level A and level B, and promotion to level B required evidence of research. It was felt that many of the 20 senior tutors would not meet this requirement, and so in 1992 a one-off promotions round that recognised teaching and past service was initiated. Of the 12 tutors who applied for level B, 9 were successful.

Awards were restructured to reflect a shift to merit-based criteria, rather than length of service.[25] The staff union pushed for promotion to professor, which was again introduced into most Australian universities, while at the local level the pressures were for gender balance and an arts/science balance on the Promotions and Tenure Committee. As the previous chapter has shown, the Leadership Development for Women programme has had a particularly significant effect.

Importantly, responsible committee members made moves to reform not only the criteria but also the procedures for assessing the merit of applicants. Aspects of an academic's performance that may once have devalued their application could now be assessed positively. The Promotions and Tenure Committee added these questions to the traditional ones about publications:

- Why has this person applied at this stage?
- What has been their service and teaching contribution?
- What might have restricted their productivity earlier?
- Has service and teaching reduced their publishing and research?

- How easy has it been to get grants in their area?
- Have there been disruptions in their career?
- How does the publication and teaching record marry with the total length of working time?

These questions interwove with one the vice-chancellor asked the committee to ponder: 'Has this candidate had ten years' teaching experience, or one year ten times over?' Yet the changes in promotion exercises were not simply a matter of changing the criteria or even the questions with which the committee perused each application.

Equally salient was change in the climate of understanding that suffused the committee's membership. From 1995 the new regime of allowing applicants to apply at any time in the year gave a sense that the committee welcomed their applications. Equally importantly, it gave time for committee members to carefully consider the applications and to discuss them more thoroughly. Meeting monthly, rather than a couple of times a year, allowed for a greater collaborative awareness, and learning how to apply a gender lens in assessing the applications was a crucial part of that process. The effectiveness of the criteria changes depended upon awareness and mutual respect developing among the members, and indeed on the members coming to know each other well enough to let down their guard and thus to debate and learn crucial new ways of thinking and assessing.

According to committee members, the change in thinking and understanding was not without long sessions of rigorous discussion. One of the Equity Managers, who was also an ex-officio member of the committee, recalls a case in the mid-1990s of a woman who was promoted on the basis of teaching and service. She had been a departmental head and an exceptional teacher, but her publications were not as outstanding as others in her discipline:

> *This sort of promotion had a crucial impact on the culture of the committee, generating rigorous debate among committee members about the concept of merit and gender issues.*

The process of debating the painstaking development of a more equitable procedure was set in motion in the early 1990s, when the professor who was later to become deputy vice-chancellor chaired the Promotions and Tenure Committee. His own early experience of being refused promotion, and of having the chair of the committee refuse to speak to him about it, had made him sensitive to the vulnerabilities of identity and self-worth that are tied up in applying for promotion. He was therefore open to the understanding that merit should be defined broadly, that academics were hard-working and meritorious individuals who should be rewarded for their efforts, and that the procedures should be completely transparent and accountable to all applicants. A woman who later joined the committee noted how important the climate of open-minded debate was to her own understanding of how the membership operated, in 'teasing out the procedures' for each individual case:

> The PTC members are completely committed to the process as high quality, compassionate, equitable. These often militate against each other and lead to teasing out the procedures, and further changes.

A key task for the committee was to sustain the open-minded yet critical expertise that was built up over several years, given that the committee membership changed somewhat every year or so:

> Each new person is welcomed into the committee and the dynamics change. The committee a few months ago had their 'let's test the new woman' phase and now they're into the 'we're feeling safe with her' time. They get a bit unsettled by too many changes.

For this interviewee, the collaborative dialogue compared well with other such committees. Nonetheless, she had no illusions that this well-tuned committee was secure from backsliding:

> I'm taking part in the process at another university this year and finding myself very angry about it. Mainly I feel

personally diminished by it and can't quite understand
why it makes me so angry. By comparison our process at
UWA feels healthy—but fragile.

When new ways of thinking and understanding are reliant
upon the insight, commitment and mutual respect of a handful of
committee members, there is a justified fear that innovation can
too easily be removed. Members of the Promotions and Tenure
Committee engaged in carefully focused relational work, both as
'compassionate' assessors of their academic colleagues and as a
group applying a new set of upgraded critieria. Because a university's
promotions committee carries high status as an internal legitimating
body, there is little danger of it being marginalised or denigrated.
Yet to some women who have contributed to that committee, new
ways of viewing the worth of academic work are constantly open to
challenge and revision.

Although the development of gender awareness in the committee was dependent upon a certain collective understanding,
assessment for promotions and tenure is still very much reliant
upon individual performance criteria. Moreover, as with any committee, its climate of openness is vulnerable to an influx of members
ignorant of the process involved. Promotion and tenure at UWA
may yet revert to more impoverished decision-making. A committee
carrying less responsibility for the accuracy of the outcomes would
be attractive to those wanting to maintain established norms that
have traditionally provided gender advantage to men. Seeking to
remedy this bias can be an unpopular and risky process, as one
interviewee attests:

> *One suggestion was you count performance across the*
> *period that a person is actually on the job, leaving out*
> *maternity leave etc. So when you looked at someone*
> *for promotion, you took the number of productive years*
> *they had been working on the job and used that as the*
> *denominator and divided that into their number of publi-*
> *cations. You actually got very, very different performance*
> *records—so these women were even more talented people.*

As you can imagine, that was one recommendation which people hated.

Many such people (i.e. men) would have gained their own promotion when merit considerations operated more narrowly. The senior male who chaired the Review of Women Academic Staff outlined the problem with retaining such systems:

We tried to get an idea of when would we approach the national standard if the current promotion rates for women continued, and it was around 2011. The reason we looked at that was because one of the biggest arguments mounted against doing anything was the 'pipeline' argument which basically went: 'Things were bad in the past. We've now corrected them. Women are flying through at a more rapid rate. It's all going to take care of itself. We just have to wait.' But to crawl up to a national average, that in itself was not considered very good, was going to take fifteen years or something like that. And of course the national average would have moved.

Conclusion

Selection and promotion policies at most Australian universities underwent considerable changes during the 1990s. Some of the change was driven by women who challenged unions, university administrators and governments to make good their own equal opportunity rhetoric. At UWA the revised promotions criteria were supported by some intensive raising of awareness as to how those criteria might be applied to best effect. This strategy was facilitated by monthly committee meetings with a core group of members, a deputy vice-chancellor who gave the committee considerable time and support, and a small group of dedicated people keen to understand how gender operated through promotions practices. Those policies have been successful in moving more women into senior positions, and therefore further away from the ivory basement.

However, our study shows that it is equally important to generate awareness of how best to implement revised merit criteria for those who remain in the basement. As noted by a senior male academic, change is easy to exaggerate:

> *There had been a bit of an impression that things were getting much better for women on campus, because you just looked at bare percentages. You might look at women as senior lecturers and you'd see that they increased by, say, 50 per cent over the last two years. But the base rates were very low, so if you imagine you've got two women and you promote a third one, then you're right at your 50 per cent increase.*

Some women have valid and substantial concerns about the stability of equity measures. If intense support for a reshaped promotion policy is insufficient to deliver a stable guarantee of gender equity, it is not hard to see why selection and search procedures, which do not benefit from such intensive elaboration and evaluation, are much less successful.

CHAPTER 7

Gaining a Voice

Jan Stuart and Joan Eveline

So when the review of general staff came about I said to the head 'Look this is the time when we start addressing everyone as staff. We are all staff and we should all attend staff meetings.' So everybody was invited to a monthly meeting.

a female member of general staff

The review of academic women (staff) is the one I noticed. That review was a watershed. Things were different after that.

a male academic

The governing body of The University of Western Australia, the Senate, called for a review or audit of gender equity for women academic staff to be conducted during 1995. This was followed by a review of women general staff in 1997. The conclusions of these reviews were not particularly surprising. Indeed, they confirmed the results of a range of other studies on these issues, which show significant gender inequities.[1]

More importantly for our study, the review process gave permission to discussion of long-held beliefs and assumptions about the role of women in universities. Pandora's box was opened: the central cultural driver of the institution was exposed and the underlying power structure of gender advantage revealed. Women were heard as representatives of the category 'women', and the equity process energised. The process drew on the everyday leadership of those who took a stance and participated, and in turn generated further opportunities for such leadership to flow on to others.

The level and range of debate surrounding the two reviews was quite different, and institutional memories of the first review (academic women) are stronger than of the second (general staff women). Those differences are a key to understanding the relationship between tower and basement.

Some reflections and theory

It can be argued that the process of review shaped cultural production at UWA as much as did the implementation of its recommendations. Looked at from this perspective, reviews exemplify a 'learning organisation', in which leadership is dispersed through participation, collaboration and debate.[2]

Almost by definition, reflection is an iterative process. Our understandings, relationships and identities are thrown into question as we respond to the demands of a changing institution and are, in turn, reshaped by those demands. Blackmore and Sachs outline what reforms can mean in universities facing the new demands of a global knowledge economy:

> As change theorists now recognise, radical reform challenges identity because it produces fundamental changes not only in structures, but also in cultures and social relationships. There are periods of transition when these challenges are particularly intense. It is at these moments when new values become embedded in work practices, cultures and structures.[3]

The concern that prompts this theorising is evidence that universities are under pressure to change from a collegial to a market model of organisation, in which values of efficiency and accountability may compromise professional integrities and academic goals. Inherent in the accountability and performance requirements of the 'new management' is the quality assurance that emphasises better teaching practice and enhanced procedures for equal opportunity.[4] For women in particular, as a number of studies show, the result is ambivalence toward the changing work practices.[5]

The context

Before the arrival of Vice-Chancellor Gale in 1990, there was complacency about UWA having one of the lowest proportions of women academics in the nation. In 1988, for example, only 16 per cent of teaching and research academic staff were female, compared to 47 per cent of the student body.

Under Gale's leadership, senior management made a commitment to gender equity and to improved human resource management in general. Nonetheless, by 1994 there was only marginal improvement in the number of women in the teaching and research staff (18.5 per cent)—and they continued to be concentrated at junior levels and largely in non-tenurable positions. Similarly, most women on the general staff were in lower level clerical positions, with a high proportion on short-term contracts.

Women on staff were increasingly frustrated with the slow rate of progress. The Status of Women Group wrote to the vice-chancellor querying the lack of improvement, as they had done on earlier occasions.[6] UWA's Equity Office and the Equal Opportunity Advisory Committee also raised concerns, as did the state government's Office of Equal Opportunity in Public Employment. A Canberra-driven discourse of gender equity, promoted by affirmative action strategies from government and unions, added further pressure.

It was in this context that the vice-chancellor in late 1994 sought Senate approval for a broad-based audit or review to determine what might account for the poor representation of women on the university staff, why there had been little progress, and what might be done. Initially it was thought that women academic and general staff could be considered simultaneously. However, early in the process it was concluded that the issues for each group were sufficiently different to require separate procedures. Review of the position of academic women took place in 1995 and that of general staff women in 1997.[7] Discussion of the recommendations of the first review took place during 1996 and of the second during 1998. The reviews were essentially cultural audits. They employed a methodology similar to that used for reviews of academic programmes and departments, drawing on committees with expert membership, both internal and external to the university. Each committee considered a wide array of background information, including written submissions, before engaging in an intensive week of dialogue with staff, both men and women, from across the campus. The review of academic women conducted follow-up interviews for a further three months. These open-ended discussions allowed staff to talk about their work at UWA and to reflect on their personal experience of gender in the workplace. In each review approximately one hundred people participated in individual interviews or group discussions, with many more taking part once discussions of the draft reports began.

Each committee prepared a draft report for discussion by the university community. Both reports were widely circulated, including placement on the World Wide Web, and comment was sought from individuals, departments and faculties.

Report on the position of academic women—the debate

This 1995 report gave public voice to a view held by many, including some men, that UWA's dominant culture was masculine in orientation and hostile to women, many of whom felt excluded from the mainstream. The accepted notion of merit was seen by many to be a male construct. One submission in particular gave a clear account of the dilemma:

Women perceive that in order to succeed in academia, their work has to become their primary focus. That is they have to behave like men...When academic worth is assessed primarily on the basis of number of publications and successful grant applications, and teaching ability is either openly or covertly de-valued, women's academic worth is de-valued.[8]

Members of the review committee determined that women should be given their own voice in the report. They moved away from comfortable third-person language to include many of the personal stories that had been related to them. They felt this was necessary to encourage meaningful debate and to get the issues on the agenda. After the report was released, the chair of the committee and the deputy vice-chancellor (both men) took every opportunity, both formal and informal, to discuss its conclusions with colleagues. This approach allowed for a diversity of voices, some of which would not normally have been heard in formal consultation.

People responded to the report at a level that is rare in busy universities. Many staff gave considerable time and thought to discussions with colleagues and preparation of written comments. As expected, the report's conclusions were not universally accepted. The views expressed by academic staff were varied, complex and occasionally acrimonious, and reflected different stages of evolution in organisational thinking. Sinclair suggests there are four stages in understanding the evolution of gender equity in organisations:

- denial—women's absence is not a business problem
- recognition of a 'problem', which is with women
- 'fixing the problem' with women-focused schemes
- commitment to change, driven from the top and marked by self-inspection.[9]

This comment from a participant in our study exemplifies that first stage—denial:

*Some departments fold their arms and say 'What prob-
lems? We haven't got any, we haven't got any women.' As
if women bring the problems.*

Formal feedback to the reviews reflected the enormous varia-
tion in views described by Sinclair. One comprehensive analysis was
more than thirty pages long; others only a few paragraphs. Their
perspectives were, on the whole, positive. One department wrote:

> writers of the report should be congratulated for such a
> comprehensive, diplomatic and subtle paper. In particu-
> lar, we have not seen before at UWA a paper which is
> imbued with the culture and ethos of inclusiveness and
> participation which it advocates, both of which can often
> be lacking in this intrinsically competitive and confronta-
> tional environment.

A few submissions, particularly from individuals, were
extremely critical of the qualitative methodology, suggesting that
it made unwarranted assumptions on a range of issues. Such submissions expressed concern that any redefinition of merit would
downgrade research and scholarship and compromise the university's mission. One respondent judged the report 'a document
in which the relationship between evidence and recommendation is the most tenuous of any I have seen in my career at the
University'.

On the basis of the feedback, the recommendations were
modified and then taken to the Academic Board, a discussion
forum for UWA's most senior academic staff. Debate there was also
heated:

> The documents before the Board are biased and give the
> impression that the writer has an axe to grind.

> There is an ideological thread underlying recommenda-
> tions which encourage heads of departments to examine
> women's scholarly approaches to knowledge.

Most of the previous impediments to equity have now been removed and there is no need or justification to give special treatment to women or other groups.

The report itself was not rewritten. It was seen to have achieved its purpose in creating debate—Pandora's box had been opened. A number of activities over the next three years supported gender equity. Some, but certainly not all, of them arose from the report's recommendations. It appears that the intense discussion, though not resulting in consensus, sparked new energy for change and enabled the flow-on effect of 'strategic opportunism'.[10]

Some initiatives, such as internal funding for the Leadership Development for Women programme, changes to academic promotion and tenure processes, search plans for qualified female candidates and a new emphasis on work and family initiatives are elaborated in other chapters. Others include the following:

Leadership development

- Members of the Academic Council, the university's key decision-making body, met for a full day to discuss the implications of the report, and committed themselves to acting on the issues.
- Members of the Academic Council attended a workshop on chairing meetings using a more inclusive style.

Policy and planning

- Equity was incorporated into the university's strategic planning process at all levels and was suggested as a standing item on faculty agendas and an addition to the performance requirements of senior administrative staff.
- Equity became a centrepiece in collective bargaining negotiations.
- Recommendations from a comprehensive review to encourage 'inclusive curricula' were taken up by some

teaching departments; an 'achieving diversity' project brought a more diverse range of employees onto the campus.

- A policy on professional workplace conduct was developed in response to a report confirming the existence of bullying, particularly of younger, often female, staff by older, more senior and usually academic staff.

Recruitment and selection

- Affirmative action appointments were made in disciplines with high female enrolments but no women academic staff.
- A requirement was introduced that all members of staff selection committees must have undertaken selection training incorporating an understanding of broad equity issues, although this was later modified to apply only to chairs of such committees.

In general, these activities were not part of any detailed and prescribed plan. Rather, there was movement on a broad front with one activity leading to another. It is only in retrospect that one can reflect on the evolutionary importance of the formal review process to the outcomes. That is not to claim that change is perceived as uniform or complete across the university. But the following measures illustrate that some of the changes for academic women have been real and meaningful (see Table 2):

- The 1997 Quality of Working Life survey found that almost 40 per cent of academic women believed that the university was a better place for them than it had been three years previously. Only 2 per cent saw it as worse, and 53 per cent of male academics saw it as better for women.[11] While the figure for women fell to 28 per cent in the 2000 survey, women were more positive than men on twelve aspects of job satisfaction. Significantly, this ran against the national trend of academic women tending to be less satisfied than men with their work environment.

- By 1997 there were 16 women full professors, compared to 2 less than a decade previously. A slight drop to 15 in 2001 reflected, to some extent, the number of senior women head-hunted for more challenging opportunities elsewhere. By 2002 it had risen again to 18.

- The promotion and retention rates for women improved, with academic participants in the Leadership Development for Women programme achieving promotion at four times the rate of non-participants.[12]

Perhaps the most powerful evidence came from women themselves. As one woman in our study commented: 'I at last feel that this is a comfortable place for women to be, where they are accepted for themselves, and where their contribution is valued'.

The report on academic women hit a nerve by describing the academic culture as 'masculine' and hostile to many women. Indeed, one response to it used the words 'competitive, individualistic, aggressive and hierarchical'. Although the criticisms of UWA's masculine culture were difficult for many male (and some female) academic staff to acknowledge, which contributed to the intensity of the debate, that debate was conducted within the context of a shared understanding about the purpose of academic work.

Table 2: The proportion of women in teaching and research and the academic staff (including research only staff)

Year	Teaching and research staff (% women)	All academic staff (% women)
1991	19	23
1995 (review year)	19	25
1997	23	30
2001	26	32

Note: Almost 40 per cent of new tenurable positions in 1997 were female appointments, compared to 10 per cent in 1990.

Lessons learned—reflections on gender

The Review of Women Academic Staff allowed examination of the central beliefs about gender and women's contributions to UWA's organisation. These beliefs, while not necessarily reflected in formal mission statements and objectives, invariably generated masculinist decisions and gendered work practices based on the 'establishment of men as the primary referent'.[13]

As the chair of the review commented: 'I was influenced directly by my experiences in interviewing people'. In an environment of controversy and debate, women and men alike felt that 'everything is in flux, and everything is possible', which unnerved some and generated hope in others. Respondents in our study saw the period surrounding the review as highly significant; for some the review was 'a watershed', for others 'a very difficult process', or 'a strategy we had to have'. For the men we interviewed in particular, it was *the* turning point in UWA culture in relation to gender matters, the time when women became an issue for the broader community of UWA. The important thing for academic women, by contrast, is that it was *the one and only* time when their concerns about UWA culture could legitimately be expressed throughout the university.

Those two interpretations link with a particular gender pattern in people's views about whether UWA culture is now more receptive on gender matters. The Quality of Working Life surveys have confirmed that men, by and large, see this shift as weighty and permanent. Women tend to describe the culture as having changed for 'the better', but that the improvement is limited and fragile—as indicated by a majority of academic women who, in 2000, saw the university as being no better.

The significance of the review to both academic and general staff women was that it provided a space in which women were invited to speak their individual and collective minds, and men were asked to listen to and discuss those views. That had never happened before. Talk of the need for 'cultural change' prompted much debate and controversy, and ensured that even in those work units where the review was scarcely discussed, these controversies were burnt into individual memories.

For men in our study, it was not so much the act of women speaking out that they recall about that first review, although that was part of it. People speaking their minds were nothing new for men in the ivory tower. Rather, many were shocked that the university leadership asked staff to regard what the women said about the culture as *legitimate* and deserving of a considered response. It can be argued that this pattern of responses—of erroneously identifying the review as UWA's first dealing with gender matters—comes directly from men's different experience. Men with responsibility for staffing were well aware that the university already had policies on issues such as child care, sexual harassment, women on committees and more women professors. What they were seeing was the first time that gender itself had become an issue. It was not the speaking out *per se* that these men recalled; it was that women's concerns were deemed important enough to become the focus of a university-wide debate.

For women academics the *crucial* nature of their concerns was not new to them. What was different was to gain a legitimate speaking position for 'women'—they were asked to hold the organisational floor, so to speak, if only for a time. The chair of the review committee, for instance, spoke of 'this number of very talented women...I mean to say they weren't bitter, they weren't totally unhappy, but they certainly had not been given a fair go'. He explicitly contrasted what happened during the review with everyday conversation: 'they were using the anonymity and the confidentiality of the review to make their feelings known, but it's not the sort of thing they would normally talk about because it would be too difficult a conversation to have.'

Women experienced that invitation to speak out about 'women's experience' as a time of cultural change. Yet the speaking out was short-lived. And it was fraught with dispute and debate, between men and women as well as between women, over just who could speak on behalf of 'women'. A weakness with the review was that it collapsed the diversity of women's ethnic and status backgrounds into a simplified category. A group of women concerned about racism felt that the focus on gender left them with nothing to say.

Report on the position of general staff women—the debate

This 1997 report revealed a very different perspective on the relative importance of women's experiences of marginalisation. Women on general staff, particularly those at middle and senior levels, argued that gender was less a barrier to their aspirations than was their position as second-class citizens in the university community. Feeling second-class is confirmed in national studies of women on general staff[14] and in research on higher education administrators.[15] As one submission to the report put it:

> being female in the University environment is not as much of a problem as being a member of the general staff. There still remains a sense of 'us' and 'them' in the University, with the contribution of the general staff to the success of the institution sometimes being under-valued. Much of this problem stems from the fact that some academic staff do not understand the roles that general staff play and fail to see that these roles provide essential support for the academic endeavours of the institution...[16]

Both men and women general staff suggested that their academic colleagues seemed to assume a master–servant relationship. Some felt their work was not appropriately valued as a contribution to the university's mission. They also expressed concern about their lack of participation in the decision-making processes of the university. At the time, the UWA Senate was the only university governing body in the nation with no representation from the general staff (although academic staff and students had formal membership), and this fact was seen as symbolic of the difference. The review committee members heard passionate calls for recognition and an equal partnership in university planning. And the review process opened an area in which general staff had previously felt silenced. As an interviewee in our study noted:

The review gave general staff women a real sense of belonging and having a contribution to make because we were asked to comment. It gave us an opportunity to discuss things and bring up things that we hadn't done before because we had been a very silent majority. There was a general feeling that as a female general staff member you could air your point of view and perhaps some notice would be taken of it.

When the report was released for general discussion, as had been the report on academic women, there was almost no debate other than that required for formal response. Why the difference in responses to the two reports? The obvious answer is that the review of women general staff was seen by members of the university community as less important than that of women academic staff by virtue of its design. The hierarchy of tower and basement had been enacted in appointments to the review process. The review committee comprised general staff, who were not the most senior members of the university. And whereas both the chair and the deputy vice-chancellor visited faculties and departments to discuss the findings of the review of academic women, there was no such follow-up of the review of general staff.

Formal responses (many fewer than for the previous report) suggested that the report had been well received by general staff, both men and women, and by the management of academic departments, but it was largely ignored by rank and file academic staff. Indeed, in a few isolated instances it was resented by academic staff, including women. Eliminating the distinction between academic and general staff in access to parking was an example. In a speech at the Leadership Development for Women graduate dinner in 2002, the deputy vice-chancellor commented that he had received 'more letters of complaint with regard to the parking issue than on any other topic before or since'.

Otherwise, the report drew little or no comment from most academic staff. Did this silence reflect a general acceptance of the conclusions, or a view that general staff are extraneous to the core business of the ivory tower? The latter appeared more probable. The feeling of being less valued was captured by a female member of general staff:

> *The general staff women's Review has not been seen as anywhere near as important as the Review of academic women's position (which had) so much follow up. We have had the recommendations from the general staff review come around in table form, and a few of the recommendations were highlighted saying 'Please discuss this within your departments and in your faculties and then we will change this and we will do that' and then another table came around and then the discussion was added, more discussion—and there has been nothing else.*

This lack of interest may well reflect a wider sense that the concerns expressed in the report on general staff women did not touch the key cultural driver of the ivory tower's mission—teaching and research. Hence, it was of less value. Yet the cry for partnership expressed by general staff was real, and continues to demand further investigation. Good human resource management requires that all staff be able to contribute optimally, and have that contribution recognised and valued.

There were some positive spin-offs from the report. There are now more senior women in the general staff, with the proportion at the two upper salary levels doubling from 17 per cent in 1994 to 35 per cent in 1997. The figure had plateaued by 2001, but senior managers point to a similar pattern for senior women academic staff. As promotional opportunities are limited by vacancies, so some senior women, general staff and academic, have opted to seek challenges beyond UWA. Some 40 per cent of general staff respondents in the 1997 Quality of Working Life survey indicated that they had seen improvements for women in the previous three years,[17] and 36 per cent reported improvements in the 2000 survey. General staff participants in the Leadership Development for Women programme have been twice as successful as their non-participating colleagues in achieving promotion.[18]

Lessons learned—reflections on organisational and cultural change

It is important to note that there are some similarities in the conclusions and outcomes of the two reports. First, both concluded that, for many members of staff, the dominant culture of UWA was not inclusive; whether for gender or status reasons, it did not allow their full participation in the university community. Secondly, both concluded that breaking down traditional patterns of attitude and behaviour was hindered by weaknesses at middle management level. Weak accountability requirements and inadequate performance management were seen as obstacles to equity and accountability.

The reviews hold lessons beyond those of improving our understanding of gender differences. The experience at The University of Western Australia—both the generally positive outcomes from the review of academic women and those less positive from the review of women general staff—poses an important question for change agents and managers. What can we learn from that experience about the process of change?

Rao et al., as well as Morgan and Senge, talk about achieving big results through doing the 'small stuff'.[19] In some ways this is the natural response when working with opportunistic or 'moving-on' behaviour. The wide array of strategies to improve working life for women staff was not part of an orderly plan but emerged from the success (or failure) of previous efforts and the rapid responses of people well prepared to manage the unexpected.[20] By definition, the changes were incremental. And they required relational effort, or what Blackmore defines as leadership: 'doing with others what cannot be accomplished by the individual alone'.[21]

While the initial improvements to human resource policies and processes were driven to some extent by demands for external accountability, the notion of an equity review was a response not only to the apparent failure of structural approaches but also to the heartfelt concerns of women across the campus. At the same time, there was change in promotions criteria for academics, and the first intake into the now very successful Leadership Development for Women programme.

The review of academic women was not a significant invest-ment of university time and resources. Yet it released considerable energy, resulting in positive outcomes for women and for UWA's identity as a more woman-friendly employer than in the past. How-ever, some serious questions must be asked about why a similar review of general staff sparked little interest in the issues. Formal responses from management were uniformly supportive, although there was no senior male whose task it was to take the debate around the various faculties. Significantly, the debate did not involve the broad population of academics, who are the central cultural drivers of the ivory tower.

The difference in response may well reflect the existence of two (at least) cultural identities within the university—'operator' and 'executive' cultures.[22] Most academic staff (the 'operator' culture) do not see general staff (the 'executive') as closely linked to the core values of the university—research and teaching. This 'invisibility' may well suggest a dysfunctional relationship—a residual 'iron cur-tain'—between the two organised groupings.

Contention over the proposed removal of carparking distinc-tions is an example of this cultural divide. While universally hailed by general staff as an important symbolic gesture of partnership, some academics felt they deserved priority access to more convenient parking bays in view of their more flexible working hours. Lurking beneath the surface were unspoken cultural (and status) differences between the two groups, which often aligned with different values placed on the work of basement and tower.

The University of Western Australia is not unique in this regard. Universities, at least in the United Kingdom and Australia, appear slow to recognise that the increasingly business-like nature of higher education has brought in highly professional and expert general staff—from financial management to public relations to human resource management—who reinforce and enlarge the executive cultures in these institutions. After experience in business and government, they are less likely to accept the traditional view that decision-making is the sole responsibility of academic staff, and that their role is as 'handmaiden', to maintain 'good processes [and thereby avoid] accountability for the much more difficult task of achieving good outcomes'.[23] These 'johnny come latelies' are more likely to see management as a shared responsibility, and to want to participate fully in decision-making. While the academic culture at UWA continues to resist what many see as the intrusion of a 'managerial' ethos, accountability remains locked in Pandora's box—for the moment.

Conclusion

Major results can indeed be achieved from incremental change. The review of academic women in particular sparked a synergy, a momentum, a critical mass which supplemented several other initiatives, principally the Leadership Development for Women programme and improved selection and promotion procedures. But it is clear from the review of general staff women that when culture is under the microscope, institutional power is critical. And, with the wisdom provided by a gender lens, one can also see that the stability of some of those changes is likely to be regarded differently by women and men.

We can conclude that using the review process as a form of cultural audit can be a useful means of exposing deeply held values and beliefs. An open, transparent process which asks people to reflect on their individual experience of organisational life can offer valuable insights and new opportunities for 'networks of leadership'. The process did help people to change how they 'perceived themselves and their world'.[24] It did increase awareness among academic women. Some are no longer simply grateful to be chosen among a significant majority of men,[25] but allow themselves to feel dissatisfied with the cultural bias that continues to favour those who most closely performed the masculinised ideal of the university's core business. Among senior academic men, the process prompted a different sense of what they could take for granted, with a majority of the group saying they could no longer 'ignore the gender issue'. And for general staff women, a sizable minority of whom felt that their status as second-class employees was being alleviated, it enhanced their sense of value.

Inequities of gender remain, as do unequal values assigned to the 'operator' class of academics and the 'executive' class of administrators. These are barriers to be overcome. In particular, the relationship between tower and basement is kept in place by the very procedures designed to overcome staff inequities: as in the different ways in which the review processes for academic and general staff women were organised, received and debated. In dealing with the gendered organisation, it is not enough to think that privileging the gender issues for one group of women is sufficient to make a lasting difference.

CHAPTER 8

Glue Work

A university which is quite content to see all its secretaries as women with an unbreakable glass ceiling on their career opportunities...is unlikely to be able to make progress towards greater gender equality among its academic staff.

Janet Finch, Vice-Chancellor, Keele University

When I first came to work here it hit me that there were three chairs that the general staff sat on in the tea room, in that corner of the room, and you didn't move from them. Then a new head decided that he was going to rearrange the furniture, which didn't leave us chairs in the corner any more. So we had to join the circle with the academic staff, and some academics stopped coming to the tea room.

Despite a rhetoric of collegiality, universities have a long history of status hierarchy, with senior academics at the top and secretaries, cleaners and casual tutors in the basement. Old chains of command are challenged by pressures to follow equity guidelines and quality management practices.[1] On the other hand, new institutional controls are encouraged by intensifying workloads, reduced funding of higher education (a 10 per cent loss in actual dollar terms in Australia between 1989 and 1999),[2] and increased demand for accountability and self-surveillance.

Entrenched in that old status hierarchy is the iron curtain between general and academic staff. That division reinforces those 'them and us' practices that an up-to-date equity agenda would wish to challenge, and devalues many of the tasks classified as general rather than academic.[3] In examining glue work in the basement, I will look not only at lower levels of general staff but also at women and men at the margins of academic work: level A lecturers, casual lecturers and tutors, contract teachers and contract researchers.

Importantly, the basement curtain between general and academic staff is no longer an iron one. The status of 'academic' and 'general' is fluid for research assistants, for example, and most staff at these lower levels share common ground in allocation of work spaces, financial rewards, job security and the value of their work. The organisation of university life is dependent on that work, on the extent to which it is feminised, and on the relational aspects of it being done so well that it disappears from sight. Glue work is the combination of servicing others and relational labour.

The concept of glue work

The everyday work of building and maintaining relationships is the glue that holds any organisation together. Although indispensable, much of that work is unseen and unsung, particularly when it is done by staff at lower levels. Having already referred to the essential but often invisible labour that turns interactional processes into relational work, I will now extend the relational theory by referring to Hoffman's idea of glue work.

Ulla Hoffman, now a well-known Swedish politician, worked as a secretary in a prestigious research institute in Stockholm in the early 1980s. Her secretarial work for her boss was invariably self-directed, involving high-level skills of negotiation, strategic planning, information and data-gathering, and quick-witted analyses of situations and people. In short, it required expert management skills. Yet her skills were frequently made to disappear, as if they were her boss's achievements rather than hers, while he claimed that his success would mean higher status for her.

Hoffman noted that it was the multiple alliances between secretaries that maintained links and relations across widely dispersed sections of the institution's functioning. Designated managers were often at odds as competition and restructuring undermined earlier forms of command and collaboration. In accounting for the continual mending of relationships, networks and interactive processes that the secretaries accomplished, Hoffman coined the term 'glue work'.[4]

Universities, like other organisations, depend upon glue work for the repairing and maintenance of human relationships, and for the smooth functioning of their human-driven systems. The fragmenting of corporate knowledge and networks after the frequent restructurings of recent years underlines this need, and has prompted the term 'corporate amnesia'.[5] At UWA it was largely up to front-line general staff to provide the glue work of re-establishing operations, work conditions and departmental relationships after they had been ruptured by restructuring. Yet when those skills are not part of an official job description, gaining recognition for them is slow.

Such face-to-face collaboration in everyday workplace practices, much of it tacit and often informal, involves skills of co-operation, facilitation and nurture, usually thought of as feminine.[6] To maintain a system which advantages those in the tower, universities depend on basement practices and skills that remain unseen, relatively unrewarded, and are judged insignificant and extraneous.

The academic work of universities conventionally uses and produces rational, objective publications that until very recently omitted personal feelings and emotional responses from study and consideration. The work of the institution, including one-to-one teaching, often means dealing with the personal and emotional. Yet much academic and management work focuses on rationality to the exclusion of emotional responses. Lloyd's work shows that the academy has, since Plato, assigned reason to the male gender and left the management of emotions to women[7]—and women are far more numerous in the basement than in the ivory tower.

As competition over knowledge production and dissemination increases, separation and hostility between university groups becomes endemic. Marceau claims, in a clarion call for reorganising universities worldwide, that 'faculties fight faculties, departments within faculties fight other departments, campuses fight campuses'.[8] The processes of glue work ensure that everyday teaching and services function smoothly and that disputes and conflicts at upper levels are contained. This glue work, carried out by general and lower level academic staff, is a key element in ensuring easy relations between one work group and another. As the faces of tutors and general staff are those with which students become most familiar, so these workers become important links to the public, small businesses, government middle managers, research managers, and officers of non-government organisations.

Universities are not the only workplaces that depend upon but discount the organisational glue that flows from relational work. Rao, Stuart and Kelleher's study of gender and diversity in work organisations across the first and third worlds showed that behaviours termed relational are ignored, undervalued and made invisible.[9] Their findings prompt such questions as:

- How much of the day's activity counts as work and how much is never seen?
- What forms of activity are systematically valued and devalued, and how do these patterns relate to gender and ethnicity?
- How does the valuing of different styles and forms of work shape the distribution of opportunities and rewards?
- How are certain forms of work, such as behind-the-scenes support, excluded from systems that account for and assess work?
- How can we reformulate these systems so that they acknowledge and reward 'invisible' work?[10]

The relevance of these questions to universities is clear, particularly the one about which activities are valued as work. Most academics place their work in very different categories to those they would apply to the administrative tasks of the departmental office staff. The front-desk work of serving and sorting students, answering phones, ordering materials, maintenance and support activities are expected to be done so well that they require no attention from academic staff. Indeed, as with household work, they are considered to be done best when they are not noticed at all.

In this 'mental model'[11] of the ideal university employee, the real work of the academic institution is research—the forming of concepts, the writing of books, the conduct of experiments—in short, the apprenticeship of the bright individual into the academic world, as a full member of the ivory tower. Sorting through the mass of students, advising them and even weeding out those not so capable of keeping this great tradition alive is necessary work but, despite the rhetoric of teaching excellence, it is not as highly esteemed. As Finch notes in the quote at the start of this chapter, the academic devaluing of this student-oriented activity leads systematically to a devaluing of much of the work performed by university academic staff.

Much of the glue work of teaching and research is left to the junior levels of academic staff and to research assistants in the general staff category. Too frequently, as work pressures increase, middle to senior academics expect to leave face-to-face teaching to junior staff. Out-of-class discussions with students, marking labs and essays and monitoring student achievement are often seen, at least in first and second year units, as routine activities needing little high-status academic attention. People in the basement carry a significant proportion of this work and, while they are undervalued, so is the work they do. The danger is that universities themselves, as teaching institutions in the public eye, risk being devalued as a result.

Dimensions of devaluing general staff

If we apply Schein's framework of operator and executive cultures [12] to the university, we see academics occupying the operator culture of teaching and research, and general staff, who tend largely to the management and servicing needs of the organisation, as part of the executive culture. Since the core work of the university is understood as research and teaching, that division into operator and executive is primary. A disturbingly complex view of what constitutes inferior and superior value becomes established, as a female member of general staff makes clear:

> *It is as if academics are put two feet above the ground. They start up there and as you get to know them they might sink or they might rise in your estimation. But a general staff woman is never two feet off the ground. As a general staff person in your dealings with academics you never feel as if you can hound them for something if they didn't do something. You politely remind them, whereas they could hound us for something. That issue of accountability is very much one-sided.*

But differences of status create further complex divisions within those two cultures. As seen from a tower perspective, the people with management responsibilities (both academic and general staff) are those given formal responsibility for others. In this view, the work of lower level general staff, even when it is providing necessary frontline functioning and systems maintenance for the university, remains subsidiary and extraneous to the 'real' work effort. This neat division is upset by emphasis on the importance of glue work in developing an inviting and creative workplace and learning institution.

General staff, no less than academics, strive for clarity and fair dealing. Their work entails negotiating new understandings, and they seek to set high standards in person to person interactions. If the work of the academics is implicitly characterised as the only 'real' work' of the university, a devaluing of important skills readily occurs.

The pictures which women paint of 'life in the front office' bear out this one-sidedness. In 1987 Tonkinson said of UWA, 'the position of secretaries is symbolic of the position of women in the University'. As one of these secretaries remarked, she was 'used to being put down'.[13] Although 'secretary' is no longer the preferred terminology, that rule still seems to apply:

> *There are so many women at Level 4 and 5 where you get treated badly in lots of ways, and it is a big part of the culture to have women in those positions and keep them in their place.*

Gendered jobs and work spaces shape staff attitudes and interactions for mid-level general staff women. One of them describes how the gender patterning of jobs sets up a certain thought process which is difficult to dislodge:

> *If you have a mindset of what is best, you tend to employ males very often because everyone who has ever done this job before has been a male and therefore only a male can do it. If you get a male secretary, quite often you think 'Oh, that is different' and then you think 'That won't matter, it is just the same.' It is just the attitude, you are so used to seeing one type of employee that what might be only a small obstacle in fact appears quite big at first.*

To describe ivory basement work as gendered is to be aware of how it is feminised and therefore devalued. To evaluate the feminising of the basement, consider these four dimensions through which the everyday devaluing of general staff work occurs:

- physical spaces provided for general staff
- responsibilities of general staff and crediting of expertise
- relative lack of encouragement for staff development opportunities
- relative lack of career opportunities

The gendering of university space

Academics above the lowest levels have a room, complete with a door that they can close when they wish. So do higher level general staff. Lower level general staff, by contrast, are usually subject to regular interruptions to their work, both through demands on their time and incursions into their working space. More women are employed in this group than anywhere else in the university. The working space itself is rarely something they can call their own:

> You find out that your office isn't your own, it is actually an extension of the academic's office. They come and sit at your desk, use your phone...you try to work round it but it makes me so frustrated. If we did the same and went to their office and sat down and started using their pens—they walk off with all your stationery, they can't see it. They have walked off with my invoices and things because they have collected them up with their own belongings—it is so frustrating.

This lack of 'owned' space can make it difficult to carry out the essential work of helping students with queries, much of which is done by the general staff:

> This office where this woman worked had the front counter and the mail boxes. People would come in and stand there and get their mail out and read it and chat to their colleagues, and they would talk across this woman, around her. And students would be coming to the counter, and she'd be trying to deal with them. There was no conception that this was somebody's workspace and they had better get out.

> Academics just walk straight in. You are on the phone with a student who is upset or needs help and people come and they sit down and start talking to you.

The work done by women in these front-line jobs, a high proportion of which demands expert relational and emotional work, is crucial to the smooth running of the whole system. It takes much of the daily administrative pressure off academic staff, who need space to prepare for teaching and to conduct their research. For higher level administrative staff, it plays a gatekeeping role, regulating and restricting access to their space and time. For general staff in lower levels, it is much more difficult to exert control over their own time and space. Some manage it only with the help of a supportive departmental or sectional head:

> With my head's support I have three hours on a Wednesday morning where I get on with more complex work and I have my door closed. Initially staff were a bit stunned and, even though I used to have a 'Please do not disturb' sign, they would still just walk in. It took them about three or four months, but now they don't. Nobody was upset about it—a lot of it is they just don't think.

For other women, the separation of academic/general staff allegiances can get in the way of the support they need:

> Heads are academics themselves and they have to work with the other academics, and they don't really want to intervene too much.

The idea of general staff as support services has a gender dimension which allocates the emotional labour to particular jobs and spaces—the jobs and spaces mostly occupied by women. For general staff the test can be how well they manage conflicts between academics:

> Overall everyone gets on well, but the general staff have to deal constantly with conflict. You know when it is going to erupt, who is going to do it, the timing. The academic staff walk away back into their rooms and shut the door, and we have to continually deal with it.

As long as general staff work is characterised as soothing and ameliorating, not as the creative centre of innovative activity, academic staff can see it as appropriate to invade this workspace freely with their own concerns:

[The head] was yelling at me simply because I was the person who was there, when what he was upset about was an academic who was just never there. This person wasn't responsible, made appointments with students and he hadn't turned up. But I was there, so the head was yelling at me and saying 'Where is he?!', in an absolute tantrum. I was shaking but I told him to stop.

Academic space is protected by a taken-for-granted régime of privacy. General staff, by contrast, have to subtly protect their workspace by manoeuvres such as rearranging the furniture:

I had an academic come in to show me something, and he happened to look at what I had on my computer screen and absolutely freaked out. He and the department head were in conflict over some issues, and he absolutely went berserk, and continued to scream his head off down the passage. So shortly after, I moved the furniture around, which made it a bit more difficult for people to walk in and see the screen. But I have had people come in and see things on my desk, and I learned very quickly to cover things up if I thought somebody could take umbrage. But it is that sense of not respecting your room, your private workspace.

The result is division into two cultures, with the divide self-confirmed from both sides:

A former admin officer said, 'Don't ever get involved in the academics' culture'. When you are in a role where you are the meat in the sandwich you can't be seen to favour this and that one—you have to play a neutral role because every academic has issues they are upset about, and I

*have observed that one day one staff member will support
an issue very, very strongly and the next day completely
change his mind.*

The division of general staff into administrative and technical
has mostly women in the first group and men in the second. Like
the bureaucrats of Whitehall (and the servants of the British upper
classes), administrative staff are expected to keep a tactful distance,
and, in many ways, their opinions to themselves:

> *When you see this conflict around you, it is best to keep
> your mouth shut and keep to yourself. That is part of the
> job, that is what we do as admin. secretaries, we have to
> be aware what is confidential and what is not and what
> information can be passed on and what shouldn't be
> passed on. You have to learn to be quiet because of what
> you overhear.*

Some administrative staff assert a right to shut out academics' disruptions but, as this dialogue demonstrates, it may take some doing:

> *If they are talking just outside my door I actually just shut
> the door. Years ago I used to feel terrible, now I just do it.*
>
> *At least you have a door to shut.*

Responsibilities of general staff and the crediting of expertise

Just as glue work is denied the protection of reserved public space,
it is likewise given little credit as a skilled performance of duties.
Rather like household work in the national economy, skills in the
work of general staff gain little reward or attention:

> *There was one woman who was responsible for putting in
> all the exam results and wanted to go and do a spreadsheet*

course because that was what they were using. She was managing, but thought she could do it better with a bit of extra training. But the head said 'No, because she is only part-time and she might not be here long, and it is $100 for the course, are we going to get our money back?' Now that woman had been employed for about seven years already in that department, and it was really a reflection on the low value they put on a person.

Not only are general staff skills and their development relatively unrecognised, but the value of those skills is determined by those without general staff competencies:

The head had a proposal where he was going to bring somebody else in above us in an administrative role to do the best parts of some of our jobs and get paid a lot more. His proposal went to an academic staff meeting, and we had heard about it, but no general staff member was able to attend even though it was going to affect our positions.

Liaising with central administration can mean that departmental general staff have a broader perspective on how the university operates, compared with many busy academics who are, of necessity, primarily focused on their specialised disciplines. Devolved structures have resulted in increased departmental responsibilities for front-office staff (such as providing a more extensive range of student information), with a corresponding increase in stress levels. Several women felt that while individual academics may appreciate the work they do, their multi-skilled abilities were not recognised. A senior male on general staff made a similar point:

The other day I had an experience in which someone senior, someone very senior, said to me 'What on earth can someone without a bachelor's degree have to offer?'

Duty statements ignore the range of skills and responsibilities of general staff members:

*We see duty statements here and they don't reflect at all
what people do. We have technical bods, but for information about how to manipulate data we ask our secretary.
But people think that all the women do is sit there and copy
type. And they overlook the student contact role, which is
essentially a PR function, and you need to know a wide
range of information to deal with all the queries. What sort
of skills and attributes do you need to do these jobs? It's
not enough to say, a pleasing personality or good verbal
skills—it's much more than that.*

There were several references to the degrading of relational work:

*There is a perception that your job is valued more highly
classification-wise if you are standing next to a piece of
machinery interacting with that than if you are standing
next to a student.*

The contributions of general staff often disappear, credited to
someone else's workload. Under the departmental system, heads of
department could gain the credits for the work of women staff in a
way that is not possible with the work of a technician:

*With secretarial type positions the head of department is
traditionally the person who owns the budget. But you have
a chat around the place and find out who does all the
work with money in departments and it is not the head of
department, it is people at level 3 and 4. Recently the duty
statements were looked at, and for a level 5 job they are
asking for all this expertise and knowledge—the people
don't only have to work independently, they have to work
at a strategic level at level 5. Now that is a female's job
and it's very demanding for the money that the women
are paid.*

Thus the actual responsibilities of key women in the department
front office can include strategic responsibilities, such as budgeting

and maintaining a regulatory overview, without this being apparent beyond the departmental head:

> *You're pretty much the senior administrator in the department, you don't have the time to be a secretary as well as the department's person, and that has become more so over the years because of the staff cutbacks in the general office and the increase in administrative work that has come through with devolution. There are also a lot of statutory regulations now to do with health and safety, equity, disability...And students now expect more of you—'I am paying'—that sort of thing.*

Even when a woman's role is clearly administrative, there is less chance that her position will be upgraded:

> *There are a few women admin officers but they are treated differently from the male admin officers. Salarywise, if you are a male you would be called a departmental manager and you would elevate yourself two levels above on the pay scales.*

Once women's skills are regarded as not worth developing, the judgement can extend to devaluing the personnel involved:

> *It makes it a little difficult at times, but we are support staff, supporting them [academics] in the purpose of the university. It doesn't mean that we should let ourselves be trampled on and not treated with respect. It is almost as if they think that we are not very intelligent.*

The devaluing of general staff capabilities can happen even at high levels of classification:

> *One boss I had was patronising in the way he would take documents I had written and go through them as though they were an undergraduate essay and make changes*

*to them, many of which were worse or were wrong. He
assumed that his approach was better than mine or that
his writing would be better than mine because he's an
academic and I'm not. This is even though my degree
probably trained me better than his did for what we're
each doing, and my experience in writing on a daily
basis is probably much greater than his.*

In extreme cases, and maybe some that are not so extreme, this lack
of respect, or 'rudeness' as some women called it, ends in what is
perceived as bullying:

*It is a culture that has tolerated bullying for a long time.
And sometimes it goes with the style in your academic
area, and academics feeling that they are so fantastic
intellectually that they can behave however they like to
those around them.*

The effects on staff development opportunities for general staff

Glue work proceeds without a recognised place and with few
rewards and, additionally, is accorded little chance for development.
UWA has given a high priority to an active and well-publicised
Organisational and Staff Development Service, which runs training
courses throughout the year. In theory, all staff are eligible to
attend. The culture of service, however, tends to limit development
opportunities for general staff. Linked to this notion of service
is, of course, a perception of what constitutes real work and
a consequent lack of rights when the work of general staff is
deemed second best. The injustice of separate outcomes is often
palpable:

*One woman was upset about not being able to go to a
conference. She had worked for the university for 20 years
and had never asked for a dollar for any training.*

Despite the university's comprehensive policies on staff development, the overall effect in some areas is that staff development for general staff is viewed quite differently from that for academics: 'Any time off for staff development is likely to be greeted with "Are you off again?"' Some women note that technical staff are given time out to update their knowledge, while administrative and secretarial knowledge is seen as being learned on the job. A gender difference in the holders of these jobs extends, it seems, to other aspects of the woman's work:

> *What really bugs me is that they haven't done an itemised comparison of the work of a lab technician and, say, an admin assistant or an admin secretary. Because the lab technician is handling a lathe which happens to be worth $200,000 then that man must be paid at a higher level. But it is not a strategic job, it is a skilled technical job. I have no grumble with him being paid at that level. What I have a problem with is not properly paying the secretary who is much more than a secretary because she is expected to do the budgeting, to do the accounts, to run the publishing, even to write things like regulations and policies, even though it goes through the head who is officially writing it.*

Here one group—academics—get the benefit of another group's work, and then dismiss that other group's skills. Equality is doubly denied. A final injustice for those whose major contribution lies in glue work readily follows—the lack of career opportunities.

Career opportunities for general staff

For reasons of family responsibilities, a balanced work life, or loyalty to a particular group, not all women in work groups, nor all men in relational work, want to move on from their current position. Yet only by moving on have general staff been able traditionally to make career moves. Although glue work gives stability and expertise to work groups in exercising these skills, career opportunities are comparatively lacking:

> *There are some people who are still classed as admin sec-*
> *retaries who actually want to come to work at 8.45 and*
> *go home at 5.15 and forget the job. They have another job*
> *when they get home. They are interested in doing a good*
> *job but not in working more than seven and a half hours*
> *per day. They have to be treated with respect, but they*
> *also should be given the opportunity to look to other things*
> *and perhaps identify a career path to show that you can*
> *actually move up through the system if you decide later*
> *that is what you want.*

Because their jobs are often accorded less value than other supposedly more technical work, they are not encouraged to seek new opportunities. Moreover, because opportunities are usually restricted within a particular department, moving up can mean moving away from a compatible work group. Like the academic whose teaching, discipline or research can become her or his life, general staff often develop deep loyalties:

> *We have to move out of our department if we want a higher*
> *level job and that's a concern, because a lot of people like*
> *their department. When you've been in a position for a*
> *long time and gained expertise and skills, women feel*
> *they should be rewarded in some way without having to*
> *move.*

Unlike the situation for academic staff, a constraint for general staff is that the process of promotion is based not on individual contribution but on the needs of the work group. General staff positions can be reclassified, but this only happens when the job itself changes:

> *Reclassification is about the job and not the person: So it*
> *is the job that is being reclassified, whereas in [academic]*

promotion, it is the person who is getting promoted, not the position.

For general staff to have access to improved career opportunities, they need the experience of acting in higher positions, which often means moving outside their departments. These secondment opportunities depend as much on networking, such as women's networks and those that grow out of the Leadership Development for Women programme, as on formal information flows. In addition, when women have busy work days, reorganising priorities to fit in tasks such as extra committee work needs clear support from the head. Such encouragement, women said, was not dependable.

UWA introduced a salary progression scheme in 1997, partly as a response to the limited opportunities for advancement among general staff. In some ways the notion of salary progression is akin to the promotion rounds available to academics. It enables staff to progress to the next level on application and annual review. To qualify, staff need to demonstrate either a change in duties (change insufficient to reclassify them to the next level), or to show that their performance is excellent, or that they have taken on additional duties. There were 31 applications for salary progression in 1999, and all were successful.[14] In 2000, 10 out of 12 applications succeeded, as did 14 out of 16 in 2001. However, among our interviewees there were some concerns about how widely this policy was accessed and pursued:

Salary progression is for people who have performed in an outstanding way, and when you look at the bell curve an outstanding performance is the top 5 per cent. So in any department the head should not put forward more than 5 per cent of their staff for salary progression, and if you have a staff of four or five, how do you pick one person to put forward for salary progression? That is the first problem. The second problem is that the university supposedly has the aim of employing outstanding staff of outstanding qualities and wants to retain them, so shouldn't they all be eligible for salary progression? The policy doesn't match reality.

In fact, there is no 5 per cent quota. Nonetheless the perception persists that only a limited number of applicants will achieve this result.

Applying for reclassification or for salary progression are processes that require time to put together the required application, time which is difficult to find in a busy nine to five job where your time and space is regularly interrupted:

> *My immediate male boss said 'I don't think you should go for salary progression because it would be so stressful'.*

> *One secretary was given lots of helpful hints by her boss to put in her reclassification form, including 'Don't forget to put down that you make teas for the departmental meetings' and 'Don't forget to put down that you keep the stationery cupboard'—all the low order things, and she made sure that she put those in. At the same time he went for a reclass. He got it and she didn't.*

> *Many times I've stood for hours photocopying applications for academics. I can't think of one academic who would say 'I will take all those and photocopy that for you and get some support going because you do your job really well'.*

When general staff decide to seek promotion they need opportunities to develop higher level skills. But persuading the head of an academic department of that is likely to be difficult, since funding and resource levels shape the level of support. Funding levels for general staff are linked to student numbers and staff in a programme group. The system that limits opportunities for general staff in the basement rests on values that perceive general staff work as secondary and subsidiary to the 'main game'.

The academic afterthoughts

Hierarchies of value and undervalue, although most marked between academic and general staff, are not confined to that division. Many of the practices that devalue the work of general staff are also present in the basement of academic jobs. This is the group of academic staff on short-term contracts, usually referred to as 'casual', and generally employed for periods of less than a year, often on a part-time basis. They are semi-acknowledged, but their employment status has not been addressed well in formal policies. As a cultural group they are a critical resource, because if current Australian workforce trends continue, and are applied in the universities, they seem likely to make up an increasing proportion of university employees.

These staff on the bottom rungs of the academic ladder are mostly women. They are pulled in and pushed out of tutoring and lecturing positions according to need. I am not referring to the respected visitors who are sometimes well paid to give occasional guest lectures and who are, according to Probert et al., mostly men.[15]

Academics on short-term contracts often carry a high level of responsibility for teaching, including co-ordination of units. Yet they are vulnerable, because their access to paid employment too often depends on who they know. The policy framework for these staff is less clear. Research shows that a number of factors contribute to the gender divide at this basement level. For example, career help is greater for men during their doctoral study.[16] Moreover, women are much more likely to face the pressures of family responsibilities, to find less family support while doing their postgraduate work, and to work in arts subjects where jobs are scarce.[17]

It seems that the level A staff in most UWA departments once included numbers of casual part-time women re-employed every year. This was changing even before the introduction in 1998 of the industrial award for continuing employment (HECE), which aims to minimise the number of staff on short-term contracts or casual employment. Today this group is mainly PhD students. Historically, level A contract positions were almost an afterthought in departmental budgets. Like casual tutors (although not quite as flexible for university employers) they formed a pool of reserve labour that was cheaper and more flexible than ongoing staff:

Departments just haven't thought about Level A as an ongoing position. So when the HECE award said that almost everybody must have an ongoing position, one immediate reaction was to cancel Level A positions.

More recently, the repeat hiring of the same contract staff year after year has all but disappeared. Although there was some evidence that a small number of departments followed this practice for the maximum allowable two years, it has been discouraged by university policy. The statistics indicate that UWA demonstrates Australian best practice in minimising levels of casual employment. Official federal statistics show UWA's casual staff at 13 per cent, which puts it roughly at the median of the Group of Eight.[18] They also show that 75 per cent of Australia's higher education institutions have higher rates of casuals than UWA.

Several of our interviewees believed that gaining an ongoing or longer term contract position at UWA depended greatly on whom you knew:

Every head of department had their protégés amongst the PhD students, who either had to be given a job in their department or they would be actively hunting for jobs for them around the place.

In some departments, where level A contract positions have disappeared and been replaced by casual tutoring, both academic administration and research output is seen to be suffering. In 2001 some departments no longer had enough ongoing, experienced teachers to adequately meet the face-to-face needs of increasing student enrolments. Casualisation of teaching leaves fewer ongoing staff to maintain the research profile of a department. The disturbing conclusion is that devaluing the relational aspects of academic work finally threatens the overall quality of academic skills.

Junior academics have lost both opportunities and status. And this increase in, and undervaluing of, casual tutoring is now being mirrored in contract research positions, where employment on 'soft money' is increasing. In 2001 women held 32 per cent of all academic positions at UWA, but only 26 per cent of those were in teaching and research jobs. A large proportion of the balance were in insecure research positions. An important national survey by Hobson, Deane and Jones, released in 2003, shows that research assistants are mainly women. It presents a bleak picture of short-term contracts, exploitation and insecurity.[19] UWA has its share of these women:

> *There is more soft money, grant money, and academic female research staff particularly are getting grant positions with almost no hope of career plans. All the policies that are in place to help make the workplace equal are not available to them because they are not on the right sort of contract. So in fact things are going to get worse as money becomes more soft.*

At the same time, overall cutbacks in staffing levels are leading to increased competition for jobs. Often tutoring is done by PhD students, who can find it hard to say no to a potential patron, particularly if that potential employer or colleague is also their supervisor. Without a policy which limits teaching load (and excludes the co-ordinating of units), doctoral students can experience difficulties completing their degree:

> *A typical level A person who is doing a PhD and is also doing lots of tutorials can find it very hard to complete their PhD and get publications so they can go up to the next level.*

Academic afterthoughts can be in for a very long period indeed of work far from the ivory tower of their dreaming. If the relational aspects of that work were valued, rather than dismissed as inferior to the prowess of solitary writing, abstract science or objective empirical work, the whole system of university activity would be healthier.

Conclusion

The mental model of the ideal university worker is shaped through micropolitical practices that masculinise that ideal while feminising the lower-level work that enables it. The academic/general staff division has kept firmly in place this judgement of what constitutes ideal and extraneous work.[20] This chapter confirms why the 1997 Review of Women General Staff at UWA was needed. There is still much to be done.

The data indicate that the strength and value of the university's work depend on the efforts of those in the ivory basement. The glue in university work relies on the corporate knowledge of loyal and experienced administrative staff who service and mediate the often volatile interactions between academics and students, academics and academics, and programme groups, schools and faculties.

Glue work involves—besides technical expertise on computers, software, printers and other machinery—maintaining staff and student records, preparing timetables, agendas and minutes, monitoring students' progress, keeping accounts, co-ordinating a range of faculty activities, passing on information in an orderly manner, and keeping abreast of university regulations and procedures. It also demands careful management of the feelings and emotions intrinsic to university work, highly developed collaborative working skills, an intricate knowledge of how the surrounding networks operate, and the skill to deploy those networks to ensure that everyday tasks are completed promptly. The work is often inherently relational, of a kind that is rarely recognised and poorly rewarded.

The university draws heavily on this glue work in the relational activities of teaching staff at lower levels, both with students and as research assistants. In their teaching, these staff act as front-line troops for programme growth, with students often choosing particular programmes within their degrees and courses because of a positive learning experience. As with many general staff, the work of lower-end academic staff is undervalued, taken for granted and invisible, as a crucial aspect of the university's self-managed identity. And the rate of this devaluing has been increasing.

The common ground shared by basement staff makes the iron curtain between academic and general staff much more permeable. In the case of general staff, their ivory basement work is feminised as a women's occupation linked to an accompanying lack of value. In the case of lower-end academics, the work is symbolically feminised as both less important and essential. Both practices produce the gendered university.

CHAPTER 9

Organising For and Against Diversity

> *One senior man says 'You can say anything here, it is a
> university'. And you feel like saying 'Did you come out of
> the cabbage patch or something?'*
>
> a female senior lecturer

A popular theory in management studies regards the ideal culture
of an organisation as unified and integrated, able to be more or
less manipulated and shaped by 'transformational' organisational
leaders and/or by improved technologies of management.[1] That
cultural engineering, or integrationist, approach rests on the assumption that there is *one* organisational culture that can be described,
assessed, rationally managed, even measured.[2] Yet countless studies
of resistance to change have taught researchers that pressure from
the top does not necessarily drive organisational behaviour.[3] Critics
also maintain that quantitative measures of culture are notoriously
unreliable.[4]

 The perspective I take follows the thought of Smircich: that it
is not so much that organisations *have* a culture that can be shaped
or measured, but that organisations *are* cultural productions.[5] The

question therefore is not whether various forms of behaviour and sets of practices have influenced UWA's culture, but what forms of behaviour and sets of practices are *produced* in that context, and how and when they are given cultural value.

Cultural productions in a university, as in any organisation, are not like cabbage patches—with neat rows of purposeful sameness. People who work and study there have many roles and a multicultural set of backgrounds—and the diversity movement argues that this is healthy for the university as organisation.[6] The process of translating government policy into something that works well with a diverse population and multifarious challenges needs a strong recognition of diversity.[7]

Earlier chapters have indicated that Commonwealth influence over universities has increased, specifically in the areas of new formulae for research funding, pressure for increased student numbers, and quality audits with extra funds tied to good rankings. Quality audits require a greater emphasis on managing staff and staff development, devolved financial management, one-line budgets and an emphasis on strategic planning.[8]

For some writers, the quality process heralded an opportunity to embed equity provisions into university management.[9] Indeed one recent book suggests that quality stems from providing equity for diverse gendered and background cultural groups, and that there can be no quality without this.[10] In most universities, equity officers and managers began in the 1990s to look to the process of defining and pursuing their strategic plans.[11] Earlier chapters have suggested how, in relation to gender matters, Canberra provided some financial incentives, through special funding mechanisms for staff development and for teaching and learning. The evidence from Crawford and Tonkinson was that UWA management showed little response to the pressure from women's groups in the 1980s.[12] It was the combination of supportive senior management, equal opportunity legislation and Commonwealth financial incentives during the 1990s that helped women to do better.

Was this combination sufficient to shape a welcoming climate in an organisation where masculinised values were entrenched and normalised? Evidence from studies by Currie et al. and Brooks and Mackinnon was that new forms of management in universities in Australia and the United States were further entrenching male advantage.[13] A decade of equal opportunity policies and procedures had not, they claim, transformed the political forms of advantage analysed in the early 1990s.[14] At UWA as elsewhere, many forms of exclusion still operate against those who do not fit the normative category of white, Oxbridge male.

Voice, visibility, diversity

Sociologists and psychologists often disagree on whether society or the individual is the best unit of analysis when examining organisational groups. Both disciplines agree, however, that we can learn as much about an organisation from observing what people do as from what they say. During our study we observed in meetings and large groups a marked gender pattern in how men and women behaved and in how well they fitted into the university space. Consider the following excerpt from our notes:

> In a recent faculty meeting I observed the gender patterns of voice and movement. I noted how men dominated the visual field: their bodies were massed in clusters round the room, they moved regularly around, talking to other men, or going to the front to make a point. The handful of women all but disappeared. Women were almost invariably alone, surrounded by male bodies; in one case there were two women together. When one of the less vocal men spoke, the men who like to speak most engaged with him, arguing for or against what he said. When one of the women spoke, no man, or woman, responded.

This gender pattern was common in the larger meetings. As agenda items were raised and discussed, shifting alliances were easy to spot. Men were invariably at their centre. With the exception of Arts faculty meetings, men swamped women numerically in most academic divisional meetings. Yet, even when the numbers were more even, the same ritual invariably occurred. Male voices dominated the air; male bodies took up most of the space. The ability to speak and to be heard is a critical source of inclusion and exclusion. Socio-linguist Tannen has studied how in-group and out-group communication styles influence the nature of talk and its impact on group decision-making:

> Those who will take a position and refuse to budge, regardless of the persuasive power to intensity of feeling among others, are far more likely to get their way...Whoever is more committed to compromise and achieving consensus, and less comfortable with contention, is more likely to give way.[15]

To the extent that these styles are likely to be apportioned by gender, it is highly likely that universities, with collegial traditions based around talk, will be environments in which gender differences in presentational style have a particularly strong impact.

The important point to make here is that the gendering of communication styles has unequal *outcomes*. Whatever may be the informal rules of an organisation or culture for gaining authority or face-saving, they are invariably geared to favour masculinised behaviour patterns (such as verbally 'standing your ground' when under pressure) even though all men may not use or gain from those behaviours.[16] Even the metaphors we use, such as 'standing your ground', presuppose norms of, for instance, physical ability—the experience or behaviour of someone in a wheelchair, for example, cannot then be categorised and is made invisible.

Diversity, then, is a lens through which to discern marginalised groups—based on gender, cultural diversity, institutional racism, sexual preference and diversity, physical or mental disability and age—and to challenge our unquestioned traditions, systems of meaning, blindspots and expectations.

Take the faculty meeting observed above. The excerpt fails to mention that all the women were white, with English as a first language, as were all but two of the men. There were no Indigenous faces at that meeting, and the way it was organised and managed would be foreign to Indigenous cultures. Moreover, the set of stairs that leads directly into the board room would be impossible for someone in a wheelchair, or who was visually impaired, to negotiate unaided. A wealth of research indicates that the outcomes of gender inequalities are matched by parallel outcomes in status and ethnic differences. The level of credibility and inclusion accorded people whose sexual orientation, religious affiliation or bodily abilities are different from the norm is as significant, if different, as for gender inequality.[17]

The ability to speak and to be heard is not simply a matter of speaking more loudly or firmly than others. Differences in status, gender, sexuality, physical or mental ability and ethnicity are shored up by certain groups being placed into categories of inadequacy—'those who are not', for example, or 'those who do not'. Provisions for larger type, hearing loops and ramps, while a first step in providing institutional recognition of presence, does not of course constitute equity in organisation.

To uncover some of the institutional ways in which marginalisation happens, we also need to examine information flows, management practices and the behaviour of groups who feel change may take away their implicit advantages. These are all cogent factors in organising, or maintaining, inequity.

A new deal for outsiders?

Several women we interviewed were very positive about the changes in gender equity they had seen happen in the 1990s. They particularly highlighted a greater sense of confidence and visibility among women, and the attitudes and language of male senior staff:

> *I remember going to a workshop for some of the senior staff, and I sat there nearly falling off my chair with joy because a number of senior men were standing up and talking the sort of stuff women had been talking for fifteen years or so. And the men had taken it on board.*

Most noticeable for some women was a change in the demeanour of male colleagues, particularly with regard to women academics:

> *The notion that we need more women professors is taken for granted.*

> *There were lots of men who were dragged kicking and screaming into the nineties who have since left, and those that remain don't have that same sort of power base any more.*

Some saw the changes as cumulative, such that as more women moved into UWA and up the levels the benefits became more marked:

> *Our numbers are still not fantastic, but...there is now a network of senior women that didn't exist before, across academic and general staff.*

For many, these changes were not limited to a specifically gender sensitivity. A number held the view that UWA was more open to diversity at the junior levels, employing more people from different ethnic and cultural backgrounds than it had in the past:

> *It's nice to walk into the reception lobby and see someone a bit different behind the counter. I think those changes are natural to people now.*

The success of UWA's Job Bank, part of the Diversity Strategy, can claim credit for the increased evidence of 'different faces'. Since it targets people for introductory and entry-level positions, the Job Bank has particularly benefited women, who have gained two-thirds of those low-level and generally short-term jobs. Interviewees who had gained such positions were usually extremely grateful. However, some expressed concern that 'the programme didn't have a lot to do with ongoing employment'. Moreover, various forms of exclusion still operated. Staff development courses, for example, took it for granted that employees were fully sighted. Anyone with impaired vision wanting to take a course on-line found that screen-reading software was still not available.

When exclusion has been a long and harsh experience, the half-open door can prompt considerable gratitude and loyalty. One of the Aboriginal women we interviewed, for example, said that observers should applaud what UWA management was doing to foster attitudinal change on Indigenous issues:

> *Our programmes speak for themselves and they have got a value to people here and throughout the state in highlighting how we are all diminished by racist attitudes. This university has got a very valid position in being a part of that attitudinal change.*

This woman identified change in the risk she would now take to assist attitudinal change:

> *When someone says something in a certain way, sometimes I think—'Excuse me, do you think that was necessary, do you feel you have to say that to me, why are you saying this?' So I put it back to them how I see it. People then think, 'Oh was I coming from that angle?'*

Making a decision to confront a colleague or acquaintance about their comments, jokes or beliefs was an important part of the process. This involved monitoring the degree to which non-Aboriginal people were becoming aware of discriminatory attitudes, and indeed of the remaining resistance:

> *You can always pick the ones that aren't aware and the ones that are actually doing it deliberately, and they know they are doing it.*

Another Aboriginal woman made it clear that she treasured the solid support she had from a few non-Aboriginal colleagues who understood the issues:

> *The good thing that I enjoy, working here, is that there are*
> *some really lovely, aware people. Some people in senior*
> *positions, but also I've had first-class interest and help*
> *from [X] and [Y] and [Z]...Some of the students too, it has*
> *been good to see them develop. UWA has given them that*
> *chance.*

But this woman still saw little sign that the UWA 'culture' had taken
Indigenous matters to heart. There was evidence that Anglo women
tended to think of women as unmarked by colour, culture, ethnicity, disability or sexual orientation. They felt that issues of women's
leadership and gender representation had gained a more secure place
on UWA agendas. One stated that there could be no going back to
an earlier way, despite some men saying they would like a return
to 'normal':

> *I don't think things can ever go back. There must be close to*
> *a hundred women now who have been through the Lead-*
> *ership programme...What would people say was normal?*
> *Does that mean that they are going to kick all the women*
> *off the committees?*

This recognition of women, with no awareness of indigeneity,
of different abilities, of linguistic, cultural and sexual diversity, has
swamped the full range beyond the norm. The statement has its
own sense of an unrealistic normality. Another participant felt that a
newfound confidence among women had placed them on a par with
the power and visibility that had been the prerogative of men:

> *I saw a quote which says 'The rooster does the crowing*
> *and the hen delivers the goods'. Now the hens are crowing*
> *too.*

A majority of men surveyed in our study and in the Working
Life Surveys said the UWA culture had improved for women. They
variously mentioned the use of gender-inclusive language, more
female students and the mainstreaming of gender equity policies.

Often, like this male departmental head, they traced the perceived change to the Review of Women Academic Staff:

> *I think most women would say this is a very different place from what it was when I came here twenty years ago. That equity review a few years back. Until then I don't think the university had done anything about gender or women... changed a lot of things.*

Another departmental head felt that the culture was different because women's issues were now on the agenda to the extent that they 'generated no heat'. Still another, who had earlier complained that his disciplinary group found it difficult to recruit women, nonetheless felt that departmental members were well aware of the issues:

> *The consciousness of the equity issue has sunk fairly deeply into people's minds, and it becomes in a sense unnecessary to explicitly raise it. The sort of level of discussion, deci-sion-making and so on that goes on in a department, you know, reflects that.*

Similarly, three of the seven male heads of department inter-viewed believed that mainstreaming equity had been a good thing because it was an issue that should be handled by management. Others preferred to deal with the question of culture as it related to the division or department under their leadership, where they felt they had more control. An executive dean, for example, felt the changes had occurred because of his efforts, not because of the policies:

> *Policies are only as good as you make them. In this faculty we had no need for equal opportunity [policies]. I've always ensured that women were employed on merit, and we've got the best record of any. Ask the women here. They'll tell you I'm always ready to listen, and we do that once a year. I don't know about the university culture, this is a complex*

place...If you look at this faculty, I don't think things have changed much because they didn't need to.

Denial of a problem marks all these cases, and denial is the first of Sinclair's four stages of organisational awareness. When the systems of meaning in an organisation are in denial, the process is seen as complete or unnecessary, as needing no further action. In reality, organising for diversity is yet at its beginning.

Unfinished business

For every good story there is another to temper its optimism. Men were likely to moderate their positive stories with complaints that the equity strategies had gone too far or were outdated in this enlightened age, as did the executive dean cited above. Women's criticisms of the slowness of change, by contrast, were usually related to the need for more effort:

> *The policies are there, but every time things are getting better I hear from other women what dreadful, dreadful things are happening in some places. Policy is being manipulated or ignored or interpreted or helped along in a self-interested way, to the point where it makes life very difficult for women.*

The story of the appointment of an Aboriginal woman illustrates the point. Her selection was met with an anonymously written document which spoke out against her credentials, claiming that she was not qualified:

> *It was faxed around to various groups and it had a little chart that they had made up. They had my name there and they had these categories which gave me a tick if I could do it, and it said if I supposedly couldn't do it. The only category in which they gave me a tick was the one which asked, 'Does she have a knowledge of Aboriginal people?'*

At this time, she received a letter from a colleague in her faculty, offering advice on how she should conduct herself in her new job:

> *He actually wrote to me telling me how to dress and behave*
> *so that I didn't damage the university's image.*

She interpreted these unwelcoming actions as being related both to her being an Aboriginal person and to her gender, because detractors showed both racist and sexist attitudes in devaluing her recognised status and leadership:

> *I think the problem with my appointment was that I ended*
> *up getting both barrels of the shotgun, racism and sexism.*
> *It was a double whammy really.*

For other women, the answer to exclusionary behaviour was sensitive policies for advancing unfinished equity business. Our interviewees used statistics to show that quantitative improvement is slow:

> *The academic staff was about 10 per cent female in the*
> *1920s, and it is still only 23 per cent women. Since the*
> *early eighties, when there were about 13 per cent, we have*
> *been charging, fighting, we have government legislation,*
> *we have policies, we have equity officers, and still now*
> *people say, 'Oh it is going to take time for this to work'.*

The gains are often swamped by competing change imperatives, and observers can see this as a sign of lack of intention (or attention) by the decision-making group. Important changes that seemed secure have since been lost in restructuring:

> *For the efforts we put in, the gains have been dispropor-*
> *tionately small and it is as though we just get something*
> *in place and the institution reorganises...a number of*
> *women were being elected to Academic Council, then*
> *they changed the structure with an increase in ex-officio*

*numbers, which meant that all the women were more or
less swept out at one blow and all these guys went in.*

Heterosexual norms operated to marginalise other women,
and some men. For example, in 1999 it became clear when our
research team analysed data in the first round of affinity groups that
sexual orientation was never mentioned. Consequently, I asked an
openly lesbian staff member if she could draw together a focus group
of lesbians. She did so, but only two women were at the time able
or willing to come. As one of those women commented, her sense
that her colleagues would be shocked by her sexuality was shaped
by heterosexism. In her work group, heterosexual partnerships were
taken for granted:

> *Our [group] has a coffee break every week and there's
> talk about families, weddings get celebrated, people say
> what they're doing on their birthday. But I'd never talk
> about my partner or where we live, or where we go for
> holidays...I've never come out to [my super ordinate],
> although I work very closely with her. She couldn't
> handle it.*

The issue of being 'out' on campus was still a crucial one in
2002, as the fledgling peer networks that accompanied the Rainbow
Project study indicated. In these groups, convened as support for
gay, lesbian, bi-sexual, transgender and intersex (GLBTI) staff and
students, many staff felt that:

> being out would be detrimental to their working lives,
> and chose to be closeted. They endured the homophobic
> tea room chat...No talk of same sex partners, no family
> photos on the desk, and minimal detail about social activi-
> ties and holidays...A feeling of discomfort, not belonging
> and not being able to be themselves.[18]

In a paper outlining both the Rainbow Project and the Ally Network
at UWA, Goody and de Vries reported:

GLBT staff have experienced UWA as an unsafe place
to be 'out' and experienced difficulty in attending group
meetings in case they were seen with other known
GLBT staff and 'outed' (having one's sexual orientation
made public against one's will) by association. They also
reported that they felt unable to attend the public launch
of the Rainbow Project for fear of being identified as
GLBT.[19]

For the publicly identified Allies in the Ally Network, the vitriol
against GLBTI staff can come as a rude awakening:

> I have been shocked not only by what people said, but by
> the fact they thought they had the right to say it...I thought
> [this campus] was a reasonably enlightened workplace.[20]

Disparaging and homophobic reactions are the mechanisms
for silencing and stigmatising GLBTI people. For people with a disability, however, one of the problems is the 'no-talk' rule that appears
to stop in its tracks many possible dialogues and most programmes
for change. A visually impaired employee described what happened
in Human Resources when he proposed some procedural changes
that would help him access web material in a form that his software
could translate: 'People are just a bit astounded, well dumbfounded
actually, about what to do'. Another employee, whose disability
confined her to a wheelchair, described the usual reaction of her
colleagues:

> it's quite a 'culture shock' for them to start with. They usu-
> ally don't know how to talk to me at all for a start, but then
> I go on as I always have and they usually loosen up and
> are able to act normally. Some get very hearty, though, or
> emotional.

Other people with physical disabilities spoke of being treated
as if they were mentally deficient or hearing impaired. 'It's as if we're
all lumped in together.' It was obvious that the need for training of

supervisors and staff, showing how to overcome a discomfort around people with a disability, had not been satisfied. All interviewees employed through the Job Bank appreciated that UWA was 'only a beginner' at employing people with disabilities, and believed that time would improve behaviours and facilities. An employee with impaired vision noted that he sometimes had offers to guide him around the campus, and that although he said he appreciated the kindness, he would appreciate more the campus having 'better way-finding systems':

> *[There are] no audio/tactile sense indicators on footpaths, no tactile map or model of the university for people who are blind, and the paths are uneven and on several different levels. That makes it hard to get around for both sighted and non-sighted people.*

This employee had found that 'developing something that was of use to everybody' was the best way to ensure change happened. One new building, for example, had no direct wheelchair access, which was a problem not only for the visually impaired but also for 'mothers with prams, people with sprained ankles, delivery men, etc.' The idea of singling out employees under the Diversity Strategy as 'different', and setting up monthly meetings where they could offer each other support, also had its limitations, he believed, since 'a diversity programme is meant to help people blend in rather than separate them out from the general population'.[21]

The effort involved in trying to blend in sufficiently to be seen as employable in the long term, plus the energy needed to manage both the job and campus and work relationships, all under a handicap not applied to others, makes it very difficult for people with a disability to voice their concerns in a wider forum than their immediate workstations. Moreover, in some cases people who spoke out about a problem that nobody else was noticing were liable to be labelled as 'the problem' if their work colleagues and supervisors were not sensitive to the issues. Gender was a classic example of this. The experience of marginalisation and exclusion meant that women were often reluctant to speak out:

You do feel scared around here actually. It can be quite dangerous speaking out. They talk about freedom of speech, but there are guys who thump the table and still talk about the 'girls in the office'.

Such discouragement can be built through a variety of experiences into a comprehensive statement of an adverse climate:

[Some] women are discouraged in a whole host of ways. They are discouraged because they are still not mentored in the same way as senior men, they are still often not encouraged to apply for promotion, they are still not assisted to set up good research teams and projects, they are discouraged from trying to get on particular committees. It just doesn't happen in the same way for women.

In extreme cases, women report what sounds like actionable discrimination:

Women in the departments are isolated, they don't hear equity issues being discussed, they hear the sneers and sniggers of their departmental colleagues and they think the Equity Office is only for trouble or something.

These stories indicate that when individuals and groups are assigned a marginal identity there is little likelihood that they will be given credibility and visibility for whatever forms of leadership they may be enacting. It is the university as organisation that loses through limitations to the leadership and initiative that might otherwise develop.

Flow of information

The devolved structure of UWA, completed in the early 1990s, was meant to ensure that departments would serve as an important interface for information. The departmental head, directly or indirectly, played a key role in what information flowed to whom. Our data reveals that there often seemed to be a gap between what was passed on to heads and what found its way to departmental members. Departments with an equity committee tended to communicate better regarding policy issues of specific interest to women. In 1999 less than 20 per cent of departments had an equity committee, and it was up to heads to ensure the information was passed on. It can be difficult for people in senior positions, who feel bombarded with information and have staff to compile it for them, to appreciate the limited access that junior-level staff have to information.

Because of this lack of access, some individuals or groups may not even be at the first level of knowledge. Who did or did not receive information was partly gendered, due both to the gendered hierarchy of male networks and to a lack of recognition by those who held information that others would find it of interest:

> *The head of department gets all these brochures and just gave them to his cronies, saying 'Look there is a scholarship going here, there is a travel grant going here'. Some of the males in the department didn't even know about these, so it was really cronyism, but it was a masculine-based one.*

In universities, one way of obtaining information is by being involved in decision-making or being on senior committees. This raises questions as to how consultation occurs, and who is privy to the information regarded as necessary for decision-making and policy formulation:

> *You are not kept informed because at lower levels you are not seen as valuable and you are not part of the decision-making.*

Once information on policies has been received, staff need to be able to act upon them—for example, on salary progression for general staff. Time and again, participants in our study mentioned departmental heads as playing a key role here. This is unsurprising, since

UWA has a long history of departmental autonomy. A significant part of this history has seen women in various academic departments isolated both from women in other departments and from a sense of the university at large.[22] A comment by a female head of department on the effects of devolution was that the larger number of committees had improved information flows:

> *In some ways communications probably are better than they were. I get the impression that twenty years ago a department was mainly run by god professors...and the decision-making was very centralised. So really only a few people at the centre knew about it, and then it would be conveyed to certain of the god professors and the rest would find out in due course, if at all. Whereas one of the products of devolution has been that there is very much more chance of finding out what is going on through more committees.*

However, the benefits of devolving information to lower levels can be limited if resources are insufficient to cater for the demand. For example, the policy of nominating and training equity advisers for all faculties means that advisers are available for counselling and information as needed. But they are often junior staff, whose ability to intervene in difficult cases is limited by their status. Furthermore, the Equity Office's limited resources means that advisers receive minimal support for their responsibilities. Thus an institutional step towards greater information flow, by bringing an additional resource into the loop, becomes ineffective when other processes of marginalisation restrict the effect on equity.

Related stories were told of management practices applying minimal attention to diversity policies. These accounts were from data gathered before the recent restructuring moves, which have replaced departmental organisation. But the stories remain relevant because they articulate how gaps between policy and implementation lead to lack of equity by excluding people from the networks of policy knowledge.

The micropolitics of management practice

Our interviews and focus groups indicated that the implementation of policy varied considerably from one department to another. Heads could employ a range of ways with which to encourage (or inhibit) the implementation of equity policies. Women gave several examples of supportive departmental heads:

> *He took the view that not only did we have to do this but we had to be seen to be doing it properly, and the policy was there for a reason and we had to meet the spirit of the policy.*

> *My head of department went around the whole depart-ment when Leadership Development for Women first came out, and spoke to every eligible female and encouraged her to apply, and that is beneficial for the work environment.*

They also told many stories about unsupportive heads:

> *I work part-time, and we have a new boss who thinks of my going to LDW as a factor against me. 'You will make sure you make up all the time, won't you? You will make sure you try to go on days when you don't work?' I don't think it is fair. LDW is staff development.*

> *I was really happy to work for the university, and I liked lots of the policies, but the reality of the department that I worked in was glaringly different to the policy.*

> *Different departments work differently...women need to understand what the dynamics are within their depart-ments, because otherwise they just get shut out and don't get what is needed to make their way up the ladder or indeed make their way out of UWA.*

In their defence, heads of department pleaded a lack of time to cover all that needs to be done:

I don't want to have to worry about those things, I have a department to run.

Several women were sympathetic to the excessive demands made of departmental heads:

Heads have a difficult job, as structurally they are the lynchpin between the management and the teaching staff.

Others felt that heads and deans needed to be assessed on their equity performance:

The whole accountability process, particularly for deans and heads, needs to be firmly embedded so there can be no backsliding and no ducking for cover where they can get away with not dealing with any of the equity issues. It has to be part of their performance review and linked to their contracts.

And some women felt that although the departmental head played a key role in larger departments, the departmental culture was crucial:

In smaller departments, one head with a poor approach can cause problems for the whole department. In larger departments, there may be counterbalances. Issues often arise through the inflexibility of departments where they have a tradition of doing things in a certain way. For example, the Work and Family policy is at the discretion of heads and this causes problems for those with inflexible managers.

While our emphasis has been on departmental or school sub-culture as a key determinant of equitable practice, it is how this interacts with the management practices of individual heads that results in a diversity-friendly or diversity-averse environment.

Diversity-friendly or diversity-averse?

The chilliness of departmental and broader culture can be reduced, therefore, to the behaviours and practices of individuals. In comparing women's stories, general patterns emerge of men's behaviour limiting the effects of equity policies. This was especially evident in male-dominated faculties and such male bastions as the University House bar—which was, some said, at the centre of UWA's information flow:

> *There is less of that male-only networking within my department now. Now that happens at Uni House, but it took me a while to realise that.*

For an Aboriginal woman, exclusionary behaviour took the form of non-verbal gestures and reactions, coupled with half-hidden comments and jokes:

> *I suppose it tends to be non-verbal, more an allusion or innuendo, a joking comment or something like that. It is sort of like hinting that I am not qualified, I don't know what I am talking about, I am impinging on other people's power bases. Things like that.*

Women frequently spoke of underground resistance, i.e. that reluctance to change was accompanied by a lack of interest or brooding compliance:

> *There remains a sizeable silent majority, some not so silent sometimes, who are less receptive to the equity changes that have come about. That kind of opinion voices itself occasionally, but it tends to be expressed more through passive resistance, not by people at the barricades and putting up banners.*

These women classified that reluctance as a grudging response to feminist compulsion:

*The effects of feminism are something that people have had
to take on board, willingly or unwillingly. It is grudgingly
seen as something that has to be—'Okay, we have to look
after these women or else they will complain'.*

Attention to the letter of the law rather than the spirit was a
theme with many dimensions:

- *silence in meetings* when equity issues arose
  Women saw that male colleagues in some situations would,
  while not overtly opposing change, covertly ignore its
  implications as far as possible:

  *At the meeting to talk about equity there was only one woman
  at the table, and all the men sat there with their arms folded
  and did not want to talk about these issues at all. You could
  tell this was the last thing anyone was interested in. There
  were no questions to speak of; it dropped like a stone.*

- *excuses* replacing action
  Several men voiced these as if equity was a bureaucratic
  requirement, like scaling student grades:

  *We don't need a separate equity committee—we have
  too many committees, too much time is taken away from
  mainstream activities and devoted to committee meetings.
  I imagine there would be strong resistance in our department to setting up yet another committee.*

- *complacency,* particularly in asserting that enough has
  been done
  This was sometimes coupled with reiteration of specific
  policies that had been implemented:

  *The culture of complacency exists in enough places with
  enough people that it makes the process of change so much
  more difficult.*

- *a sigh of relief*
  An expression of hope that the university was back to normal again:

  Now a man is at the top, they say 'Oh it's okay, that will go through, because he is a man and he understands these things'. All the men in our department are very happy that a man is now at the top because they say 'Many more things will be done in the university now, like all those things that we had before'. So the culture is slipping back.

Some men did recognise a need to think through this set of problems and to move on to a new way of conceiving how to deal with them:

> *I favour open management, everything transparent—you know, no secrets, don't manage by having more information than the person that you are trying to manage. I think there is still a bit of that...that is one of the cultural changes that I think is pretty important that we should have.*

According to Storey, the study of culture is often the review of 'a terrain of "incorporation" and "resistance": one of the sites where hegemony is won or lost'.[23] By using a diversity lens, we no longer characterise the practices identified above as cases of individual bosses resisting change. Rather, we recognise them as the outcome of widespread cultural patterns in which gender, racism, heterosexism and norms of bodily ability are produced or 'done'.

Recent work on human resources shows that inattention to such patterns brings institutional liabilities.[24] It was noted from North American studies by Cox that organisations which do not manage human diversity well invariably perform less well on a range of organisational measures.[25] An Australian study by Bertone and Leahy suggests that the conservative approach to multiculturalism flowing from federal government policy is influencing workplaces to follow conservative ideological forms with regard to employees' diversity. Until those workplaces move beyond the novelty value of diversity and link it to the stronger language of consistent equity, institutions will not receive the full benefit that a diverse population promises. In a conservative climate, small wins for diversity can loom large. The University of Western Australia has taken small steps on the path to making diversity a force for equitable change, and has rightly won awards for so doing. Yet organising for diversity has, from the indications of our study, much further to go. However, our study does give hope that the broad and varied population doing the ivory basement work is achieving voice and visibility.

CHAPTER 10

Work/Life

*Some of these men who have grown-up children, or maybe
their wives have never worked, they have no idea about the
constant struggle for some women to get to work, to find
child care, to do all these things. All I get is 'Oh, it's your
choice to have children'.*

a female lecturer

From the late nineteenth century, women entering universities began
to challenge two time-honoured gender stereotypes—the straitjacket
for women as society's nurturers and the fear of women as change
agents.[1] Indeed the birth rate for those early academic women proved
they could be as non-maternal as any man. In Australia the contra-
ceptive effect of academic engagement continues, with 20 per cent
of women with a bachelor degree or higher being childless, which
is more than double the rate for women with no post-schooling
qualifications.[2]

Decline in motherhood is not now confined to academic
women. In 2001 the total fertility rate in Australia, at 1.73, was the

lowest on record. One in four women will remain childless and those who do have children are having fewer and coming to motherhood later.[3] There is also research indicating that men wish to spend more time with their families.[4] Yet when policymakers turn to the topic of work and family, they tend to associate it with women. They see childcare places as a women's issue, parental leave as a women's issue, part-time work as a women's issue, job sharing as a women's issue, household work as a women's issue.

There are sound practical reasons for that focus on women, since women tend to do all of those things, and to a much greater extent than men.[5] Despite the practical benefits, however, treating work and family matters as a women's issue leaves an unsolved social and conceptual problem—one which has haunted equal opportunity policy from the outset. Developing policy that will help women with childcare, maternity leave and part-time jobs does nothing to encourage men to take up their share of family matters.

Or does it? In Australia, former National Party leader Tim Fischer, Microsoft executive Daniel Petre, Australian Council of Trade Unions Secretary Bill Kelty and cricket pace-bowler Paul Reiffel are among the high-profile men whose decisions to put their families ahead of their careers have generated metres of media column-space. Yet such men are a select minority. Few fathers, and even fewer mothers, have the parliamentary pension, the company board seat, the share entitlements or the product endorsements to ensure that 'quality plus quantity time' with their children is a realistic and gender-equal choice. In a study of the emotional lives of success-ful male managers, Pahl found that they rated family life as more important to them than work.[6] Yet they rarely followed through in developing intimacy with wives and children through engaging in the domestic and childcare labour necessary for such intimacy. Other research shows that the expectation that fathers will do more childcare exceeds their actual involvement.[7]

It is important to make sense of current Australian work and care arrangements within the context of increasingly globalised pro-duction. Lying outside the restraints of national standards and in the absence of international controls, global capital, as Pocock remarks, can be footloose and 'quite literally—care-free'.[8] Global competition forces nationally based companies to comply with the lowering of standards and wage relativities that multinational corporations can access through their capacity to go where labour supply is plentiful and cheap. Increases in hours and intensity of work, coupled with a swift rise in under-employment, plus casualised and insecure work are the outcomes in OECD countries. All this reduces the quality of family lives and perpetuates a system wherein women do the bulk of the unpaid and underpaid labour.

The university campus, however, is viewed as one of those rare workplaces where a more equal sharing of family work can occur. Many university departments can point to the man or two, usually an academic, who arranges his day so he picks up the children on the way home, or does the morning drop-off. On occasion, usually during school holidays, he brings them into the office, or decides to work from home. He even has the right to paid parental leave, although few seem to take it up. In this chapter, therefore, we ask how this development is tackled at UWA, largely by comparing the picture for women. A survey of the extant work and family research indicates that we should not expect too much equality, and that family work forms a major rationale for why women are relegated to the ivory basement.

The Australian family snapshot

Most women and men have family responsibilities for some period during their working lives. There is a stark gender difference, however, in how those responsibilities are balanced with work. Countless studies reveal that the domestic arrangements of male and female workers give the lie to the myth that equality has been achieved. A 2001 study by Pocock shows similar results to that of Bittman a decade earlier: that there was much more juggling than balancing occurring, and that most of the burden still fell on women.[9] In Australia, policy changes have accompanied equity legislation, with the union movement, the women's movement and enterprise bargaining all playing a role. Overwhelmingly, however, the evidence suggests that policy changes have been insufficient to counter the gender division of work and family lives.

At the beginning of the 1990s Australian Equal Employment Opportunity and Affirmative Action programmes signalled that workers with family responsibilities must be considered in the employment relationship. In addition, the Australian government ratified Convention 156 of the International Labour Organisation, 'Workers with Family Responsibilities', in 1990. Soon after, the Australian Council of Trade Unions won its parental leave test case. That decision granted twelve months of unpaid parental leave, the right to part-time work for parents during the child's first two years, and one week of paternity leave for a father at the time of his child's birth.[10] Such developments led MacDonald to suggest that Australia's relatively higher fertility rate can be attributed to family-friendly workplace policies.[11]

The question, however, is to whom in the family do those policies prove most friendly. There is little sign that men are taking an equitable role in childcare. The provision of unpaid parental leave, for example, has proved ineffectual in persuading fathers to participate. A comprehensive study shows no rise in men taking paternity leave between 1993 and 1995, and that twice as many men took bereavement leave as took parental leave.[12]

The crucial issue for a number of writers is father-child disengagement.[13] It is claimed that men are losing the war to remodel the masculinity of fatherhood, but they are also suffering the angst of a generation of men who have lost control of their destiny.[14] Although prompted by justified concerns about male suicide, violence and unemployment, such studies tend to inflate and universalise the problems of men and, as Hearn argues, to construe the crisis of masculinity as a social problem of unprecedented moment.[15] Such studies generally ignore the fact that most conflicts over family responsibilities stem from a still-resistant workplace in which, as Pocock shows, a strict division between work and family is normalised.[16] To what extent do these findings apply to the University of Western Australia?

Policy and promises

By 1999 UWA had developed a wide range of policies to assist staff balance work and family responsibilities. These policies included access to flexible work hours, including job sharing, part-time work, flexi-time, leave to care for sick children, 42/52 and 48/52 schemes[17] and home based work. They also included the sponsorship of two childcare centres (one of which received government funding but used university premises) and the recent upgrading of one of them.

A written guideline had, until 1991, disallowed children on campus. Vice-Chancellor Fay Gale had it removed when a lecturer complained about a student breast-feeding in class. In 1993 the vice-chancellor championed the enterprise bargaining process of ensuring paid maternity leave for general staff, which brought them in line with academic women. Along with her team of equity and human resource managers, she also promoted job sharing, and funded a project that interviewed women on campus who were already job sharing so as to build a model for others.

Our study indicates that most staff believe that the university's flexible work policy, and policies on work and family, are excellent. However, their ability to take advantage of these policies is often limited by lack of support from a manager or head of department, and the constraints of increasing workloads due to cost-cutting.

A number of submissions to the review of women academic staff in 1995 expressed concern about the inefficacy of the work and family policies, as the report noted:

> It is clear that men and women often follow very different career paths. For a variety of reasons, including family responsibilities…many academic women feel less competitive in a system which has developed from assumptions about availability, interests and progression rates that are characteristics of male careers.[18]

Consequently, the initial report made an overall recommendation that UWA should do more:

The Committee was of the view that the university must define itself as a more family-friendly environment which supports all staff in their parenting roles...While it was acknowledged that the university has done much to support activity in this area, there are further ways to address issues of supporting staff with children.[19]

Specific recommendations included support for job sharing and part-time work, increased opportunities to work from home, and extended leave for parents wishing to care for children.

The general staff review, released in 1997, acknowledged that policy advances had been made but argued that accessibility was still seen as a problem:

Access to these arrangements however, is determined at the local level and staff reported there were often difficulties in doing so. Where part-time work had been successfully negotiated, incumbents reported feeling that their decision to do so was perceived by supervisors as disinterest in a career, in the university or in meaningful participation in working life.[20]

The report recommended that supervisors be encouraged to support staff wishing to take advantage of policies to assist them in their work and family choices.

A system of budget devolution was instituted between 1993 and 2002 whereby each department took responsibility for managing its own budget. In that context, encouragement to implement policies largely took the form of persuasion through documents and occasional pep talks. The *Work and Family Guide for Staff* was first published in 1998. It outlines the policies that assist staff to balance work and family, and provides information on implementation. The two main avenues have been part-time work and job-sharing arrangements.[21]

Another booklet, *Job Sharing: A Viable Option* (mid-1990s) featured several job-share pairs—including the Equity Managers, who had job-shared since 1990. It gave departments hints on how to do the same for those who requested it. However, five years after its publication, women were still reporting problems in achieving a job-share arrangement. Less than ten job shares were running in 2000. Along with moving to part-time work without being seen as lacking interest in the job, negotiation of a job share seems to be a hard battle to win. One of our general staff interviewees saw her successful job-share arrangement as contingent on the goodwill of her head of department:

> *One thing I remember about Fay Gale was how much she supported the issue of job sharing. Because I was one of the first to get a job-sharing position. She came along with others and interviewed us and we told them how it worked, and they generated their policy on that to a large extent I think. And you know what Fay Gale said? That we needed to get men to start doing this, too, that we would know we had succeeded when we had men doing the job sharing. I thought that was so positive. To give my head of department his due, he was very supportive of us going for a job-sharing position too.*

She described what happened when her head of department changed:

> *Our current head has done everything he could to do away with the job-sharing arrangement. When the woman I shared with left, it was touch and go getting another person into that position. [The department head] said I'd have to go too, because what the department needed was a full-time person who was always there when you needed it. I said we were always there. We covered for each other if one was on leave and we covered if the other was ill or something. That's more than you can say for a full-timer.*

Putting men into women's shoes?

Not all men empathise with the 'dual burden' of paid work and what many still see as women's responsibilities for the home. More understanding may come from those who have working wives or, especially, daughters who want to combine family and work. Women who had experienced a shift in male sensitivity expressed very positive views about the policy:

> *I've had support from my current boss who himself has very small children, so he has some understanding because his wife wants intellectual stimulation from her workplace, she wants to go on making a contribution, but she also wants quality time with her children, and quality childcare. So he is willing to consider alternatives such as an interesting part-time job.*

But often even sympathetic men have a restricted range of experience and, in consequence, a limited view:

> *The family thing really is not understood by a male. We have one here who is shooting up to the top of a career, doing very well academically, and we are delighted to have him in the department. But his wife drives him to work, gives him a cut lunch. It would be so easy if you didn't have home responsibilities or a husband to look after.*

In *The Missing Chapters*, Crawford wrote of a double standard in attitudes to men and women who take on childcare.[22] Men were congratulated; women were not. And the picture has changed little. A common occurrence at late afternoon committee meetings exemplifies this double standard. When a man says 'I have to go now, taking Johnnie to T-Ball' he receives plaudits and appreciation. A woman saying the same thing gets either no response or the glance that says 'You're not quite full-time like the rest of us'. A senior female academic picks up the story:

*All the men I know who are at the same level all work at
night and weekends and they all have young kids. I'm
finding increasingly that I'll go to the meetings say at four
o'clock thinking 'Oh, I've got to pick the kids up at five',
and it will be male professors who will say 'I hope you don't
mind—I've got my mobile on, my child is going to call at
you know, a quarter to five'. And I think 'Oh, good, thank
heavens for that. Somebody else has made the excuse, and
the meeting will finish by then.'*

Are there more men doing that?

*It has become more acceptable for men to say that. But it is
indicative of the fact that everybody is completely worked
out and that having a family life is a legitimate and valued
excuse.*

Is it the same for women?

*Women might feel more uncomfortable about using it as
an excuse...There is always a tendency to assume that as
a woman you would stand up for it but that your opinion
is not valued, somehow you are put down because you are
a woman. [They think] that you can't cope somehow. So it
is good when men say, 'Sorry, it was my turn to take the
kids to the crèche'.*

Examples of this double standard were repeated in four of our
focus groups and several of the individual interviews. One woman
on the general staff, whose husband was an academic, intimated that
some men were well aware of the dynamic. She outlined a discussion
she had had with her husband about how colleagues respond when
it was his turn to do the childcare:

*He said 'I feel actually quite good when I say I have to be
home with the kids. I feel people respect me for that, and I
don't think they respect women for it at all.'*

The 'greedy institution' [23]

Questions about what counts as 'work' and how to be a good or committed employee are exacerbated by the intensifying work conditions in universities.[24] Many of our respondents said that these new pressures had lessened the quality of their lives and their efforts. UWA's Working Life surveys show that workload is ranked as one of the four top concerns by all groups of staff. Our study showed a similar concern among most academic women:

> *I was supposedly half time. This meant I worked five full days a week but I didn't have to work evenings, weekends.*

> *Everybody is overworked, and everybody is becoming concerned that [the] quality of what they are doing is not what it ought to be. People feel dissatisfied with that...frustrated because they feel they have to put more work in but they have less time to do it, the end outcomes are not as good as they used to be.*

Dissatisfaction might be coupled with resignation:

> *There's a sense of 'The problem is there, but everyone has it and there isn't any money to do anything about it, we'll just ignore it and hope it will go away.'*

Some gave in to new norms, however difficult to swallow that may be:

> *There is this thing about corporate culture which thinks you are pretty good if you are here at 7.00 and not home until 7.00.*

Women and men responded to this overload by prioritising their tasks and responsibilities so that the pressures hurt as few people as possible in the short term:

> *Sometimes it is stressful if you have a school event or a sick child that you need to get away to, but it is not worth stressing out about because then you don't do a good job here and you don't do a good job at home and you just don't enjoy life.*

> *I have things in my in-tray that have been there for months...I don't feel cynical about it, I have decided that you can only do so much and if you want to stay sane then there are some things that you have to decide are not that important.*

The men we interviewed were more likely to take a heroic stance to stress and overwork:

> *If you're not handling the stress or the work then it's time to get out. I have no time for people who say it's all getting too much...if people can't get their work done and have the weekend for recovery then they shouldn't be doing this job.*

At least one man resolved the stress by shouting at his staff:

> *I like doing things that the others say can't be done or that look impossible. I can get hot under the collar about the red tape though. I handle that by letting off steam.*

How do you do that?

> *I shout a bit, let them know I want something done now. They've got used to that around here. You ask my staff. I might upset them at times when I go off the deep end, but they all respect me. I'm very good to them in lots of ways.*

Revealingly, his female staff tolerated his 'letting off steam' by rationalising that 'he's just like that'. Stress, adrenaline and masculine sexuality can be a potent cocktail for some men:

Stress? I love it, thrive on it. I work best when it's all coming at once. Doesn't everyone?

The male norm of success

Men's priorities are affected by how they are expected to respond to workplace norms. Traditionally these have not, for university scholars any more than for, say, politicians or bishops, involved them in what Haavind and Andenaes call the 'running wheel' distractions[25] familiar to any mother:

> *A lot of the very successful academics have a particular style of work and I am starting to think it is a very male style of work...now I am starting to think, maybe I should be looking somewhere else for my model because I am in a discipline that is extremely male-focused and not collaborative.*

For academics, a degree of flexibility in working hours can make the juggling of work and family more manageable than in other occupations. Two women gave family responsibilities as their reason for leaving professional careers outside academia.

Despite supportive policies, general staff who are part-time (or job share) because of family responsibilities often feel that they are second class citizens. They feel more vulnerable to cuts, and believe that upward progression is often not possible because they will be blocked from managerial roles. As a female member of general staff noted, these negative outcomes are particularly evident when they involve children:

> *I had a very young child and a very sick child. But when I asked if I could go part-time, the head of department and the dean were both very concerned about precedent because I was the first person who had asked to do this... That was one of the times when I felt that the policies were in place but weren't quite working.*

When it is a question of maternity leave, the effects bite differently for general and academic female staff:

> *I sit on university-wide groups, and it seems that although we have policies like the one where you can come back part-time from maternity leave, if you are general staff you can't, it is almost impossible and it is put down to the needs of the job.*

> *Although you do get maternity leave, with an academic job inevitably you have work you must do, especially if you are trying to do research. So every maternity leave I've had PhD students around the house, theses to read...Work still came home.*

But this type of discrimination is not inevitable. Supportive job supervisors can and do adjust expectations so that what seemed insurmountable can even begin to look beneficial. A female manager noted:

> *In this department we have really generous provision regarding flexi-time—we have two women here on 0.7 and 0.8 appointments because they have children, and within that they are very flexible so that they can arrange over that number of hours, shuffle it around, share it with other staff, and if their kids are sick then there is no problem sort of shuffling it around.*

Whether it is childbirth, parenting, illness, or stopping to talk to a colleague in another department, norms of behaviour are codified in ways that benefit men and women who champion a masculine model of work. The meanings given to these activities, as either advancing or burdening the institution, shape not only the gendering of women and men but also the work they do, the work practices they follow and the responsibilities they take on.

The masculinised workplace

In their stories of who does what work, women criticised a narrow valuation of what should be counted as 'work'.

Having children should be a plus on your CV, not a black mark.

Much of the discussion about flexible working conditions focuses on responsibilities for children. Almost all such responsibilities are assumed to be the sole province of female employees. In this discourse is a hidden concept of compensation, wherein the woman is expected to relinquish her expectations of career in return for what she does in the home with children:

Women are often told that they shouldn't expect to have it all.

This perceived benefit of family responsibilities then justifies placing women's working conditions—status, salary—in a lower position than men's:

It is clear that many academic women, because of their family responsibilities, remain on short-term contracts and at the lower level of academic promotions, and there are sections of the university that are seriously unbalanced compared to the private sector.

The sectors with fewer women include, of course, those with greater influence: specifically, more senior and more highly paid staff with greater work responsibilities:

The biggest problem is to get more women into senior positions so that they can bring their influence to bear on the culture. To do that you face an enormous degree of conflict in the women's role in family and work, and how do you accommodate that 10–15 year period when they are needed between childbirth and children becoming independent?

Those who do survive and manage to reach high levels in Australia often demonstrate either skills or good fortune beyond those required of either their male contemporaries or women in other countries:

> *When I did staff exchange at a south-east Asian university, I was having this discussion with the various managers of the different sections and they asked me 'Do you have domestic helpers in Australia?' and I said 'What??' Then one said 'How do you possibly cook, clean, work, do the shopping, and look after the children?' and I sat there and for probably all of two minutes I was starting to defend this, and then I thought to myself 'Yes, how do we?'*

Facing these dilemmas, women felt that the typical male response maintains a duality of career expectations and structures:

> *The young woman had been speaking to the sub-dean who had said 'Why don't you go part-time?', and she said 'I am a single mother and can't afford to go part-time, I have to get my qualifications'. So the male academic staff around the place continue to be advising women to go home and look after [their] children, rear them and get that out of the way and then you do your studies, instead of saying 'How can we make this possible for you?'*

Loyalty to the job or the staff?

Work and life do not have to be mutually exclusive. Several women gave accounts of how the tension was being resolved. Interestingly, senior women were the most consistently optimistic, arguing that diversity may lead to greater productivity by enhancing the loyalty of employees:

*If an employer, you don't just give lip service to policy, you
actually get more out of your staff in skills, knowledge and
loyalty, and if you allow them flexibility they go the extra
mile. You find that they take work home, they work the day
they are supposed to have off and they come in to catch up
when it suits them.*

This applies to all aspects of flexible work, from job sharing to
maternity to provisions for diversity:

*From my experience of having a range of people share, if
you have two people on 0.5 you are going to get about 1.2
worth of performance from them...the experience is that
you get more for your money, you get very loyal staff.*

*For Indigenous people, family issues are always important,
so if we make allowances for cultural issues people feel they
have been respected and then work overtime.*

Trust seems to be the key. Employees with different circumstances and experiences are relating in ways that generate
understanding, rather than making a hierarchical response based
primarily on monetary exchange. In collegial terms, we need to
like our workplace and to know that people's contribution will be
rewarded according to their circumstances:

*People have to like working in their workplace, and the
way to get more productive work out of people is not to
punish them. It should be that when they come to work
they feel happy and they feel like they are being treated as
people and they feel like they are being respected. We are
in danger of losing that.*

The supportive manager

Women we interviewed spoke of the 'luck' of having a supportive boss. Even in the supposedly collegial atmosphere of a university, women learn to expect little empathy for how they juggle work and family lives. Consequently, when a boss does demonstrate such understanding, women respond with heartfelt appreciation:

> *I have always been fortunate in that every head I've had has been sympathetic to family needs as well as work needs, so that when the children were young and one of them was sick and I had to go, there was never a grumble or a problem...I was never made to feel you shouldn't be here if you can't manage your family and work.*

> *When my mother was dying my head of department could not have been more supportive. I sometimes had to drop everything and run off to tend to her, but no one complained. I made up the time at night or whatever.*

Lack of support

Hidden assumptions about the spheres of work and home, and who should primarily occupy them, were out of step with the reality of working lives. All interviewees, women and men, noticed when individual bosses showed support for people with family responsibilities. Yet when bosses showed a *lack* of support for such practices, or when policies proved ineffective, men in particular were unlikely to notice. Consider this man's response to a question about what might hinder women's careers in his field:

> *I think the standard problem is that they tend to have babies at some time. Which means they leave the workforce.*

Don't they come back?

*Some do. I mean the trend now is you leave for three weeks
and come back. I'm afraid I'm a bit old-fashioned, I don't
like that idea very much.*

Have you had women in your department who come back
that quickly?

*Three at least...one was a senior research fellow. Very
senior. I never think of those in terms of the academics
because we have our permanent academics and then
there is the research staff. A lot of the research staff are
academic appointments and they are always on contracts
and they have to make their money by publishing.*

Are women falling behind because of the work culture?

*I think so...I mean if you're not here, you're not perform-
ing, then if you're not performing you're not showing
people that you can do things. Therefore you are falling
behind. I mean girls have got to make up their mind. What
do they want to do?*

Two years off is such an obstacle that women can't
recover?

*This is a science-based department. And our science is
changing very rapidly...if you're away for three years you
certainly do fall behind. You have to retrain. I think it
really depends on the person. Some people are brilliant
and they can do it quite easy. Some people are not so brilliant, they can't expect to be automatically...I think it's the
expectation of an automatic progression that causes the
problems possibly.*

This exchange illustrates the first of two patterns we found of
perceptions about how the lack of support for women with family
cares arises. Motherhood is considered a choice of the woman, with

little to do with the father or society. And the problem is primarily defined as disruption of the workplace by the demands of working mothers, as this reaction indicates:

> *If it was you that was sick, no-one would mind much. If it was your mother who was sick no-one would mind, even if it was your spouse who was sick no-one would mind. But if it is your children, this brings in the wider society's view that this is a problem.*

The second pattern of misconception is about what constitutes a family. Aboriginal staff are likely to have extended families, while some staff are responsible for the care for elderly parents. These responsibilities tend to have little meaning for bosses who see their primary role as guarding the institution's rights:

> *When dealing with Indigenous people, men or women, because their family structure is so large and extended it is an enormous stress. Commitment and workload to the family situation is often much more than in a non-Aboriginal family situation.*

> *Taking time off for responsibilities such as parent-care is a less acceptable form of absence. Many secretaries are at the age where they have these responsibilities; but their age and responsibilities also mean they need to keep the job they have. So they won't argue with their head.*

Single women with no children are usually seen as people without family responsibilities. The expectation is that they should take up the masculine model and always be available for work. There appears to be a growing belief among childless people that their rights are being infringed by funding and support for family leave of various kinds. Some deplored what they saw as a tendency for parents to bring children into the office during school holidays:

It's getting beyond a joke. One colleague decided if the kids were going to be here he would bring in his dogs, there they were, tied up under the desk...So I said, 'Look, I've got a pony at home. I'll bring him in and the kids can gallop him up the corridor.'

Conclusion

Uncovering the ways in which work is gendered has been a key project for the movement for equity and diversity. In relation to work and family concerns, it has ranged from naming work as paid and unpaid to defining family responsibilities as a crucial component of working lives.[26] Equal opportunity has required us to face up to the greedy institution. In particular, we must ask how we as employees and managers shape and enact our identities so as to convince ourselves that we really want a workaholic lifestyle.[27]

The stories we have related show that the core work of the university is gendered, as are working conditions and work–family arrangements that consign women to the ivory basement. The work/family collision, as Pocock describes it, is 'being imposed on a landscape that is inscribed with ancient patterns of gender that promise women and men different outcomes'.[28] While it is played out in individual organisations, such as a university, its ramifications and the forces that drive it are global.

Conclusion

Joan Eveline and Jen de Vries

I am arguing for a view from a body...versus a view from above, from nowhere...Only the god trick is forbidden.

Donna Haraway, 'Situated knowledges', 1988

Our study of how one Australian university has dealt with equity and diversity offers what one enthusiastic reviewer called 'a case study of the possible, an inspiration in less enlightened times'. Evaluation was not our aim. Nonetheless, there are lessons here about what can be achieved when foresight, commitment, collective voice and expertise cohabit with a generous dose of good fortune in leadership, external pressures and funding sources. There are also warnings that gender inequality can be locked in a time warp, constrained by nostalgia for a golden age when women's sphere was limited to kitchens, kindergartens and keyboards.

Women at UWA, like those at most universities in Australia[1] and overseas,[2] are still grossly under-represented at upper levels and in disciplines such as engineering and medicine that are associated with men. In asking why universities in The Netherlands remain 'modern monasteries', Benschop and Brouns suggest the Dutch academy relies for its male dominance on an 'Olympus' model of the sciences:

> The dominant representation of the brilliant researcher is a young man, in solitude high on top of the Olympus, distanced from everyday practices, glittering at the top of an esoteric scientific community.[3]

The detachment and hierarchy of the Olympus model bears a strong resemblance to the ivory tower, note Benschop and Brouns. They suggest that Dutch academics climb down from their Mount Olympus, which in any case is in danger of crumbling beneath them, and institute transparent recruitment and promotion practices. That will produce the staff diversity and the innovative teaching and research practices now necessary for survival.

We have gone a step beyond concern with the blindspots and limitations of the Olympus model. We have highlighted the contested and shifting relationship between basement and tower in a search for clues about how the micropolitics of leadership and community shape the wider university environment. The lessons those clues convey—about small wins and complacency, commitment and misconceptions, compliance and struggle—are relevant to all organisations and institutions.

Relevance

The ivory tower, divorced from societal influence and domestic cares, is an image that harks back to the traditions of Oxbridge, where division between 'gown' and 'town' allowed students to avoid paying their bills, and where dons, tutors and an all-male student body enjoyed complete freedom from the domestic responsibilities of meals, cleaning and bath-times.[4] Needless to say, the Oxbridge colleges employed generations of ivory basement workers—cooks, cleaners, provosts and low income students who earned their keep by serving meals.

Now as then, universities are more than ivory towers. Academic communities, as Goodall reminds us, 'exist within a complex web of families, friendships, departments, academic institutions, cities and states, educational hierarchies, professional organisations, and world histories, all of which can and do influence us'.[5] The benefits and perils of that influence flow both ways between university and wider society, and the rate of flow has been increased by mass higher education and growing pressures for community-linked research.

Like most public and private organisations in post-industrial societies, Australian universities are caught in a frenzy of restructuring. The intention of this restructuring is to help them cope with more students and fewer resources, while also demonstrating the relevance of academic research to applied studies generating marketable products. A throw-away society, in which demand for certain kinds of labour and professional expertise shifts rapidly, fosters critics of the relevance of universities as teaching institutions. Running counter to such critiques is the escalating proportion of local,[6] and sizable numbers of international, students who vote with their feet and enrol in Australian university courses.

Universities must learn how to build on that learning society. If they fail, they will indeed have lost their unique role as disinterested arbiters of the truth and wisdom needed for sustainable communities. Their challenge is to harness our growing appetite for learning in order to combat the economic and industrial changes that are denuding and fragmenting sustainable communities in universities and suburbs alike. Neither new forms of information technology nor the latest restructure will sufficiently advance that cause. Collaborative team-work will fail also, so long as universities continue to model a system which rewards entrepreneurial individualism and ignores or devalues companionate support.

The decrease and restructuring of university workforces reflects that of many Australian workplaces. Both academic and general staff must develop complex and flexible skills and knowledge, as old divisions between employment categories shift and blur. Academics are no longer the sole or privileged occupants of the ivory tower, and the basement now includes more levels of academic work. The tensions caused by such shifts affect the morale and satisfaction levels of both individuals and groups.

At UWA, for example, some former academic departmental heads (all men) have complained of being shouldered aside by school managers with insufficient academic background to judge the effect of their budgetary decisions on teaching and research. The school managers (half of them women) have retorted that academics have little or no training in management, and that change heralds institutional efficiency. Such tensions and debates shift attention away from the glue work that repairs damaged relationships and broken networks. Yet relational work not only transcends the academic/general staff division but also binds and nurtures a disparate and diverse university community.

This blurring of the old demarcations between basement and tower is incorporated into equity and diversity considerations, which are pursued as a way of showing that universities are in touch with the wider community. The present urgent need to promote the relevance of universities and to develop community would seem to require the demolition of old hierarchies based on access and privilege. Such courageous acts must begin at home, in the organisational form and human resource practice of universities themselves.

UWA is part way down that track. Demarcations between academic and general staff have been reduced, casualisation limited, teaching staff on contract positions moved into tenure, and most female staff ensured entitlement to development and support programmes. Yet the lines between academic and general staff remain firmly drawn. Equal representation in university decision-making is far from a reality, most general staff are still excluded from programme and faculty meetings, and most academic staff are strongly resistant to any decrease in the differential value between academic and general staff work.

While the academic/general staff demarcation may become increasingly pertinent as university communities seek to avoid being torn asunder, it is not the only concern in the ivory basement. There are other hierarchies of recognition and reward, which operate essentially through assumptions about relevance. The micropolitics of relevance often has more to do with status, power and position than with experience and expertise. It is crucial to ask the following questions. Whose experiences and expertise are judged most relevant to decision-making? Whose jobs and contributions are judged extraneous to the university's future? The usual answers are not only devices for differentiating between the occupants of tower and basement but are also ways of doing gender.

What would a university look like if existing judgements about relevant and extraneous work were to be dismantled? Clearly, the essential ivory basement work, whether by women or men, academic or general, would be recognised and rewarded. Success, corporate knowledge and innovation resulting from years of doing glue work would be seen as leadership. A woman with ten years' experience in running a department's finances and resolving student crises would not have to bow to an academic's invasion of her workspace. Academic programme meetings would discuss and appreciate the intricacies of relational work. A tutor's ability to inspire learning would be no less rewarded than analytical skill with theoretical texts. And work on equity and diversity would rate alongside research and teaching on academic councils. Such a university community would offer an invaluable model of justice and fairness.

Innovation

Many university managers and leaders see innovation in research and teaching as the answer to tight finances and charges of irrelevance. Teaching innovation focuses on responsive curricula and on extending international and distance education. Research promises a competitive edge through innovative science, technology and management practices which will gain the attention of business and industry.[7] Some academics in management roles regard 'innovation' as synonymous with good research. In her assessment of Australian university research, Marceau asserts that 'Innovation is now recognised as *the* driver of growth in the twenty-first century'. She argues that research in our universities must take the OECD route 'implied by acceptance of competition via innovation and technological advance [which] maximises higher-skilled, higher-paid employment and improved living standards'.[8]

Australian management circles more widely assert that our science and technology is insufficiently innovative to give competitive advantage. What is needed first and foremost, say high-profile managers and consultants, is a blueprint for wide-ranging innovation in management practice.[9] But has the concept of innovation in higher education been cheapened by overuse? From one perspective, the 'cult of innovation' devalues proven 'teaching research and administration methods, and those who practice them'.[10] Marginson warns that universities use the discourse of 'innovation in research' at their peril. He argues that such thinking comes from a management push for continuous organisational change, which reduces the creative and fluid processes of research to formulaic responses, and equates them with 'changing a funding formula or creating a new level of management'.[11]

While we struggle over terminology, the world is changing rapidly. In the search for a responsive research practice for gendered organisations, Martin and Collinson offer 'jazz improvisation'. Improvisation, they suggest, signifies the political and intellectual struggle, fuelled by conditions and voices from the margins, that accompanies ground-breaking research.[12] Our approach is similar. We have turned on its head the 'god trick'[13] of the view from the ivory tower, and given serious attention to the view from the basement below.

Marceau shows important leadership in arguing that research must build on established fluid networks to develop diverse and creative solutions. But her view from above is restricted. She posits an ivory tower of collaborative research communities as the model not only for financing and managing research but also for the beneficial organising of teaching and administration. This top-down view renders invisible the collaborative improvisation that already exists across universities. Indeed, the ivory basement perspective reveals intricate criss-crossing networks of local and organisational knowledge that build and sustain competence within the basement. Marceau fails to see that mobile, fluid and isolated research communities would be unsustainable without the glue work of a stable, secure body of resources, assistants, teachers and administrators. Her blindspot characterises the view from above.

It is neither naive nor irrelevant to recognise that innovation is intricately linked with leadership and staff development. The linkages take the form of creative configurations of consultative decision-making, reward systems that encourage relational and emotional skills, and a sense of sustainable community which welcomes all forms of diversity.

The promotion of innovative, creative and collaborative effort is the backbone of leadership. Indeed leadership reflects and shapes innovation. As universities are swept along by the tide of neo-liberal reforms, there seems to be no room for such leadership. But perhaps the leadership we crave does exist, and a lack of innovative thinking leads us to call it by another name—such as team work or collaboration. Because collaboration does not privilege the individual, the leadership it fosters is likely to be invisible. But today's complex organisations cannot afford to be so near-sighted as not to recognise how people change their institutions through everyday innovation and improvisation.[14]

'Post-heroic' leadership in strong distributive and inclusive forms is occuring in universities today. We have outlined some of the forms it has taken at UWA. The ultimate test of universities will be whether they recognise and reward those innovations in leadership.

UWA has long taken pride in its research reputation. It has now made considerable progress in instituting promotion procedures, training and support mechanisms—including collaborative team work—that highlight the importance of teaching. Yet, inequities remain. Despite considerable advances in academic promotion practices, teaching is still less rigorously assessed than is research, and research still dominates in selection for higher positions. Moreover, those who co-ordinate either research or teaching carry more weight than those who work face-to-face with students or research objects. At the lower levels of teaching and research, those with a powerful sense of vocation and well-honed skills in generating leadership and community are not recognised and given authority. Universities and workplaces generally are failing to acknowledge glue work.

We will know that innovative leadership is crucial to universities when men's networks reward relational skills and emotional intelligence, and when men and women together challenge the myth of individual achievement. We will know that universities have more deeply addressed the value difference between teaching and research when promotion and tenure committees call on as many external referees for teaching as they do for research. We will know that innovation has grown deep roots when teamwork and collaboration are seen as major forms of leadership and when a demonstrated commitment to equity and diversity is required in candidates for senior staff. When institutional prestige comes from inspiring and nurturing students and colleagues—then we will know that improvisation and innovation are building dynamic and sustainable communities.

Autonomy

A rapid increase in the number of tertiary students should be a source of pride to Australians, and especially to those who work in universities. Yet public funds to support this growth are dwindling. The price of success is larger classes, reduced curricula, fewer support staff, teaching overloads and highly stressed academics. Free markets, wealth creation and competitive advantage provide the rationale for self-managed universities. Yet it is clear that governments in the wealthy English-speaking world are keeping a tight budgetary rein on their public universities in a push for user-pays services.[15] Institutional autonomy is being challenged, and professional autonomy over the integrity of scholarship and the maintenance of high standards is under pressure.[16]

Currie et al. have established that academic women were more likely to be in non-mainstream areas of teaching and research. They were thus less likely to be affected by establishment pressures to compromise their professional integrity. But they conclude that, as long as that professional integrity is 'pitched at the level of the individual scholar' and not at wholesale institutional practices, academics find it difficult to maintain an appropriate distance from economic and strategic interests.[17]

In order to overcome that close association between professional autonomy and individualism, the values of autonomy and integrity must be linked to democratic and collaborative participation. Such an attempt was made at UWA, in relation to the promotion and tenure committee; and a coalition of academic and administrative staff used the same coupling in designing and executing a staff development programme for women. Yet despite strong support from the vice-chancellery, these initiatives have not been extended into other areas of university practice, such as budgetary decision-making, selection procedures and quality assurance. Hence the fear of many women that any gains may be fragile. Many also question how far the turn to diversity management in universities, which was seen as an opportunity to enlarge those collaborative initiatives, has been successful.

Many universities are tackling budgetary problems by competing in the market for international fee-paying students. A consequent management task is to persuade teachers and administrators to develop skills responsive to diversity. However, the danger is that 'multiculturalism is not about the opening up of knowledge but a strategic advantage used to attract students—multiculturalism thus becomes one of the weapons of globalization'.[18] Moreover, while this competition has increased the need for responsive equity and diversity management, many equity and diversity functions have been mainstreamed. Steering at a distance from downsized and centralised equity offices is often counterproductive.[19]

Corresponding pressure is being brought to align staff composition more closely with student populations. The vast majority of those people employed to date under UWA's diversity strategies are either general staff or lower level academic staff. Only time will tell whether these strategies will enable professional autonomy to be secured through collaborative and democratic enterprise.

Our study highlights an overall sense at UWA that awareness of equity and diversity issues has noticeably increased. The issues are on the agenda, people are no longer surprised when the terms 'gender equity' and 'diversity' are used, and challenging concerns can be voiced. Yet adherence to policy is patchy, and minorities are expected to conform to the dominant cultural group, not least by being clustered at the bottom of the organisation. The steps taken to welcome Indigenous people, and gays and lesbians, have been small indeed. And the middle and senior staff ranks show a startling homogeneity: almost all are white males, mostly of European–Australian background. However, as Inayatullah asserts, the university 'still offers an alternative to how to organize life and provide self and group identity outside the cold model of the corporatist organization or the bureaucratic state system'.[20]

When universities have incorporated the values of integrity and professional autonomy into democratic practice, these will be the signs. Active equity and diversity practices will be the unremarkable norm. All women and minorities will know their rights and entitlements and be able to build alliances that do not threaten their sense of having unique identities. Faculties will no longer be male-controlled dominions. Debate over inclusivity will be vigorous, informed and not overridden by other 'more important' issues. Evidence of relational experience and ability will be an indispensable criterion for judging merit. Fresh approaches to creativity and innovation will be core values. People selecting for teams will no longer choose others like themselves. And the topic of 'men' and masculinities will be a normal part of management and business studies curricula.[21] Only then will we know that collaborative and democratic autonomy has succeeded.

Renewal

Few of us can flee the task of managing the pace and breadth of global change in our local jobs and professions. Job insecurity and incessant juggling of family responsibilities—alongside longer hours, increased workloads and demands for a growing toolkit of technological and team skills—are the manifestations of constant instability. The everyday stresses encountered by our much-vaunted 'battler' are now the lot of most workers.

Over the four-years of our interviews, concern about workloads and their effect upon quality of life became an increasing theme. An associate professor told us: 'I used to work long and hard to get ahead, now I do it to survive'. Women in level 3 and 4 general staff positions told similar stories of overtime decreasingly offset by time-out in quieter periods. Said one: 'Everything's so new [yet] I don't find time to renew myself'. Restructuring, with its new tasks, longer hours, intensified pressures and flexible spread of duties, has undermined opportunities for renewal and revitalisation.

The technological fix does nothing to mend the cracks in collaborative community that inevitably accompany restructuring. In universities, Web-based learning and electronic mail systems allow not only ivory tower academics but also a select group of general staff the freedom of working from home. It is no longer sufficient to shut the office door when deadlines and commitments call. Yet taking work home further denudes university corridors of the communities that sustain innovative research and teaching. It also encourages the idea that work time can encroach on private time without adverse ramifications for individuals and communities.

New technologies of information and management represent for some the promise of nirvana. They confidently predict that old habits of juggling work and family and devaluing diversity will be overcome by flexible work practices, dual career families, greater choice for women to stay at home, flat and decentralised organisations, and virtual communications with less opportunity for gender and racial stereotyping.[22] Yet the internet and e-mail have ensured that work is possible 24 hours a day, and university workers, in tune with the broader employed population, are working longer hours than ever before.

Families, communities, health and safety all suffer from this galloping workaholism.[23] Yet for those without hands-on family responsibilities, the rewards can be high. Long hours and being indispensable 'can often become planks to a privileged identity, evidence of status and importance'.[24] Showing that a job can be done part-time seriously undermines such claims to substance, which may explain why part-time work has been so strongly rejected as an option for senior managers, including those in unions.[25] At UWA, some excellent policies for workers with family responsibilities have done little to inhibit deeply held assumptions about gender and gender roles, which privilege the sphere of work over the sphere of home and family. Collective action is the cornerstone of effective workplace resistance,[26] but when staff work 55 to 70 hours a week, the collegiality that sustains such action all but disappears.[27] Inevitably, the renewal of healthy and fulfilled selves, family and community, and the collegiality of the workplace, all suffer. These will be the signs that work practices that inhibit the renewal of self and community have been transformed. Men and women at the top will job-share or work part-time. Women and men using family friendly policies will be seen in an equally positive light, and policy provisions will be used equally by both genders. It will be exceptional to be denied part-time work or paid parental leave. Heroic dedication to working long hours at the cost of family, community and leisure will cease to symbolise a productive workplace. The unacknowledged and undervalued work of women will not be shoring up illusions of individual achievement. When academics do not assume that 'you have to work extra to stay afloat', and to say 'I have a weekend' is not a radical statement, we shall be able to say that the greedy institution is no longer dominant over our lives.

Conclusion

We have foregrounded university women and men who enrich their workplaces with fresh ideas and companionate, democratic values. They harness collaborative leadership to confront powerful and unjustified patterns of exclusion in their own and others' everyday working lives. We have told the stories of people who, with courage, loyalty and wisdom have challenged the damaging effects of under-staffing, ever-widening responsibilities and unrealistic performance criteria. They all promote sustainable and inventive communities in their university and beyond. Their actions are often hidden from view. Yet from their ivory basement perspective we can learn not only about survival but also about innovation, leadership, creativity and renewal.

APPENDIX 1

Methodology

Ethnography, embodied through a wide range of disciplinary applications, has featured in social science research for most of the twentieth century. While in Britain the rich tradition of ethnographic method grew out of social anthropology,[1] its United States pedigree can be traced to symbolic interactionism[2] and is linked to the Chicago School of sociology from early in the century.[3] The harvest of this diversity was tension between different strands of the ethnographic tradition. As intellectual attention refocused onto postmodernism and globalisation, some of the earlier debates over generalisability and validity subsided and new controversies over voice and positionality took their place.[4]

My position on validity is to recognise the partiality of all knowledge production.[5] That means that in common with many postmodernist and feminist researchers, I view with scepticism those studies claiming to provide *the* truth, or to be value-free. As McRobbie reminds us, 'no research is carried out in a vacuum. The very questions we ask are always informed by the historical moments we inhabit.'[6] It does not follow that one must throw out all criteria for judging the validity and worth of research. Along with Haraway,

I state my own feminist position and values so that readers can see how the knowledge I have a hand in shaping is situated and framed. I am more concerned to claim credibility by showing the complexity of social relations than by establishing unchallengeable truth claims.[7] Despite their many differences, all ethnographers share the view that social knowledge is won in the field rather than in the library.[8] Field studies, therefore, are the bedrock of ethnographic method. In Atkinson's words, ethnography is 'grounded in a commitment to the first-hand experience and exploration of a particular social and cultural setting on the basis of (though not exclusively by) participant observation'. This flourishing tradition is widespread:

> [it is found] in nursing and health studies, in studies of work and organizations, in science and technology studies, in human geography, in social psychology, in educational research, cultural, media and theatre studies, and many other domains of empirical research.[9]

In the design and execution of the research for this book, the premises and concerns of ethnographies of work and organisations occupied a primary place. Ethnographic studies of work emphasise labour processes, organisations, occupations and industries.[10] They ask questions about power and control over the work effort, about the relationship between workers, managers and their workplaces, and sometimes about the gendered nature of work organisation.[11] That combination of concerns has underpinned our study, and has been linked with questions of leadership, invisible labour and recognition of voices from the margins.

In addition to participant observation, and in common with the ethnographic approach, the research team used interviews, focus groups, documentary analysis and descriptive statistics. I called the focus groups 'affinity groups' because they drew together people with similar interests and work experiences. There were 192 participants in 17 affinity groups. We also conducted 97 individual interviews. Because a major goal was to give voice to women's experiences and views, the majority of the individual interviews were with women in the middle and lower ranks of academic and general staff. About a quarter were with staff in positional leadership: men and women on the governing board (Senate), in the vice-chancellery and senior administration, as well as deans, departmental heads and departmental managers. As most of these were men, we compensated by interviewing every woman in a senior management position.

Concern for context and complexity leads me to place importance on a reflexive process of data analysis and writing in which participants can play a part. In this research, the feedback mechanisms included short reports to, and discussions with, a variety of groups and participants, along with seminars and presentations to the wider university community. Although not designed as action research, material was sometimes deployed quite swiftly by participants to inform and reshape university policy. Comments from participants in feedback sessions were assessed for inclusion in the writing, along with comments on early drafts from eighteen participants in both senior and junior positions. The final drafts were disseminated and reshaped in the light of comments and advice from ten of those people, linked with a research team and an advisory body totalling twelve.

I make no claim that this form of feedback and input creates an equal relationship between researcher and researched. However, a partnership whose partipants have the right to a say and a right of reply is in line with the principles of lengthy and complex participation that inform most contemporary ethnography. As noted in a recent ethnography handbook, 'It is this sense of social exploration and protracted investigation that gives ethnography its abiding and continuing character'.[12]

On the crucial score of anonymity, this book departs from established ethnographic tradition. As Walford points out, anonymity is widely accepted as part of the ethnographer's access strategy. Pseudonyms are widely promised and given to protect organisations against unwanted exposure and researchers against libel claims. Yet as Walford demonstrates, when the findings turn out to be controversial, pseudonyms offer no protection.[13] The careful detailing of the organisation's specifics is a founding component of ethnography. As it may take news reporters, other researchers or lay readers very little effort to identify the ethnographic subject, attempts at anonymity often fail miserably.

The promise of anonymity for a research site may benefit the researchers more than the researched. As Walford writes, 'researchers are able to hide poor evidence behind the pseudonyms without the researched being able to make a challenge'.[14] Although the majority of our participants were given an interview code, and therefore anonymity, I decided that it would improve the study to identify for the reader both the university and a small group of senior staff. That decision helped prompt regular checks to ensure accuracy of reporting. Although a few details of personal and professional relationships did not make it into the book, the overall reporting shows a higher degree of collaborative precision.

Ethnography's emphasis on participation and observation demands a close encounter between the researcher and the object of study. Lengthy and intensive study of localised knowledge and sense-making has always generated highly contested terrain for ethnography, and researchers aligned with the quantitative sciences have challenged its validity on the grounds that it lacks generalisability. Ethnographers have responded by arguing that their goal is depth rather than breadth, a depth which they claim their accusers are prepared to sacrifice.[15] Hammersley notes that, with the growth in qualitative research in Britain over the past half-century, debates over generalisability have declined. A growing concern with the global has taken their place. It challenges the relevance of the local and the small-scale, causing ethnographers to argue that 'the local mediation of global processes' provides a fresh and important validation of ethnographic studies.[16]

In our interviews and affinity groups, discussion of the local, organisational context mingled with wider issues of university restructuring, work intensification, staff development and diversity of cultural backgrounds. To deal with this complexity, transcripts were coded and sorted by theme. The research team also tracked the logic of each speaker's account and the dynamics of each affinity group by analysing the transcripts as discrete units. Combining these techniques allowed us to tease out the main themes, and the mix of fact and feeling, in people's responses.

Women of all ranks spoke clearly and eloquently. It is hoped that the methods we used give full weight to their voices.

Interviewers: Genevieve Calkin, Joan Eveline, Rachel Robertson, Frances Rowland, Judy Skene

Affinity group facilitators: Marie Finlay, Joan Eveline, Pat Klinck, Maria Osman, Rachel Robertson, Frances Rowland, Judy Skene

APPENDIX 2

Critical Dates

1983   Status of Women Group formed at UWA
1984   Equal Opportunity Act (WA)
1986   UWA appoints Equal Opportunity Officer in response
            to Equal Opportunity Act (WA)
1986   Affirmative Action (Equal Employment Opportunity for
            Women) Act (Cwlth)
1988   Postdoctoral Re-entry Fellowship Introduced at UWA
            to assist women with careers interrupted by family
            responsibilities
1989   Administrative Secretaries Group formed at UWA
1990–97   Professor Fay Gale completes term as Vice-Chancellor
            at UWA, during which there is a marked increase in
            women professors and in the participation of women in
            key decision-making committees and roles. Gale was
            the first female chair of the Australian Vice-Chancellors
            Committee (1996–97)
1993 (Oct.) Governing Board, UWA, adopts Equal Opportunity in
            Employment and Education Policy

1994 (Aug.)   Leadership Development for Women Programme at UWA commences
1995–96   Review of the Position of Women on Academic Staff, UWA
1997–98   Review of the Position of Women on General Staff, UWA
1999   Equal Opportunity for Women in the Workplace Act (Cwlth) supersedes Affirmative Action (Equal Employment Opportunity for Women) Act, 1986

NOTES

Introducing the Ivory Basement

1   Brooks and Mackinnon (eds), *Gender and the Restructured University*, p. 1.
2   Bailyn, 'Academic careers and gender equity', pp. 137–53.
3   Martin and Collinson, 'Over the pond and across the water', pp. 259–60.
4   Brooks and Mackinnon (eds), *Gender and the Restructured University*; Inayatullah and Gidley (eds), *The University in Transformation*; Currie and Newson (eds), *Universities and Globalization*.
5   Eveline, 'The politics of advantage'.
6   Higher Education Quality Council, Report, *Choosing to Change*, London, HEQC, 1994, p. 315.
7   Morley, *Organising Feminisms*, p. 5.
8   ibid., p. 4.
9   Pocock, *The Work/Life Collision*, citing the 2001 HILDA survey.
10   Connell, 'Charting futures for sociology'.
11   T. Coady, 'Universities and the ideals of inquiry' in Coady (ed.), *Why Universities Matter*, pp. 3–25.
12   To establish this ethnographically requires micropolitical analysis of individual workplaces and individual events in depth, as in my work on women miners ('Surviving the Belt Shop Blues'; 'The worry of going limp'; Eveline and Booth, 'Gender and sexuality in discourses of managerial control and politicians'; Eveline and Booth, 'Who are you, really?').
13   Rimmer and Palmer, 'Future research in managing human diversity', p. 11
14   Currie and Newson (eds), *Universities and Globalization*; Coady, (ed.), *Why Universities Matter*; Tudiver, *Universities for Sale*.
15   York Stories Collective (ed.), *York Stories*, p. x.
16   Brewer, *Ethnography*.
17   Walford (ed.), *Debates and Developments in Ethnographic Methodology*.
18   The personal and political dimensions of this casts some research into a different category, as in my study (from 1996 to 1999) of women leaders in Western Australia, which became a popular collection of personal stories reflecting on the ambiguous project, occurring at the time, of celebrating Western Australia's centenary of women's suffrage (Eveline and Hayden, *Carrying the Banner*).
19   I have found this invaluable in studies of the police service and of mining, where the gendered organisation results in particularly vivid accounts of sexual harassment, racism and gender-bias, and where an action research methodology is integral to the data gathering (Eveline and Harwood,

'Challenging the gendering of police work', fifteenth World Congress of Sociology, Brisbane, 6–13 July 2002; Paper 3903, Joint Session of RC01, RC06 and RC32, 'Gender, work and family issues in predominantly male occupations' <www.sociology2002.com/203.94.129.73/timetable.html>; Eveline, 'Normalization, leading ladies and free men').

20   Mulkay, *The Word and The World*, p. 239.

21   P. Crawford, 'A partial story: women on the academic staff at UWA', in Crawford and Tonkinson, *The Missing Chapters*, p. 11.

22   Haraway, 'Situated knowledges'.

23   Some examples: Wright, *Managerial Leadership*; Bass, *Leadership and Performance Beyond Expectations*; Kotter, *A Force for Change*; Sims and Lorenzi, *The New Leadership Paradigm*.

24   Eveline, 'The politics of advantage'.

Chapter 1: The New Knowledge Economy

1   J. Brett, 'Competition and collegiality', in Coady (ed.), *Why Universities Matter*, pp. 145–6.

2   Coaldrake and Steadman, *On the Brink*.

3   Slaughter and Leslie, *Academic Capitalism*; Currie and Newson (eds), *Universities and Globalization*; Tudiver, *Universities for Sale*; Inayatullah and Gidley, *The University in Transformation*; Coady (ed.), *Why Universities Matter*.

4   Eccles and Nohria, cited in Knights and Wilmott (eds), *The Reengineering Revolution*, p. 50.

5   Knights and Wilmott (eds), *The Reengineering Revolution*.

6   K. Grint and P. Case, 'Now where were we?: BPR lotus eaters and corporate amnesia', in Knights and Wilmott (eds), *The Reengineering Revolution*, pp. 26–49.

7   Probert, ' "Grateful slaves" or "self-made women": a matter of choice or policy?'.

8   P. B. Altback, 'An international academic crisis: the American professoriate in comparative perspective', *Daedalus*, 126 (4), 1997, p. 332.

9   Hirst, *Globalisation in Question*.

10   Currie et al., *Gendered Universities in Globalized Economies*, pp. 19–25.

11   Connell, 'Charting futures for sociology', esp. p. 301.

12   Hirst and Thompson, 'Globalisation and the future of the nation state'.

13   Hodson and Sullivan, *The Social Organization of Work*, pp. 407–9.

14   Connell, *'Charting futures for sociology'*, pp. 301–2.

15   Blackmore and Sachs, 'Women leaders in the restructured university', p. 46.

16   Tonelson, *The Race to the Bottom*.

17   J. Marceau, 'Australian universities: a contestable future', in Coady (ed.), *Why Universities Matter*, pp. 216–17.

18   M. Gibbons et al., *The New Production of Knowledge*.
19   Slaughter and Leslie, *Academic Capitalism*, p. 37, cited in Brooks and Mackinnon (eds), *Gender and the Restructured University*, p. 2.
20   A. Brooks, 'Restructuring bodies of knowledge', in Brooks and Mackinnon (eds), *Gender and the Restructured University*; Currie and Newson (eds), *Universities and Globalization*; Prichard et al. (eds), *Managing Knowledge*.
21   J. Marceau, 'Australian universities: a contestable future', in Coady (ed.), *Why Universities Matter*.
22   Gibbons et al., *The New Production of Knowledge*, p. 70.
23   Connell, 'Charting futures for sociology', p. 302.
24   Gibbons et al., *The New Production of Knowledge*, esp. pp. 7–8.
25   Marginson, *Markets in Education*; J. Marceau, 'Australian universities: a contestable future', in Coady (ed.), *Why Universities Matter*.
26   Mackinnon and Brooks, *Gender and the Restructured University*, p. 3.
27   Gibbons et al., *The New Production of Knowledge*, p. 71.
28   J. Brett, 'Competition and collegiality', in Coady (ed.), *Why Universities Matter*, p. 154.
29   Gibbons et al., *The New Production of Knowledge*, p. 11.
30   ibid.
31   ibid.
32   Currie et al., *Gendered Universities in Globalized Economies*.
33   Brooks and Mackinnon (eds), *Gender and the Restructured University*, p. 15.
34   Blackmore and Sachs, 'Women leaders in the restructured university', p. 47.
35   P. Karmel, 'Funding universities', in Coady (ed.), *Why Universities Matter*, p. 167.
36   Blackmore and Sachs, 'Women leaders in the restructured university', p. 47.
37   P. Karmel, 'Funding universities', in Coady (ed.), *Why Universities Matter*, p. 160.
38   Currie et al., *Gendered Universities in Globalized Economies*, p. 19.
39   Dawkins, J., *Higher Education: A Policy Statement. The White Paper*, Canberra, Australian Government Publishing Service, 1988, pp. 10–11, cited in ibid., p. 20.
40   J. Molony, 'Australian universities today', in Coady (ed.), *Why Universities Matter*, pp. 73–4.
41   P. Karmel, 'Funding universities', in Coady (ed.), *Why Universities Matter*, p. 162.
42   Currie et al., *Gendered Universities in Globalized Economies*, p. 20.
43   S. Marginson, 'Research as a managed economy: the costs', in Coady (ed.), *Why Universities Matter*, p. 198.
44   Currie et al., *Gendered Universities in Globalized Economies*, pp. 20–21.

45   Marginson, *Markets in Education*, p. 21.
46   P. Karmel, 'Funding universities', in Coady (ed.), *Why Universities Matter*, p. 161.
47   ibid., p. 162.
48   J. Molony, 'Australian universities today', in Coady (ed.), *Why Universities Matter*, p. 77.
49   P. Karmel, 'Funding universities', in Coady (ed.), *Why Universities Matter*, pp. 167, 162.
50   Harris, 'Changing patterns of governance'.
51   Currie et al., *Gendered Universities in Globalized Economies*, p. 31.
52   S. Marginson, 'Research as a managed economy: the costs', in Coady (ed.), *Why Universities Matter*, p. 209.
53   J. Marceau, 'Australian universities: a contestable future', in Coady (ed.), *Why Universities Matter*, pp. 216, 220, 225.
54   Weick, 'Educational organizations as loosely coupled systems'.
55   Sydney, Melbourne, Adelaide, Western Australia, Queensland and Tasmania.
56   Adelaide, ANU, Melbourne, Monash, New South Wales, Sydney, Queensland, Western Australia.
57   In 2003, UWA had 3981 postgraduates (graduates) and 12,357 under-graduates enrolled.
58   Weick, 'Educational organizations as loosely coupled systems'.
59   The restructure was proposed on academic grounds, 'to minimise academic and organisational boundaries and encourage growth in new research areas'. 'Economies of scale' were also envisaged, through 'reduction in numbers of departments'. (UWA, 'The University of Western Australia restructure update', *Research News*, 3, 2002, p. 7.)
60   P. Crawford, 'A partial story: women on the academic staff at UWA', in Crawford and Tonkinson, *The Missing Chapters*, p. 15.
61   S. Marginson, 'Research as a managed economy: the costs', in Coady (ed.), *Why Universities Matter*, p. 192.
62   J. Marceau, 'Australian universities: a contestable future', in Coady (ed.), *Why Universities Matter*, p. 225.

Chapter 2: The Search for Answers
1   J. Gidley, 'Unveiling the human face of university futures', in Inayatullah and Gidley (eds), *The University in Transformation*, p. 243.
2   Pocock, *The Work/Life Collision*, citing the 2001 HILDA survey, p. 258.
3   Cited in S. Inayatullah, 'Corporate networks or bliss for all: the politics of the futures of the university', in Inayatullah and Gidley, *The University in Transformation*, p. 223.
4   Mackinnon, *Love and Freedom*.
5   Acker, 'Hierarchies, jobs, bodies'.

6   Hearn and Parkin, 'Gender and organisations'.
7   Acker, 'Hierarchies, jobs, bodies', p. 152.
8   Bailyn, 'Academic careers and gender equity', p. 143.
9   Kolb and Meyerson, 'Keeping gender in the plot'.
10   K. Carrington and A. Pratt, *How Far Have We Come?: Gender Disparities in the Australian Higher Education System*, Information and Research Services, Department of the Parliamentary Library, Canberra, 2003, p. 1.
11   A. Witz et al., 'Organised bodies'; Kolb and Meyerson, 'Keeping gender in the plot'; Hearn and Parkin, 'Gender and organisations'; Acker, 'Hierarchies, jobs, bodies'.
12   Eveline, 'Surviving the belt shop blues'.
13   West and Zimmerman, 'Doing gender'.
14   ibid., p. 23.
15   Fenstermaker and West, *Doing Gender, Doing Difference*.
16   Pringle, 'Denial and embrace', p. 5.
17   Sawicki, *Disciplining Foucault*, pp. 21, 25.
18   Morley, *Organising Feminisms*, p. 5.
19   ibid., pp. 4–5.
20   ibid., p. 6.
21   Fletcher, *Disappearing Acts*.
22   Coaldrake and Steadman, *On the Brink*.
23   T. Coady, 'Universities and the ideals of inquiry', in Coady (ed.), *Why Universities Matter*.
24   Morley and Walsh (eds), *Feminist Academics*; Astin and Leland, *Women of Influence, Women of Vision*.
25   Morley, *Organising Feminisms*.
26   Palmer, 'Diversity management'.
27   Bacchi, 'The seesaw effect'.
28   Rimmer and Palmer, 'Future research in managing human diversity'.
29   Eveline and Todd, 'Teaching managing diversity'; Bertone and Leahy, 'Multiculturalism as a conservative ideology'.
30   A. Oakley, 'Foreword', in Brooks and Mackinnon, *Gender and the Restructured University*, p. xi.
31   Gherardi, *Gender, Symbolism and Organizational Cultures*, pp. 12–13.
32   ibid., p. 13.
33   Bacchi, 'Changing the sexual harassment agenda', p. 78.
34   Weick, 'Educational organizations as loosely coupled systems'.
35   Smircich, 'Concepts of culture and organizational analysis'.
36   Martin, *Cultures in Organizations*.
37   Dahlerup, 'From a small to large minority: women in Scandinavian politics'.
38   Eveline and Booth, 'Holes in the ivory basement'.
39   Fletcher, *Disappearing Acts*.

40   Meyerson, *Tempered Radicals*.

41   Meyerson and Scully, 'Tempered radicalism and the politics of ambivalence and change'.

Chapter 3: Leading in the Basement

Some of the material in this chapter was published in J. Eveline and B. Goldflam, 'The networking queens: advancing women's status in a conservative work environment', *Proceedings*, eleventh International Women in Leadership conference, Edith Cowan University, 26–8 November 2002.

1   Blackmore and Sachs, 'Women leaders in the restructured university'.

2   Marginson, 'Steering from a distance'.

3   Donald, *Sentimental Education*; Marginson, *Markets in Education*; Blackmore and Sachs, 'Women leaders in the restructured university'.

4   S. Marginson, 'Research as a managed economy: the costs', in Coady (ed.), *Why Universities Matter*, pp. 186–213.

5   Yeatman, 'The new contractualism and the politics of quality management', p. 126.

6   Blackmore and Sachs, 'Women leaders in the restructured university', p. 49.

7   ibid., p. 50.

8   Fletcher, *Disappearing Acts*, p. 31.

9   Bryman, 'Leadership in organizations'.

10   Sinclair, *Doing Leadership Differently*.

11   Fletcher, 'The greatly exaggerated demise of heroic leadership'.

12   Blackmore, *Troubling Women*.

13   Fletcher, 'The greatly exaggerated demise of heroic leadership'.

14   Blackmore, *Troubling Women*.

15   Fletcher, 'The greatly exaggerated demise of heroic leadership'.

16   Astin and Leland, *Women of Influence, Women of Vision*, p. 116.

17   Blackmore, 'Educational leadership', p. 123.

18   Yeatman, 'The gendered management of equity oriented change in higher education'.

19   Limerick and Lingard (eds), *Gender and Changing Educational Management*.

20   Industry Taskforce on Leadership and Management Skills, *Enterprising Nation*.

21   Sinclair, *Doing Leadership Differently*.

22   Fletcher, 'The greatly exaggerated demise of heroic leadership', p. 1.

23   Goleman, *Emotional Intelligence*.

24   Blackmore and Sachs, ' "Zealotry or nostalgic regret"?', pp. 491–2.

25   For an account of these values as part of a 'professional politics', see
      Edwards, *Changing Place*.
26   Smith, *Writing the Social*, pp. 196–8.
27   P. Crawford, 'A partial story: women on the academic staff at UWA', in
      Crawford and Tonkinson, *The Missing Chapters*.
28   Astin and Leland, *Women of Influence*.
29   P. Crawford, 'A partial story: women on the academic staff at UWA', in
      Crawford and Tonkinson, *The Missing Chapters*, p. 37.
30   M. Tonkinson, 'Women on the general staff: telling their own story' in
      Crawford and Tonkinson, *The Missing Chapters*, p. 73.
31   Gale and Goldflam, *Strategies to Address Gender Imbalance in Numbers
      of Senior Academic Women*.
32   Eisenstein, *Inside Agitators*; Eveline, 'Feminism, racism and citizenship
      in twentieth century Australia'.
33   Gale, 'Taking on the academy'.
34   P. Crawford, 'A partial story: women on the academic staff at UWA', in
      Crawford and Tonkinson, *The Missing Chapters*.
35   ibid.
36   ibid.
37   Astin and Leland, *Women of Influence*.
38   Crawford and Tonkinson, *The Missing Chapters*.
39   Ferree and Martin (eds), *Feminist Organizations*.
40   Astin and Leland, *Women of Influence*, p. 66.
41   Meyerson, *Tempered Radicals*.
42   ibid.
43   S. Ackroyd and P. Thompson, *Organizational Misbehaviour*, London,
      Sage, 1999.
44   Dahlerup, 'From a small to large minority'.
45   Cockburn, *In the Way of Women*.
46   UWA, *Creating Opportunities: An Evaluation of the Leadership Develop-
      ment for Women Programme 1994–1997*, 1998; *Core Programme
      Evaluation: Leadership Development for Women*, 2002.
47   UWA, *LDW Programme*, 1994.
48   Sullivan et al. (eds), *The Rainbow Project: Perspectives on Sexuality
      at UWA*, Perth, The University of Western Australia, Guild of Under-
      graduates, 2002, p. iii.
49   See also Wyn et al., 'Making a difference'.
50   Dahlerup, 'From a small to a large minority'.
51   Blackmore and Sachs, 'Women leaders in the restructured university',
      p. 49.
52   H. Bloland, 'Postmodernism and higher education', *Journal of Higher
      Education*, 66 (5), 1995, pp. 521–70, cited in Blackmore and Sachs,
      'Women leaders in the restructured university', p. 46.

Chapter 4: Tacking in the Tower

1 UWA registered near the bottom on most tables comparing women in senior leadership. QUT: *Advancing the AVCC Action Plan for Women, Comparative DEST Data for All Australian Universities*, 2003.

2 Rosener, *Women's Competitive Secret*.

3 Bond, 'What price leadership'.

4 S. Powell, 'Dame Leonie gets "limp" comment rebuff', *Australian*, 8 August 1995, p. 1.

5 Eveline, 'The worry of going limp'.

6 Fletcher, 'The greatly exaggerated demise of heroic leadership', p. 2.

7 ibid., p. 3.

8 Gardiner and Tiggemann, 'Gender differences in leadership style, job stress and mental health in male- and female-dominated industries'.

9 Sinclair, *Doing Leadership Differently*, p. 109.

10 C. Pollitt, *Managerialism and the Public Services: The Anglo-American Experience*, London, Blackwell, 1990; Eccles and Nohria, *Beyond the Hype*.

11 Yeatman, 'The new contractualism and the politics of quality management', p. 203.

12 Knights and Willmott (eds), *The Reengineering Revolution*.

13 T. Peters, 'Why can't a man be more like a woman?', *Portfolio*, February 1991, pp. 21–35.

14 Helgeson, *The Female Advantage*.

15 Wyn et al., 'Making a difference', p. 442.

16 Yeatman, 'The gendered management of equity oriented change in higher education', pp. 23–4.

17 For examples, see M. David and D. Woodward (eds), *Negotiating the Glass Ceiling: Careers of Senior Women in the Academic World*, London, Falmer Press, 1998; Kolodny, *Failing the Future*; E. Ramsay, 'Managing within the malestrom', in Brooks and Mackinnon (eds), *Gender and the Restructured University*.

18 R. Munford and S. Rumball, 'Managing innovatively', in Brooks and Mackinnon, *Gender and the Restructured University*, pp. 142.

19 ibid., p. 141.

20 Wyn et al., 'Making a difference', p. 442.

21 Sinclair, *Doing Leadership Differently*, pp. 128, 127.

22 Wyn et al., *Gender and Education*, p. 442.

23 Blackmore and Sachs, 'Women leaders in the restructured university', p. 63.

24 Acker, 'Carry on caring'.

25 Blackmore and Kenway, 'Gender and the green paper'; Gale and Lowe, *Changing Australia*; Blackmore, 'More power to the powerful'.

26 Crawford and Tonkinson, *The Missing Chapters*.

27   Rupert Bunny, *Chloe at the Pool*, oil, now in the Lawrence Wilson Art Gallery, UWA.
28   J. Reid, *Tribute to Professor Fay Gale*, National Colloquium of Senior University Women, University of Sydney, 19 March 1998, p. 7.
29   *West Australian*, 1990. A 'blow-in' in Australian vernacular is an unexpected and transitory visitor.
30   Cockburn, *In the Way of Women*; Thornton, *Dissonance and Distrust*; Crawford and Tonkinson, *The Missing Chapters*; Astin and Leland, *Women of Influence*; Ozga and Walker, 'Women in education management'; Kolodny, *Failing the Future*.
31   Reid, *Tribute to Professor Fay Gale*, p. 6.
32   Currie et al., *Gendered Universities in Globalized Economies*, p. 120.
33   See research by Blackmore and Sachs, Currie et al., and Wyn.
34   Gardiner and Tiggemann, 'Gender differences in leadership style'.
35   However, see Acker and Feuerverger, 'Doing good and feeling bad'.
36   Wyn et al., 'Making a difference'.
37   Thornton, *Dissonance and Distrust*.
38   ibid.
39   ibid., p. 287.
40   D. Knights and H. Willmott, *Management Lives: Power and Identity in Work Organizations*, London, Sage, 1999.

Chapter 5: Inside Agitators?

1   Sawer, 'Why has the women's movement had more influence on government in Australia than elsewhere?' in F. G. Castles, *Australia Compared*, Sydney, Allen & Unwin, 1991, pp. 258–77.
2   Eisenstein, *Inside Agitators*, p. xii. The term underwent a sharp increase in use as other countries took it up, and Eisenstein suggests the meaning was often distorted to encompass any woman in a government bureaucracy. She claims an accurate definition is: 'a woman, feminist by personal conviction, who works within a government bureaucracy at a senior level to advance the status of women in society'.
3   A term coined by Hernes for the public policy devoted to women's interests developed following the 1975–85 UN Decade for Women (Hernes, *Welfare State and Women Power*).
4   S. Dowse, 'The women's movement fandango with the state: the movement's role in public policy since 1972', in C. Baldock and B. Cass (eds), *Women, Social Welfare and the State in Australia*, Sydney, Allen & Unwin, 1984; Franzway et al., *Staking a Claim*; Sawer, *Sisters in Suits*; Watson (ed.), *Playing the State*; Yeatman, *Bureaucrats, Technocrats, Femocrats*; Eisenstein, *Inside Agitators*.
5   Eisenstein, *Inside Agitators*.
6   ibid., pp. 86–100; Sawer, *Sisters in Suits*.

7   Blackmore, *Troubling Women*; Rao et al. (eds), *Gender at Work.*

8   Eisenstein, *Inside Agitators*, p. 218 n. 9. The ALP gained 54 per cent of votes from women in the 29–35 age group, and the coalition 38 per cent.

9   H. Eisenstein, *Gender Shock: Practising Feminism on Two Continents*, Allen & Unwin, 1991.

10 C. Wieneke, 'Equal employment opportunity in Australia: a practitioners perspective', *Equal Opportunities International*, 10 (1), 1991, pp. 1–10.

11 Wieneke and Durham, 'Regulating the equality agenda: EEO in higher education'.

12 Currie, 'The emergence of higher education as an industry', p. 2.

13 Currie, 'Restructuring employment', p. 49.

14 Currie, 'Women and award restructuring in universities', p. 7.

15 FAUSA, *Annual General Meeting 1990: Report on Award Restructuring*, FAUSA, 1990, p. 2.

16 Currie, 'Women and award restructuring in universities'.

17 ibid.

18 The Australian Technology Network (ATN) Women's Executive Development programme (WEXDEV) offers a comprehensive model with combined inhouse and nationally co-ordinated activities and opportunities for senior women. See Australian Vice-Chancellors' Committee, *Women and Leadership Programmes in Australian Universities: Summary of Responses to AVCC Questionnaire*, AVCC Secretariat, 2001.

19 Curtin, South Australia, Queensland University of Technology, Royal Melbourne Institute of Technology and University of Technology Sydney.

20 A staff development fund established by the National Tertiary Education Union and the federal Department of Education and Training. A criterion for funding was affirmative action for women.

21 S. Milligan and L. Genoni, *A Report of an Evaluation of the Women in Leadership Program: Edith Cowan University*, Edith Cowan University, 1993.

22 C. Pyner, *Shaping the Culture: Women in Leadership Program 1993*, Edith Cowan University, 1994.

23 Interview with J. Hutchinson, Head of Organisational Development, Edith Cowan University, 1991–95, August 2003.

24 C. Burton, An Equity Review of Staffing Policies and Associated Decision-making at Edith Cowan University, unpublished, 1994.

25 Junior female staff (at associate lecturer and lecturer levels) were matched with female mentors at more senior levels (senior lecturer and associate professor). Seventeen pairs were initially established, with 4 mentors having 2 mentees each. By the end of the project, 14 pairs remained, with 3 mentors having 2 mentees each. (F. Rowland and A. Butorac, *Mentoring Junior Academic Women 1995: Project Evaluation*, Murdoch University, 1996, p. 3.)

26   C. Chesterman, *Integrating Executive Development for Women: How 5 Australian Universities Collaborated to Enhance and Embed Leadership Activities for Women*, Sydney, ATN WEXDEV, April 2003, p. 14.
27   ibid., pp. 14–15.
28   ibid., pp. 8–15.
29   Bryman, 'Leadership in organizations', p. 278.
30   de Vries, 'Creating opportunities'.
31   The University of Western Australia, *Creating Opportunities: An Evaluation of the Leadership Development for Women Programme 1994–1997*, 1998.
32   ibid., p. iv.
33   Castleman et al., *Limited Access*.
34   Crawford and Tonkinson, *The Missing Chapters*.
35   The University of Western Australia, *Creating Opportunities*, p. iii.
36   de Vries, 'Creating opportunities'.
37   Data from the AVCC Action Plan website, August 2003, using 2002 figures. See <http://www.avcc.edu.au/policies_activities/university_management/uni_women_action_plan/>
38   ibid. Two of these on a cost recovery basis only.
39   de Vries, 'Creating opportunities'.
40   Gale, 'Who nurtures the nurturers?' p. 294.
41   Kolb and Meyerson, 'Keeping gender in the plot', p. 137.
42   The University of Western Australia, *Core Programme Evaluation, Leadership Development for Women*, 2002.
43   ibid.
44   Massey, 'Politics and space/time'.
45   Mitchell, 'The end of public space?'.
46   Both men were in acting positions at that time. One has since gained the position substantively.
47   This group comprises executive deans, deans, heads of department and departmental managers.
48   The University of Western Australia, *Leadership Development for Women Programme, Strategic Plan*, 1999.
49   Kolb and Meyerson, 'Keeping gender in the plot', p. 137.
50   The University of Western Australia, *Leadership Development for Women Programme*, 1994, p. 1.
51   Fraser, *Justice Interruptus*.
52   The University of Western Australia, *Leadership Development for Women Programme, Strategic Plan*, 1999.
53   See Kolb and Meyerson, 'Keeping gender in the plot', pp. 134–9, for an account of how a gender lens can help to show the traps of 'fix the women' and 'valuing the feminine'.
54   Equal Opportunity for Women, Employer of Choice for Women Award, 2003.

55   International conference attendance and a 2000 study tour of similar
        initiatives in the United Kingdom, Europe, Canada and the United States
        indicate that Australian universities are at the cutting edge in this area.
        LDW is considered to star on a number of key criteria: a long-standing
        cohort programme covering all women staff; the breadth of support
        and training offered and the long-term backing it receives from senior
        management (J. de Vries, 'What they are doing about leadership develop-
        ment overseas', presentation, Centre for Staff Development Forum, UWA,
        December 2000).

Chapter 6: The Elasticity of Academic Merit

1   Smith, *Writing the Social*, p. 204.
2   Eveline, 'The worry of going limp'.
3   Eveline, 'Heavy, dirty and limp stories'.
4   Hall and Sandler, *The Classroom Climate*, p. 5.
5   Cockburn, *In the Way of Women*.
6   Eveline, 'The politics of advantage'.
7   Martin and Collinson, 'Over the pond and across the water', p. 248.
8   Steinpreis et al., 'The impact of gender on the review of curricula vitae
        of job applicants and tenure candidates'.
9   Currie et al., *Gendered Universities in Globalized Economies*, use Eveline,
        'The politics of advantage', to show how the normalisation of gender
        advantage results in a gendered university.
10   Fletcher, *Disappearing Acts*.
11   J. Finch, 'Foreword: Why be interested in women's position in academe?',
        p. 134.
12   West and Zimmerman, 'Doing gender'; Benschop and Brouns, 'Crumbling
        ivory towers'.
13   Burton, *Redefining Merit*.
14   Bagilhole, 'How to keep a good woman down'; Burton, *Gender Equity
        in Australian University Staffing*.
15   Queensland University of Technology, *Advancing the AVCC Action
        Plan for Women: Comparative DEST Data for All Australian Universi-
        ties*, 2003. UWA registers near the bottom on most tables. In part this
        may be because the figures are compiled as full-time equivalents (FTEs)
        rather than as individuals, and UWA has a number of part-time female
        academics.
16   As did its predecessor, the Federation of Academic Staff Associations.
17   Promotion procedures had altered to include weightings that allowed
        areas such as service in the community and outside experience to be
        counted (Currie, 'Women and award restructuring in universities', p. 13).
18   C. Burton, An Equity Review of Staffing Policies and Associated Decision-
        making at Edith Cowan University, unpublished, 1994, p. 46.

19   Interview, Head of Organisational Development 1990–95, Edith Cowan University, 2003.
20   J. Everett, 'An analysis of gender discrimination in academic rank at Australian universities', *Australian Journal of Management*, 19 (2), 1994, pp. 159–77.
21   Gale, 'Academic staffing'.
22   Probert, Ewer and Whiting, *Gender Pay Equity in Australian Higher Education*, National Tertiary Education Union, Melbourne, 1998.
23   The University of Western Australia, Promotions and Tenure Committee, *Annual Report to Senate*, 1996.
24   Todd and Bird, 'Gender and promotion in academia'; Booth and Eveline, 'Companionate leadership in the case of academic promotions', 2001.
25   Currie, 'Restructuring employment'.

Chapter 7: Gaining a Voice
Much of this chapter was previously published in Stuart, 'The position of women staff at the University of Western Australia'.
1   Burton, *Gender Equity in Australian University Staffing*; Castleman et al., *Limited Access*; Probert, Ewer and Whiting, *Gender Pay Equity in Australian Higher Education*.
2   Senge, *The Fifth Discipline*.
3   Blackmore and Sachs, 'Women leaders in the restructured university', p. 54.
4   Luke, *Globalization and Women in Academia*.
5   Blackmore and Sachs, 'Women leaders in the restructured university'; Currie et al., *Gendered Universities in Globalized Economies*; L. A. Kretting, 'Intertwined discourses of merit and gender: evidence from academic employment in the USA', *Gender, Work and Organization*, 10 (2), 2003, pp. 260–78; R. Thomas and A. Davies, 'Gender and new public management: reconstituting academic subjectivities', *Gender, Work and Organization*, 9 (2), 2002, pp. 372–97.
6   P. Crawford, 'A partial story: women on the academic staff at UWA', in Crawford and Tonkinson, *The Missing Chapters*.
7   The Review of Academic Staff Women was chaired by Professor Bob Wood of the UWA Department of Management. Members were Kay Rollinson, Equity Manager from the University of Adelaide and Marcia Neave, Professor of Law at Monash University. The Review of General Staff Women was chaired by Christine Richardson of the Faculty of Agriculture. Members were Owen Hicks from the Centre for Staff Development and Karen Thompson of the State Government, Office of Equal Opportunity in Public Employment. Jan Stuart acted as Executive Officer to both reviews.

8   The University of Western Australia, *The Position of Women Academic Staff at the University of Western Australia: A Review of Equity (Draft Report)*, 1995, p. 11.

9   Sinclair, *Trials at the Top*, p. 19.

10   Morgan, *Imaginization*.

11   The University of Western Australia, *Working Life Survey (Draft Report)*, 1997.

12   The University of Western Australia, *Creating Opportunities: An Evaluation of the Leadership Development for Women Programme 1994–1997*, 1998.

13   Currie et al., *Gendered Universities in Globalized Economies*, p. 46.

14   McLean, 'Hearing from the forgotten workforce'; Burton, *Gender Equity in Australian University Staffing*.

15   Moodie, *Leaping Tall Organisational Boundaries in a Single Bound*; McInnis, Academics and Professional Administrators in Australian Universities.

16   The University of Western Australia, *The Position of Women General Staff at the University of Western Australia: A Review (Draft Report)*, 1997.

17   UWA, *Working Life Survey*, 1997.

18   UWA, *An Evaluation of the Leadership Development for Women Programme 1994–1997*.

19   Morgan, *Imaginization* and *Images of Organization;* Senge, *The Fifth Discipline*; Rao et al., *Gender at Work*.

20   Weick and Sutcliffe, *Managing the Unexpected*.

21   J. Blackmore, 'Educational leadership: a feminist critique and reconstruction' in J. Smyth (ed.), *Critical Perspectives in Educational Leadership*, London, Falmer Press, 1989, p. 123.

22   Schein, *Three Cultures of Management*.

23   Morgan, *Images of Organization*.

24   Senge, *The Fifth Discipline*, p. 12.

25   Crawford, 'A partial story: women on the academic staff at UWA' in Crawford and Tonkinson, *The Missing Chapters*.

Chapter 8: Glue Work

1   Yeatman, 'The new contractualism and the politics of quality management'.

2   S. Marginson, 'Cash cure for campus blues', *The Australian,* 9 May 2000, p. 13.

3   Wieneke, 'Managing women'; Whyley and Callender, 'Administrative and support staff in higher education'.

4   Hoffman, *Sekretaren Bakom Allt.*

5   K. Grint and P. Case, 'Now where were we?: BPR lotus eaters and corporate amnesia', in Knights and Wilmott (eds), *The Reengineering Revolution*, pp. 26–49.
6   Cox and Leonard, *From Umm to Aha!*
7   Lloyd, *The Man of Reason.*
8   J. Marceau, 'Australian universities: a contestable future', in Coady (ed.), *Why Universities Matter*, p. 225.
9   Rao et al., *Gender at Work.*
10   Kolb and Meyerson, 'Keeping gender in the plot', p. 132.
11   Senge, *The Fifth Discipline.*
12   Schein, *Three Cultures of Management.*
13   M. Tonkinson, 'Women on the general staff: telling their story', in Crawford and Tonkinson, *The Missing Chapters*, pp. 64–5.
14   The University of Western Australia, *Equal Opportunity Annual Report*, 1999.
15   Probert et al., *Gender Pay Equity in Australian Higher Education.*
16   Wieneke and Durham, 'Regulating the equality agenda'.
17   Burton, *Gender Equity in Australian University Staffing.*
18   Commonwealth, Department of Education, Science and Training, 2002.
19   J. Hobson, E. Deane and G. Jones, 'Technology's Handmaiden: Fact or Fiction?', unpublished paper presented at Women, Research and Publication conference, ATN WEX-DEV, Curtin University, 25–27 June 2003.
20   Castleman and Allen, 'The forgotten workforce'.

Chapter 9: Organising For and Against Diversity

1   The debates over transformational v. 'transactional' leadership range from Burns, *Leadership*, to Kotter, *A Force for Change.*
2   For a criticism of this notion, see Martin, *Cultures in Organizations.*
3   Rao et al., *Gender at Work.*
4   Martin and Frost, 'The organisational culture war games'.
5   Smircich, 'Concepts of culture and organizational analysis'.
6   Prasad et al., *Managing the Organizational Melting Pot.*
7   Luke, *Globalization and Women in Academia.*
8   Currie et al., *Gendered Universities in Globalized Economies*, p. 117.
9   Yeatman, 'The new contractualism and the politics of quality management'.
10   Luke, *Globalization and Women in Academia.*
11   Burton, *Gender Equity in Australian University Staffing.*
12   Crawford and Tonkinson, *The Missing Chapters.*
13   Currie et al., *Gendered Universities in Globalized Economies*; Brooks and Mackinnon (eds), *Gender and the Restructured University.*
14   Eveline, 'The politics of advantage'.

15   Tannen, *Gender and Discourse.*
16   Cockburn, *In the Way of Women*; Wacjman, *Managing Like a Man.*
17   Cockburn, *In the Way of Women*; Prasad et al., *Managing the Organizational Melting Pot.*
18   de Vries, 'The last acceptable prejudice?'.
19   Goody and de Vries, 'Straight talk about queer issues', p. 5.
20   Cited in de Vries, 'The last acceptable prejudice?'.
21   Minow argues that unless we take as our norm for planning the needs of people with disabilities, we will never overcome the marginalisation that our current systems of meaning produce for large sections of the population (Minow, *Making All the Difference).*
22   P. Crawford, 'A partial story: women on the academic staff at UWA', in Crawford and Tonkinson, *The Missing Chapters.*
23   Storey, *What is Cultural Studies?*
24   Bertone and Leahy, 'Multiculturalism as a conservative ideology'.
25   T. H. Cox Jnr, *Cultural Diversity in Organisations.*

Chapter 10: Work/Life

1   Mackinnon, *Love and Freedom*, pp. 1–12.
2   Australian Bureau of Statistics figures for 1996, cited in Pocock, *The Work/Life Collision*, p. 27.
3   ibid., pp. 26–7 (ABS figures).
4   M. Bittman and J. Pixley, *The Double Life of the Family: Myth, Hope and Experience*, Sydney, Allen & Unwin, 1997.
5   A recent Australian study indicates that men's contribution to housework has shown no increase between 1986 and 1997, although women are also doing less (Baxter, 'Patterns of change and stability in the gender division of labour in Australia, 1986–1997').
6   R. Pahl, *After Success*, Cambridge, Polity Press, 1995.
7   McBride and Darragh, 'Interpreting the data on father involvement', p. 491.
8   Pocock, *The Work/Life Collision*, p. 46.
9   ibid.; Bittman, *Juggling Time.*
10   H. Glezer, 'Fathers are parents too: parental leave in Australia', *Family Matters*, 27, 1990, p. 24.
11   P. MacDonald, *Gender Equity, Social Institutions and the Future of Fertility,* Working Papers in Demography 69, Canberra, Research School of Social Sciences, Australian National University, 1997; MacDonald, 'Contemporary fertility patterns in Australia'.
12   Kilmartin, 'Are Australian workplaces family-friendly?'.
13   J. Levine, address to the Work and Family: Beyond 2000 conference, Department of Productivity and Labour Relations, Perth, 12 May 1998.
14   R. Bly, *Iron John*, Shaftesbury, Dorset UK, Element Books, 1990.

15   Hearn, *Men in the Public Eye.*
16   Pocock, *The Work/Life Collision.*
17   Whereby employees work 42 or 48 weeks per year but spread their pay over the full 52 weeks.
18   The University of Western Australia, *The Position of Women Academic Staff at The University of Western Australia: A Review of Equity (Draft Report)*, 1995, p. 17.
19   ibid., p. 18.
20   The University of Western Australia, *The Position of Women General Staff at the University of Western Australia: A Review (Draft Report)*, 1997, p. 19.
21   Job shares are more applicable to general staff because it is easier for academic staff to negotiate a fractional appointment.
22   P. Crawford, 'A partial story: women on the academic staff at UWA', in Crawford and Tonkinson, *The Missing Chapters.*
23   Currie et al., *Gendered Universities in Globalized Economies*; Franzway, *Sexual Politics and Greedy Institutions.*
24   Currie et al., *Gendered Universities in Globalized Economies.*
25   Haavind and Andenaes ('Care and responsibility for children') argue that mothers are socialised into carrying a 'running wheel' in their heads, a planning and reminder mechanism of all that they need to do at home, while concentrating on their jobs.
26   Cockburn, *In the Way of Women*; Waring, *Counting For Nothing*; Pocock, *Having A Life.*
27   Hochschild, *The Time Bind.*
28   Pocock, *The Work/Life Collision*, p. 263.

Conclusion

Jen de Vries provided the initial notes for the futuristic wish list included in the four main sections of this chapter. She, Michael Booth, Jan Stuart and Barbara Goldflam gave valuable feedback and editing suggestions on the chapter overall.

1   Brooks and Mackinnon (eds), *Gender and the Restructured University*; Currie et al., *Gendered Universities in Globalized Economies.*
2   Finch, 'Foreword: Why be interested in women's position in academe?'; I. Milojevic, 'The crisis of the university: feminist alternatives for the twenty first century and beyond', in Inayatullah and Gidley (eds), *The University in Transformation*, pp. 175–86.
3   Benschop and Brouns, 'Crumbling ivory towers: academic organizing and its gender effects', p. 207.
4   As late as 1905 a college was built at Cambridge without bathrooms, 'since students were only there for eight weeks at a time' (college guide, 2003).

5   Goodall, 'Casing the academy for community'.

6   Almost half of all Australians undertake tertiary learning during their
        lives (P. Karmel, 'Funding universities', in Coady (ed.), *Why Universities
        Matter*, p. 167).

7   Coaldrake and Stedman, *On the Brink*, pp. 116–17.

8   J. Marceau, 'Australian universities: a contestable future', in Coady (ed.),
        Why Universities Matter, p. 217.

9   Karpin, *Enterprising Nation*.

10   T. Coady, 'Universities and the ideals of inquiry', in Coady (ed.), *Why
        Universities Matter*, p. 18.

11   S. Marginson, 'Research as a managed economy: the costs', in Coady
        (ed.), *Why Universities Matter*, p. 200.

12   Martin and Collinson, 'Over the pond and across the water'.

13   Haraway, 'Situated knowledges'.

14   Meyerson, *Tempered Radicals*.

15   Slaughter and Leslie, *Academic Capitalism*.

16   S. Miller, 'Academic autonomy', in Coady (ed.), *Why Universities Matter*,
        pp. 110–31.

17   Currie et al., *Gendered Universities*, p. 188.

18   S. Inayatullah, 'Corporate networks or bliss for all', in Inayatullah and
        Gidley (eds), *The University in Transformation*, p. 227.

19   C. Bacchi, 'Managing equity: mainstreaming and diversity in Australian
        universities', in Brooks and Mackinnon (eds), *Gender and the Restruc-
        tured University*, p. 120.

20   Inayatullah, 'Corporate networks or bliss for all', in Inayatullah and
        Gidley (eds), *The University in Transformation*, p. 223.

21   A. Sinclair, 'Gender = men + women: why men's experiences should be
        part of management studies', *Mt Eliza Business Review*, Summer/Autumn
        2000/2001, pp. 9–16.

22   Spearritt and Edgar, *The Family-Friendly Front*; C. Hakim, *Work/Lifestyle
        Choices in the Twenty First Century: Preference Theory*, Oxford, Oxford
        University Press, 2000.

23   Pocock, *The Work/Life Collision*.

24   Sinclair, 'Gender = men + women', p. 14.

25   J. O'Reilly and C. Fagan (eds), *Part-Time Prospects: An International
        Comparison of Part-time Work in Europe, North America and the Pacific
        Rim*, London Routledge, 1998; Franzway, *Sexual Politics and Greedy
        Institutions*.

26   McKinley and Taylor, 'Power, surveillance and resistance'.

27   J. Brett, 'Competition and collegiality', in Coady (ed.), *Why Universities
        Matter*, pp. 144–58.

Appendix 1: Methodology

1   Brewer, *Ethnography*, pp. 11–12.
2   Walford (ed.), *Debates and Developments in Ethnographic Methodology*.
3   P. Rock, 'Symbolic interactionism and ethnography', in Atkinson et al. (eds), *Handbook of Ethnography*, pp. 26–38.
4   M. Hammersley, 'Ethnography and the disputes over validity', in Walford (ed.), *Debates and Developments in Ethnographic Methodology*, pp. 7–22.
5   Reinharz, *Feminist Methods in Social Research*; Denzin and Lincoln (eds), *Handbook of Qualitative Research*.
6   McRobbie, cited in Morley, *Organising Feminisms*, p. 12.
7   Haraway, 'Situated knowledges'.
8   P. Rock, 'Symbolic interactionism and ethnography', in Atkinson et al. (eds), *Handbook of Ethnography*, p. 29.
9   P. Atkinson, 'Editorial introduction', in Atkinson et al. (eds), *Handbook of Ethnography*, pp. 4, 5.
10   V. Smith, 'Ethnographies of work and the work of ethnographers', in Atkinson et al. (eds), *Handbook of Ethnography*, pp. 220–33.
11   Cockburn, *In the Way of Women*.
12   Atkinson, 'Editorial introduction', in Atkinson et al. (eds), *Handbook of Ethnography*, p. 5.
13   G. Walford, 'Why don't researchers name their research sites?' in Walford (ed.), *Debates and Developments in Ethnographic Methodology*, pp. 95–106.
14   ibid., p. 100.
15   Brewer, *Ethnography*, p. 78.
16   ibid., p. 180.

SELECT BIBLIOGRAPHY

Acker, J. 'Hierarchies, jobs, bodies: a theory of gendered organizations', *Gender and Society*, 4 (2), 1990, pp. 139–58.

Acker, S. 'Carry on caring: the work of women teachers', *British Journal of Sociology of Education*, 16 (1), 1995, pp. 21–36.

Acker, S. and Feuerverger, G. 'Doing good and feeling bad: the work of women university teachers', *Cambridge Journal of Education*, 26, 1996, pp. 401–22.

Ackroyd, S. and Thompson, P. *Organizational Misbehaviour*, London, Sage, 1999.

Astin, H. S. and Leland, C. *Women of Influence, Women of Vision*, San Francisco, Jossey–Bass, 1991.

Atkinson, P., Coffey, A., Delamont, S., Lofland, J. and Lofland, L. (eds), *Handbook of Ethnography*, London, Sage, 2001.

Australia, Department of Employment, Education, Training and Youth Affairs, *The Higher Education Management Review* (the Hoare Report), 1996 <http://www.deet.gov.au/pubs/hedmanrv.htm>.

Bacchi, C. 'Changing the sexual harassment agenda', in A. Mackinnon and M. Gatens (eds), *Gender and Institutions: Welfare, Work and Citizenship*, Cambridge, Cambridge University Press, 1998, pp. 75–89.

—— 'The seesaw effect: down goes affirmative action, up comes workplace diversity', *Journal of Interdisciplinary Gender Studies*, 5 (2), 2002, pp. 64–83.

Bagilhole, B. 'How to keep a good woman down: an investigation of the role of institutional factors in the process of discrimination against women academics', *British Journal of Sociology of Education*, 14 (3), 1993, pp. 261–74.

Bailyn, L. 'Academic careers and gender equity: lessons learned from MIT', *Gender, Work and Organization*, 10 (2), 2003, pp. 137–53.

Bass, B. M. *Leadership and Performance Beyond Expectations*, New York, Free Press, 1985.

Baxter, J. 'Patterns of change and stability in the gender division of labour in Australia, 1986–1997', *Journal of Sociology*, 38 (4), 2002, pp. 399–424.

Benschop, Y. and Brouns, M. 'Crumbling ivory towers: academic organising and its gender effects', *Gender, Work and Organization*, 10 (2), 2003, pp. 194–212.

Bertone, S. and Leahy, M. 'Multiculturalism as a conservative ideology: impacts on workforce diversity', *Asia Pacific Journal of Human Resources*, 4 (1), 2003, pp. 101–15.

Bittman, M. *Juggling Time: How Australian Families Use Time*, Canberra, Australian Government Publishing Service, 1991.

Blackmore, J. 'Educational leadership: a feminist critique and reconstruction' in J. Smyth (ed.), *Critical Perspectives in Educational Leadership*, London, Falmer Press, 1989, pp. 93–129.

—— 'More power to the powerful: corporate management, mergers and the implications for women of the reshaping of the "culture" of Australian tertiary education', *Australian Feminist Studies*, 15, 1992, pp. 65–89.

—— *Troubling Women: Feminism, Leadership and Educational Change*, Buckingham, Open University Press, 1999.

Blackmore, J. and Kenway, J. 'Gender and the green paper: privatisation and equity', *Australian Universities' Review*, 31 (1), 1988, pp. 49–56.

Blackmore, J. and Sachs, J. 'Women leaders in the restructured university', in A. Brooks and A. Mackinnon, *Gender and the Restructured University*, Buckingham, Society for Research into Higher Education / Open University Press, 2001, pp. 45–66.

—— '"Zealotry or nostalgic regret"? Women leaders in technical and further education in Australia: agents of change, entrepreneurial educators or corporate citizens?', *Gender, Work and Organization*, 10 (4), 2003, pp. 478–503.

Bond, S. 'What price leadership: professional lives of women leaders in Canadian universities', Women, Research and Publication conference, ATN WEXDEV, Curtin University, Perth, 25–27 June 2003.

Booth, M. A. and Eveline, J. 'Companionate leadership in the case of academic promotions', refereed proceedings, 10th International Women in Leadership conference, Esplanade Hotel, Fremantle, Edith Cowan University, 2001, pp. 6–13.

Brewer, J. D. *Ethnography*, Buckingham UK, Open University Press, 2000.

Brooks, A. and Mackinnon, A. (eds), *Gender and the Restructured University*, Buckingham, Society for Research into Higher Education / Open University Press, 2001.

Bryman, A. 'Leadership in organizations' in S. Clegg, C. Hardy and W. Nord (eds), *Handbook of Organization Studies*, London, Sage, 1996, pp. 276–92.

Burns, J. M. *Leadership*, New York, Harper and Row, 1978.

Burton, C. *Redefining Merit*, Canberra, Australian Government Publishing Service, 1988.

—— *Gender Equity in Australian University Staffing*, Evaluations and Investigations Program, Higher Education Division, Department of Employment, Education, Training and Youth Affairs, 1997.

Castleman, T. and Allen, M. 'The forgotten workforce: female general staff in higher education', *Australian Universities' Review*, 38 (2), 1995, pp. 65–9.

Castleman, T., Allen, M., Bastalich, W. and Wright, P. *Limited Access: Women's Disadvantage in Higher Education Employment*, National Tertiary Education Union, Melbourne, 1995.

Coady, T. (ed.). *Why Universities Matter*, Sydney, Allen & Unwin, 2001.

Coaldrake, P. and Steadman, L. *On the Brink: Australia's Universities Confronting their Future*, Brisbane, University of Queensland Press, 1998.

Cockburn, C. *In the Way of Women: Men's Resistance to Sex Equality in Organizations*, London, Macmillan Education, 1991.

Connell, R. 'Charting futures for sociology', *Contemporary Sociology*, 29 (1), 2000, pp. 291–6.

Cox, E. and Leonard, H. *From Umm to Aha!*, Canberra, Australian Government Publishing Service, 1991.

Cox T. H. Jnr, *Cultural Diversity in Organisations: Theory, Research and Practice*, San Francisco, Barrett–Koehler, 1993.

Crawford, P. and Tonkinson, M. *The Missing Chapters: Women Staff at the University of Western Australia, 1963–1987*, Perth, Centre for Western Australian History, University of Western Australia, 1988.

Currie, J. 'The emergence of higher education as an industry: the second tier awards and award restructuring', unpublished paper.

—— 'Women and award restructuring in universities', paper presented at Women in Leadership, second national conference, Edith Cowan University, Perth, 1–3 December 1993.

—— 'Restructuring employment: the case of female academics', *Australian Universities' Review*, 38 (2), 1995, pp. 49–54.

Currie, J. and Newson, J. (eds). *Universities and Globalization: Critical Perspectives*, London, Sage, 1998.

Currie, J., Thiele, B. and Harris, P. *Gendered Universities in Globalized Economies*, Maryland, Lexington Books, 2002.

Dahlerup, D. 'From a small to a large minority: women in Scandinavian politics', *Scandinavian Political Studies*, 11 (4), 1988, pp. 275–98.

Denzin, N. K. and Lincoln, Y. S. (eds). *Handbook of Qualitative Research*, London, Sage, 1994.

de Vries, J. 'Creating opportunities: the difference a women's leadership programme can make', in C. Wiedmer (ed.), *Sound Changes: An International Survey of Women's Career Strategies in Higher Education*, Zurich, Frauenstelle/Office of Equal Opportunities at the University of Zurich, 2002, pp. 133–9.

—— 'The last acceptable prejudice?', *UWA News*, 1 July 2002.

Donald, J. *Sentimental Education*, London, Verso, 1992.

Eccles, R. and Nohria, N. *Beyond the Hype: Rediscovering the Essence of Management*, Boston, Ma., Harvard University Press, 1992.

Edwards, R. *Changing Place: Flexibility, Lifelong Learning and a Learning Society*, London, Routledge, 1997.

Eisenstein, H. *Inside Agitators*, Sydney, Allen & Unwin, 1996.

Eveline, J. 'The politics of advantage', *Australian Feminist Studies*, special issue: Women and Citizenship, 19, 1994, pp. 129–54.

—— 'Normalization, leading ladies and free men: affirmative actions in Sweden and Australia', *Women's Studies International Forum*, 17 (6), 1994, pp. 157–68.

—— 'Surviving the belt shop blues: women miners and critical acts', *Australian Journal of Political Science*, 30, 1995, pp. 91–107.

—— 'The worry of going limp: are you keeping up in senior management?', *Australian Feminist Studies*, 11 (23), 1996, pp. 65–79.

—— 'Heavy, dirty and limp stories: male advantage at work' in M. Gatens and A. MacKinnon (eds), *Gender and Institutions: Welfare, Work and Citizenship*, Cambridge, Cambridge University Press, 1998, pp. 90–106.

—— '"Whither the new father?" Male managers and early child care in Australia and Sweden', *Journal of Interdisciplinary Gender Studies*, 6 (1), 2001, pp. 3–20.

—— 'Feminism, racism and citizenship in twentieth century Australia', in P. Crawford and P. Maddern (eds), *Women as Australian Citizens: Underlying Histories*, Melbourne, Melbourne University Press, 2001, pp. 141–77.

—— 'Developing women leaders or generating a new campus culture?' in Institute for the Service Professions (eds), *Journeys in Leadership: Reflections, Redirections*, refereed papers, 10th international Women in Leadership conference, Esplanade Hotel, Fremantle, 14–15 Nov. 2001, pp. 28–36.

Eveline, J. and Booth, M. 'Who are you, really? feminism and the female politician', *Australian Feminist Studies*, 12 (25), 1997, pp. 105–18.

—— 'Images of women in Western Australian politics: the suffragist, Edith Cowan and Carmen Lawrence', *Women and Citizenship: Suffrage Centenary; Studies in Western Australian History*, 19, 1999, pp. 29–47.

—— 'Gender and sexuality in discourses of managerial control', *Gender, Work and Organization*, 9 (5), 2002, pp. 556–78.

—— 'Holes in the ivory basement: the essential but devalued work of women in the restructuring university', refereed proceedings, 11th International Women in Leadership conference, Edith Cowan University, 26–28 November 2002, pp. 35–48.

Eveline, J. and Goldflam, B. 'The networking queens: advancing women's status in a conservative work environment', refereed proceedings, 11th International Women in Leadership conference, Edith Cowan University, 26–28 November 2002, pp. 49–60.

Eveline, J. and Hayden, L. (eds). *Carrying the Banner: Women, Leadership and Activism in Australia*, Perth, UWA Press, 1999.

Eveline, J. and Todd, P. 'Teaching managing diversity', *International Journal of Inclusive Education*, 6 (1), 2002, pp. 33–46.

Fenstermaker, S. and West, C. *Doing Gender, Doing Difference: Inequality, Power and Institutional Change*, New York, Routledge, 2002.

Ferree, M. M. and Martin, P. Y. (eds). *Feminist Organizations: Harvest of the New Women's Movement*, Philadelphia, Temple University Press, 1995.

Finch, F. 'Foreword: Why be interested in women's position in academe?', *Gender, Work and Organization*, 10 (2), 2003, pp. 133–6.

Fletcher, J. K. *What's Love Got to Do with It?*, CGO Working Paper Series no. 4, Boston, Center for Gender in Organizations/Simmons College of Management, 1998.

—— *Disappearing Acts: Gender, Power and Relational Practice at Work*, Cambridge, Mass., MIT Press, 1999.

—— *The Greatly Exaggerated Demise of Heroic Leadership: Gender, Power and the Myth of the Female Advantage*, CGO Insights, Briefing Note no. 13, Boston, Center for Gender in Organizations / Simmons College of Management, 2002.

Franzway, S. *Sexual Politics and Greedy Institutions: Union Women, Commitments and Conflicts in Public and Private*, Sydney, Pluto Press, 2001.

Franzway, S., Court, S. D. and Connell, R. W. *Staking a Claim: Feminism, Bureaucracy and the State*, Sydney, Allen & Unwin, 1989.

Fraser, N. *Justice Interruptus: Critical Reflections on the Post-Socialist Condition*, New York and London, Routledge, 1997.

Freeman, J. 'From seed to harvest' in M. M. Ferree and P. Y. Martin (eds), *Feminist Organizations: Harvest of the New Women's Movement*, Philadelphia, Temple University Press, 1995, pp. 397–408.

Gale, F. 'Academic staffing: the search for excellence', *Vestes*, 23, 1980, pp. 3–8.

—— 'Who nurtures the nurturers?: senior women in universities', *Winds of Change: Women and Culture in Universities*, conference proceedings, Sydney, 1998, pp. 290–5.

—— 'Taking on the academy', in J. Eveline and L. Hayden (eds), *Carrying the Banner: Women, Leadership and Activism in Australia*, Perth, UWA Press, 1999, pp. 136–44.

Gale, F. and Goldflam, B. *Strategies to Address Gender Imbalance in Numbers of Senior Academic Women*, Perth, University of Western Australia, 1997.

Gale, F. and Lowe, I. *Changing Australia: The Boyer Lectures 1991*, Sydney, ABC Publications, 1991.

Gardiner, M. and Tiggemann, M. 'Gender differences in leadership style, job stress and mental health in male- and female-dominated industries', *Journal of Occupational and Organizational Psychology*, 72, 1999, pp. 301–15.

Gherardi, S. *Gender, Symbolism and Organizational Cultures*, London, Sage, 1995.

Gibbons, M., Limoges, C., Nowotny, H., Schwartzman, S., Scott, P. and Trow, M. *The New Production of Knowledge*, London, Sage, 1994.

Goleman, D. *Emotional Intelligence*, New York, Bantam Books, 1995.

Goodall H. Jnr. 'Casing the academy for community', *Communication Theory*, 8 (4), 1999, pp. 465–94.

Goody, A. and de Vries, J. 'Straight talk about queer issues', HERDSA conference proceedings, 2002.

Haavind, H. and Andenaes, A. 'Care and responsibility for children: creating the life of women creating themselves', unpublished paper, Department of Psychology, University of Oslo, 1992.

Hall, R. M. and Sandler, B. *The Classroom Climate: A Chilly One for Women*, project on the Status and Education of Women, Association of American Colleges, Washington D.C., 1982.

Haraway, D. 'Situated knowledges: the science question in feminism and the privilege of partial perspective', *Feminist Studies*, 14 (3), 1988, pp. 575–99.

Harris, P. 'Changing patterns of governance: developments in Australian public hospitals and universities', *Policy Studies*, 20 (6), 1999, pp. 255–72.

Hearn, J. *Men in the Public Eye: The Construction and Deconstruction of Public Men and Public Patriarchies*, London, Routledge, 1992.

Hearn, J. and Parkin, W. 'Gender and organisations: a selective review and a critique of a neglected area', *Organisation Studies*, 4 (3), 1983, pp. 219–42.

Helgeson, S. *The Female Advantage: Women's Ways of Leadership*, New York, Doubleday, 1990.

Hernes, H. *Welfare State and Women Power: Essays in State Feminism*, Oslo, Norwegian University Press, 1987.

Hirst, P. *Globalisation in Question: The International Economy and the Question of Governance*, London, Pluto Press, 1996.

Hirst, P. and Thompson, G. 'Globalisation and the future of the nation state', *Economy and Society*, 24 (3), 1995, pp. 409–22.

Hochschild, A. R. *The Managed Heart: Commercialization of Human Feeling*, Berkeley, University of California Press, 1983.

—— *The Time Bind: When Work Becomes Home and Home Becomes Work*, New York, Metropolitan Books, 1997.

Hodson, R. and Sullivan, T. *The Social Organization of Work*, Belmont NY, Wadsworth/Thomson Learning, 2002.

Hoffman, U. *Sekretaren Bakom Allt: en Väg till Synliggörande* (secretaries behind it all: a way toward making them visible), Stockholm, Arbetslivscentrum, 1987.

Inayatullah, S. and Gidley, J. (eds). *The University in Transformation: Global Perspectives on the Futures of the University*, Westport Calif., Bergin & Garvey, 2000.

Karpin, D. *Enterprising Nation: Renewing Australia's Managers to Meet the Challenge of the AsiaPacific Century*, Australian Government Publishing Service, 1995.

Kerfoot, D. and Knights, D. 'Managing masculinity in contemporary organizational life: a "man"agerial project', *Organization*, 1998, 5 (1), pp. 7–26.

Kilmartin, C. 'Are Australian workplaces familyfriendly?', *Family Matters*, 44, 1996, pp. 36–7.

Knights, D. and Willmott, H. *Management Lives: Power and Identity in Work Organizations*, London, Sage, 1999.

Knights, D. and Willmott, H. (eds). *The Reengineering Revolution, Critical Studies of Corporate Change*, London, Sage, 2000.

Kolb, D. and Meyerson, D. 'Keeping gender in the plot: a case study of The Body Shop', in A. Rao, R. Stuart and D. Kelleher, *Gender at Work: Organizational Change for Equality*, West Hartford Pa., Kumarian Press, 1999, pp. 129–54.

Kolodny, A. *Failing the Future: A Dean Looks at Higher Education in the Twenty-First Century*, Durham DC, Duke University Press, 1998.

Kotter, J. P. *A Force for Change: How Leadership Differs from Management*, New York, Free Press, 1990.

Limerick, B and Lingard, B. (eds). *Gender and Changing Educational Management*, Rydalmere NSW, Hodder Education, 1995.

Lloyd, G. *The Man of Reason: 'Male' and 'Female' in Western Philosophy*, London, Methuen, 1998.

Luke, C. *Globalization and Women in Academia: North/West, South/East*, Mahwah N.J., Lawrence Erlbaum Associates, 2001.

McBride, B. A. and Darragh, J. 'Interpreting the data on father involvement: implications for parenting programs for men', *Families in Society*, 1995, 25, pp. 490–7.

MacDonald, P. 'Contemporary fertility patterns in Australia: first data from the 1996 census', *People and Place*, 6 (1), 1998, pp. 1–13.

McInnis, C. 'Academics and professional administrators in Australian universities: dissolving boundaries and new tensions', unpublished paper, Centre for the Study of Higher Education, University of Melbourne, 1998.

McKinley, A. and Taylor, P. 'Power, surveillance and resistance: inside the factory of the future', in P. Ackers, C. Smith and P. Smith (eds), *The New Workplace Trade Unionism: Critical Perspective on Work and Organization*, London, Routledge, 1996, pp. 279–300.

Mackinnon, A. *Love and Freedom: Professional Women and the Reshaping of Personal Life*, Melbourne, Cambridge University Press, 1997.

McLean, J. 'Hearing from the forgotten workforce: the problems faced by general staff women working in universities', *Australian Universities' Review*, 39 (2), 1996, pp. 20–7.

Mant, A. *Intelligent Leadership*, Sydney, Allen & Unwin, 1997.

Marginson, S. *Markets in Education*, Sydney, Allen & Unwin, 1997.

—— 'Steering from a distance: power relations in Australian higher education', *Higher Education*, 34, 1997, pp. 63–80.

—— *Harvards of the Antipodes? Nation–building in a Global Environment*, Winter Lecture Series, University of Auckland, 21 July 1998.

Martin, J. *Cultures in Organizations: Three Perspectives*, New York, Oxford University Press, 1992.

Martin, J. and Frost, P. 'The organisational culture war games: a struggle for intellectual dominance', in S. R. Clegg, C. Hardy and W. R. Nord, *Handbook of Organisation Studies*, London, Sage, 1996, pp. 599–621.

Martin, P. Y. and Collinson, D. 'Over the pond and across the water: developing the field of gendered organizations', *Gender, Work and Organization*, 9 (3), 2002, pp. 245–65.

Massey, D. 'Politics and space/time', *New Left Review*, 196, 1992, pp. 65–84.

Meek, V. and Wood, F. *Higher Education Governance and Management: An Australian Study*, Evaluations and Investigations Program, Higher Education Division, Department of Employment, Education, Training and Youth Affairs, 1997.

Meyerson, D. *Tempered Radicals: Everyday Leadership Transforming Organizations*, Cambridge Mass., Harvard University Press, 2001.

Meyerson, D. and Scully, M. 'Tempered radicalism and the politics of ambivalence and change', *Organization Science*, 6 (5), 1995, pp. 585–600.

Minow, M. *Making All the Difference: Inclusion, Exclusion and American Law*, Ithaca, Cornell University Press, 1990.

Mitchell, D. 'The end of public space?: people's park, definitions of the public, and democracy', *Annals of the Association of American Geographers*, 85 (1), 1995, pp. 108–33.

Moodie, G. 'Leaping tall organisational boundaries in a single bound', paper presented to 18th AITEA conference, Adelaide, 1994.

Morgan, G. *Imaginization: The Art of Creative Management*, Thousand Oaks Calif., Sage Publications, 1993.

—— *Images of Organization*, Thousand Oaks Calif., Sage Publications, 1997.

Morley, L. *Organising Feminisms: The Micropolitics of the Academy*, London, Macmillan, 1999.

Morley, L. and Walsh, V. *Feminist Academics: Creative Agents for Change*, London, Taylor and Francis, 1995.

Mulkay, M. *The Word and The World: Explorations in the Form of Sociological Analysis*, London, Boston, Allen & Unwin, 1985.

National Tertiary Education Union, 'How diverse and specialised do Australian universities need to be?', briefing paper, NTEU, May 2003.

Ozga, J. and Walker, L. 'Women in education management', in B. Limerick and B. Lingard (eds), *Gender and Changing Educational Management*, Rydalmere NSW, Hodder Education, 1995, pp. 34–43.

Palmer, G. 'Diversity management: past, present and future', *Asia Pacific Journal of Human Resources*, 41 (1), 2003, pp. 13–24.

Pocock, B. *Having A Life: Work, Family, Fairness and Community in 2000*, Adelaide, Centre for Labour Market Research, 2001.

—— *The Work/Life Collision*, Sydney, Federation Press, 2003.

Prasad, P., Prasad, A. and Mills, A. *Managing the Organizational Melting Pot*, Thousand Oaks Calif., Sage Publications, 1998.

Prichard, C., Hull, R., Chumer, C., and Willmott, H. (eds), *Managing Knowledge*, Basingstoke UK, Macmillan, 2000.

Pringle, J. K. 'Denial and embrace: issues of gender and sexuality in senior women managers', unpublished paper, 3rd International Gender, Work and Organization conference, Keele University, June 2003.

Probert, B. '"Grateful slaves" or "self-made women": a matter of choice or policy?', Clare Burton Memorial Lecture, Hyatt Regency Hotel, Perth, 10 September 2001.

Probert, B., Ewer, P. and Whiting, K. *Gender Pay Equity in Australian Higher Education*, National Tertiary Education Union, Melbourne, 1998.

Rao, A., Stuart, R. and Kelleher, D. *Gender at Work: Organizational Change for Equality*, West Hartford Pa., Kumarian Press, 1999.

Reinharz, S. *Feminist Methods in Social Research*, Oxford, Oxford University Press, 1992.

Rimmer, M. and Palmer, G. 'Future research in managing human diversity: an overview', *Asia Pacific Journal of Human Resources*, 41 (1), 2003, pp. 6–12.

Rosener, J. *Women's Competitive Secret: Women Managers*, New York, Oxford University Press, 1995.

Russell, A. 'Individual and family factors contributing to mothers' and fathers' positive parenting', *International Journal of Behavioural Development*, 21, 1997, pp. 111–32.

Sawer, M. *Sisters in Suits: Women and Public Policy in Australia*, Sydney, Allen & Unwin, 1990.

——— 'Why has the women's movement had more influence on government in Australia than elsewhere?' in F. G. Castles, *Australia Compared*, Sydney, Allen & Unwin, 1991, pp. 258–77.

Sawicki, J. *Disciplining Foucault: Feminism, Power and the Body*, New York, Routledge, 1991.

Schein, E. H. *Organizational Culture and Leadership*, San Francisco, Jossey–Bass, 1985.

——— *Organizational Learning: What is New?*, The Society for Organizational Learning, 1997, <http://www.solne.org/res/wp/10012.html>.

——— *Three Cultures of Management: The Key to Organizational Learning in the 21st Century*, The Society for Organizational Learning, 1998, <http://www.solne.org/res/wp/three.html>.

Senge, P. M. *The Fifth Discipline: The Arts and Practice of the Learning Organization*, Sydney, Random House, 1990.

Sims, H. P. and Lorenzi, P. *The New Leadership Paradigm*, Newbury Park UK, Sage, 1992.

Sinclair, A. *Trials at the Top: CEOs Talk about Men, Women and Australian Executive Culture*, Australian Centre, University of Melbourne, 1994.

——— *Doing Leadership Differently: Gender, Power and Sexuality in a Changing Business Culture*, Melbourne, Melbourne University Press, 1998.

——— 'Gender = men + women: why men's experiences should be part of management studies', *Mt Eliza Business Review*, Summer/Autumn 2000/01, pp. 9–16.

Slaughter, S. and Leslie, L. *Academic Capitalism: Politics, Policies and the Entrepreneurial University*, Baltimore MD, Johns Hopkins University Press, 1997.

Smircich, L. 'Concepts of culture and organizational analysis', *Administrative Science Quarterly*, 28, 1983, pp. 339–58.

Smith, D. *The Conceptual Practices of Power: A Feminist Sociology of Knowledge*, Toronto, University of Toronto Press, 1990.

—— *Writing the Social: Critique, Theory and Investigations*, Toronto, University of Toronto Press, 1999.

Spearritt, K. and Edgar, D. *The Family Friendly Front: A Review of Australian and International Work and Family Research*, Melbourne, National Key Centre of Industrial Relations, 1994.

Steinpreis, R., Anders, K. and Ritzke, D. 'The impact of gender on the review of curricula vitae of job applicants and tenure candidates: a national empirical study', *Sex Roles*, 41 (7/8), 1999, pp. 509–28.

Storey, J. *What is Cultural Studies?: A Reader*, London, Arnold, 1996.

Stuart, J. 'The position of women staff at The University of Western Australia: some reflections on the outcomes and process of two reviews of gender equity', *International Review of Women and Leadership*, 5 (4), 1999, pp. 46–56.

Tannen, D. *Gender and Discourse*, New York, Oxford University Press, 1994.

Taylor, S. and Tyler, M. 'Emotional labour and sexual difference in the airline industry', *Work, Employment and Society*, 14 (1), 2000, pp. 77–95.

Thornton, M. *Dissonance and Distrust: Women in the Legal Profession*, Melbourne, Oxford University Press, 1995.

Todd, P. and Bird, D. 'Gender and promotion in academia', *Equal Opportunities International*, 19 (8), 2000, pp. 1–16.

Tonelson, A. *The Race to the Bottom: Why a Worldwide Worker Surplus and Uncontrolled Free Trade are Sinking American Living Standards*, Boulder Colo., Westview, 2000.

Tudiver, N. *Universities for Sale*, Toronto, James Lorimer and Co., 1999.

Wacjman, J. *Managing Like a Man*, Cambridge, Polity Press, 1999.

Walford, G. (ed.). *Debates and Developments in Ethnographic Methodology*, Oxford, Elsevier Science, 2002.

Waring, M. *Counting For Nothing*, Sydney, Allen & Unwin, 1988.

Watson, S. (ed.). *Playing the State: Australian Feminist Interventions*, London, Verso, 1990.

Weick, K. 'Educational organizations as loosely coupled systems', *Administrative Science Quarterly*, 21 (1), 1976, pp. 1–19.

—— 'Small wins: redefining the scale of social problems', *American Psychologist*, 39 (1), 1984, pp. 40–9.

Weick, K. and Sutcliffe, K. M. *Managing the Unexpected: Assuring High Performance in an Age of Complexity*, San Francisco, Jossey–Bass, 2001.

West, C. and Zimmerman, D. 'Doing gender', in J. Lorber and S. Farrel (eds), *The Social Construction of Gender*, Thousand Oaks Calif., Sage Publications, 1991, pp. 13–37.

Whyley, C. and Callender, C. 'Administrative and support staff in higher education: their experiences and expectations', Report 4: National Committee of Inquiry into Higher Education, Report 4 (Dearing Report), 1997, <http://www.ncl.ac.uk/ncihe/report4.htm>.

Wieneke, C. 'Managing women: positioning general staff women in Australian universities', *Journal of Tertiary Education Administration*, 17 (1), 1995, pp. 5–19.

Wieneke, C. and Durham, M. 'Regulating the equality agenda: EEO in higher education', *Australian Universities' Review*, 35 (2), 1992, pp. 30–5.

Winefield, A., Gillespie, N., Stough, C., Dua, J. and Hapuararchchi, J. *Occupational Stress in Australian Universities: A National Survey*, National Tertiary Education Union, 2002.

Wright, P. *Managerial Leadership*, London, Routledge, 1996.

Wyn, J., Acker, S. and Richards, E. 'Making a difference: women in management in Australian and Canadian faculties of education', *Gender and Education*, 12 (4), 2000, pp. 435–47.

Yeatman, A. *Bureaucrats, Technocrats, Femocrats: Essays on the Contemporary Australian State*, Sydney, Allen & Unwin, 1990.

—— 'The gendered management of equity oriented change in higher education', in D. Baker and M. Fogarty (eds), *A Gendered Culture*, Melbourne, Victorian University of Technology, 1993, pp. 14–27.

—— 'The new contractualism and the politics of quality management', Women, Culture and Universities: A Chilly Climate?, National Conference on the Effects of Organisational Culture on Women in Universities, conference proceedings, Sydney, University of Technology, 19–20 April 1995.

York Stories Collective, *York Stories: Women in Higher Education*, Toronto, Tsar Publications, 2000.

INDEX